SCHOOL LEADERSHIP IN DIVERSE CONTEXTS

School Leadership in Diverse Contexts demonstrates the centrality of context to understanding school leadership. It offers varied portrayals of leadership in a diverse range of distinct settings. Each chapter highlights the prominence of context in understanding the realities of school leadership, focusing on issues and influences that school leaders face, strategies school leaders adopt to deal with the complexities of their work and conceptualisations of school leadership relevant to the context.

An impressive array of international experts examine this neglected area of research by considering school leadership in nine heterogeneous contexts, providing rich and varied portrayals of school leadership and suggesting ways in which the leadership may be enhanced.

School Leadership in Diverse Contexts is an ideal book for undergraduate and postgraduate students, particularly those studying units in educational leadership, comparative education and educational policy. Similarly, undergraduate and postgraduate students engaged with development studies, history, sociology, law and human geography will be attracted to this text.

Simon Clarke is Professor and Deputy Dean in the Faculty of Education, The University of Western Australia, Australia.

Tom O'Donoghue is Professor of Education in the Graduate School of Education, The University of Western Australia, Australia.

SCHOOL LEADERSHIP IN DIVERSE CONTEXTS

Edited by
Simon Clarke and Tom O'Donoghue

Routledge
Taylor & Francis Group
LONDON AND NEW YORK

First published 2016
by Routledge
2 Park Square, Milton Park, Abingdon, Oxon OX14 4RN

and by Routledge
711 Third Avenue, New York, NY 10017

Routledge is an imprint of the Taylor & Francis Group, an informa business

British Library Cataloguing in Publication Data
A catalogue record for this book is available from the British Library

Library of Congress Cataloging in Publication Data
Names: Clarke, Simon (Simon R. P.), editor of compilation. |
O'Donoghue, T. A. (Tom A.), 1953-
Title: School leadership in diverse contexts / Simon Clarke and
Tom O'Donoghue.
Description: Abingdon, Oxon ; New York, NY : Routledge is an imprint of the
Taylor & Francis Group, an Informa business, [2016] |
Includes bibliographical references and index.
Identifiers: LCCN 2015016243| ISBN 9781138817319 (hardback) |
ISBN 9781138817326 (pbk.) | ISBN 9781315745633 (ebook)
Subjects: LCSH: Educational leadership—Cross-cultural studies. | School
management and organization—Cross-cultural studies.
Classification: LCC LB2806 .C514 2016 | DDC 371.2—dc23
LC record available at http://lccn.loc.gov/2015016243

ISBN: 978-1-138-81731-9 (hbk)
ISBN: 978-1-138-81732-6 (pbk)
ISBN: 978-1-315-74563-3 (ebk)

Typeset in Bembo and Stone Sans
by Florence Production Ltd, Stoodleigh, Devon, UK
Printed in Great Britain by Ashford Colour Press Ltd, Gosport, Hants

FSC www.fsc.org MIX Paper from responsible sources FSC® C011748

CONTENTS

1

INTRODUCTION

Simon Clarke and Tom O'Donoghue

The understanding and practice of leadership are often contested. Also, they can vary significantly from context to context. As a result, academics, policy makers and educational leaders, including school leaders, need to spend a significant amount of time deliberating on the crucial importance of considering matters of context alongside leadership theories when engaging with school improvement for any particular setting. Herein lays the fundamental premise underpinning the overall thrust of the present work.

The central concern of this book is with the way in which school leadership is understood and practised in a diverse range of distinctive contexts. This consideration is demonstrated most persuasively by means of rich and varied portrayals of school leadership as it is pursued in widely differing settings. In doing so, the book, we believe, contributes greatly to understanding of the nuances of school leadership as they are shaped by distinct environments and the ways in which this leadership may be enhanced.

To date, empirical research into leadership of educational organisations, and particularly schools, has tended largely to ignore the emphasis placed by those like Gronn and Ribbins (1996) since the 1990s, on the importance of being sensitive to context. On this, Dimmock (2005, p. 82) commented as follows nearly ten years ago: 'It is depressing to find so many scholars in the field who feel qualified to write about leadership while divorcing it from, and even ignoring, the specific contexts within which it is exercised.'

It is fair to say that his observation still largely holds true today. At the same time, however, there are some indications of change. For example, a number of insights have emerged from investigations into leadership in small, remote schools (Clarke and Wildy, 2004) into the idiosyncratic characteristics of leadership in multi-ethnic (Walker, 2004) and faith-based schools (Sullivan, 2006) and into leadership in 'schools facing challenging circumstances' (Chapman and Harris, 2004). In similar a vein, our most recent work has considered the complexity of school leadership as it is exercised in post-conflict settings (Clarke and O'Donoghue, 2013). We argue, however, that there are many other distinctive environments which warrant closer academic attention because of their implications for the situated understanding and exercise of school leadership. This book, therefore, incorporates portrayals of nine very different contexts to provide rare insights into the diversity of approaches to school leadership that are mediated by specific settings. Each depiction of school leadership lends a distinctive edge to scholarly discussion about the influence a particular context can have on the agency of leaders. Collectively, the depictions illuminate critical aspects of conceptualisations and practices of school leadership.

Given that the specific focus of this book is on school leadership as it is understood and practised in distinctive contexts, we considered that an effective way to provide the broadest array of appropriate settings was to invite a number of recognised experts to write on the topic in relation to the particular contexts with which they have been most concerned in both their academic and professional work. For this purpose, we were keen to encourage combinations of authors comprising practitioners and researchers. Each contributor approached (listed below) agreed to participate and, in relation to his or her respective setting, to provide a chapter accommodating each of the following key considerations:

- The issues and influences that school leaders face as they perform;
- their day-to-day work within the given context;
- the nature of the context within which these issues and influences arise;
- the strategies that school leaders adopt to deal with the complexities of their work within their contexts;
- the reasons why these strategies are adopted;
- possible conceptualisations of school leadership that may be germane to the given distinctive environment.

Overall, the book consists of twelve chapters. Following this chapter, Chapter 2 presents the broad background to the remaining chapters in the book, each of which deals with school leadership as it is understood and practised in a distinctive context. In particular, the chapter examines what is meant by context (both in-school context and out-of-school context) and its component parts. It goes on to outline the thrust of the tradition in comparative education which stresses that the possibility of any set of educational ideas and practices proposed for any context being adopted successfully is maximised when attention is paid to the nature of that context. Consideration is then given to how those involved in educational leadership can benefit not only from taking into account each of these two matters, but also by deliberating on the extent to which other sub-branches within educational scholarship have paid attention to them and the consequences that have followed. The possibility that much school leadership practice for the future could be unsuccessful if leaders are not sufficiently sensitive to context provides the justification for considering the sorts of cases reported in the chapters that follow.

Chapters 3 to 11 are written by the invited contributors. They were guided in their writing by the key considerations outlined above. At the same time, they were given latitude to bring their own individual mode of presentation to bear as much as possible. On this, we point out that while some chapters are focused on an individual school within its context, others are more general in their examination of schools that are located in distinctive settings.

Chapter 3, by Bruce Barnett and Howard Stevenson, is concerned with leading high poverty urban schools while dealing with such context-specific factors as a multiplicity of economic, emotional and social challenges. Professor Barnett is a Professor in Educational Leadership and Policy Studies at the University of Texas at San Antonio, USA. Previously, he worked at the Far West Laboratory, Indiana University, and the University of Northern Colorado. Howard Stevenson is a Professor of Educational Leadership and Policy studies at the University of Nottingham. He has extensive experience directing doctoral programmes and collaborative action research projects in schools.

Chapter 4, by Karen Starr, is concerned with leading small, remote schools while dealing with such context-specific factors as isolation and the community. Professor Starr is Foundation Professor in School Development and Leadership, Deakin University, Melbourne, Australia. She was a school principal for fifteen years in South Australia and Victoria and was Chief Writer of South Australia's Curriculum, Standards and Accountability Framework (SACSA).

Chapter 5, by Gilbert Karareba, Simon Clarke and Tom O'Donoghue, is concerned with leading schools in circumstances attributable to conflict and trauma while dealing with such context-specific factors as the provision of education in situations where survival and livelihood priorities are overwhelming. Gilbert Karareba is from Rwanda. He is currently an International Postgraduate Research Scholarship holder at The University of Western Australia (UWA), where he is undertaking his Ph.D. studies in the Graduate School of Education. Simon Clarke is a Professor in the Faculty of Education, The University of Western Australia, where he teaches, supervises and researches in the substantive area of educational leadership. Tom O'Donoghue is also Professor of Education in the Graduate School of Education, The University of Western Australia. He is an elected Fellow of the Royal Historical Society and a Fellow of the Academy of Social Sciences in Australia and a former President of the Australian and New Zealand History of Education Society.

Chapter 6, by Anthony Kelly, is concerned with challenges in leading schools in historically tense, diverse community settings. Professor Kelly is the Head of Southampton Education School at the University of Southampton, where he specialises in educational effectiveness and improvement; in particular, as it relates to educational leadership, governance and policy analysis. Previously, he was a school head in Ireland.

Chapter 7, by Fiona Walton, Joanne Tompkins, Jukeepa Hainnu and Denise Toney is concerned with such context-specific factors as language, culture, health, attendance, racism, and family and peer relationships while leading indigenous schools. Fiona Walton is an Associate Professor in the Faculty of Education at the University of Prince Edward Island (UPEI), Canada. She worked in the Northwest Territories from 1982 to 1999, holding positions of leadership as a special education consultant, supervisor of schools, teacher education instructor, and director of curriculum and school services. Joanne Tompkins has worked as an associate professor in the Faculty of Education at St Francis Xavier University (StFX), Nova Scotia, Canada since 1996. She worked as a teacher, consultant, principal and teacher educator in Pangnirtung, Hall Beach, and Cape Dorset in the Northwest Territories from 1982 to 1995. Jukeepa Hainnu was born in Clyde River, Nunavut, and received her education in both English and Inuktitut at the local school. Hired as a Classroom Assistant in 1982, Jukeepa went on to complete her Bachelor of Education from McGill University in 1984 and her Master of Education at the University of Prince Edward Island in Charlottetown in 2007. Jukeepa taught for many years, becoming a co-principal in 1998 and principal in 2008. Denise Toney is a member of the Eskasoni Mi'kmaw community in Cape Breton, Nova Scotia. She is a fluent speaker of the Mi'kmaw language and a strong believer in the place of language and culture in schools. She is currently the principal of Eskasoni Middle School. Denise received her Bachelor of Arts from Cape Breton University and her Bachelor of Education from St Francis Xavier University (1990). She holds an M.Ed. in Curriculum and Instruction (2003) and an M.Ed. in Administration and Policy from St Francis Xavier University (2012).

Chapter 8, by Ralph Townsend, is concerned with leading exclusive private schools in dealing with such context-specific factors as complex governance and the relentless pressure to achieve. Dr Townsend has been Headmaster of Winchester College in England since 2005. He was previously Headmaster of Oundle School (1999–2005) and before that Headmaster of Sydney Grammar School (1989–1999).

Chapter 9, by Christopher Chapman, is concerned with leading autonomous state schools while dealing with such tensions as that which exists between enhanced autonomy and increased accountability in an especially fluid policy environment. Professor Chapman was appointed Professor of Educational Policy and Practice at the University of Glasgow in January 2013. Prior to this he was Professor of Education at the University of Manchester, and previously held academic and research posts at the universities of Nottingham and Warwick.

Chapter 10, by Qian Haiyan and Allan Walker, is concerned with leading schools in Communist China while adapting to neoliberal pressures. Qian Haiyan is an Assistant Professor in the Department of Education Policy and Leadership, Hong Kong Institute of Education. Her research focuses on understanding school leadership and educational change in the Chinese societies. Allan Walker is Joseph Lau Chair Professor of International Educational Leadership, Dean of Faculty of Education and Human Development and Director of The Joseph Lau Luen Hung Charitable Trust Asia Pacific Centre for Leadership and Change at The Hong Kong Institute of Education. His research focuses on expanding knowledge of school leadership in Chinese and other Asian societies and disseminating this internationally.

Chapter 11, by Jim Ryan and Stephanie Tuters, is concerned with leading diverse schools in dealing with such context-specific factors as constructing and nurturing an inclusive school culture. Professor Ryan is a professor in the Department of Theory and Policy Studies at The University of Toronto, Canada, and is co-director of the University's Centre for Leadership and Diversity (CLD). Prior to his present appointment he worked at Lakehead University where he was involved in teacher education and graduate studies. Stephanie Tuters is a doctoral candidate at OISE/University of Toronto, in Ontario, Canada. Her doctoral research examines the experiences of elementary teachers who engage in equity work.

Chapter 12, by Simon Clarke and Tom O'Donoghue, provides a synthesis of the previous chapters. The focus of the chapter is on highlighting similar, different and unique ways in which school leadership is understood and practised between and among the distinctive contexts featured in the overall commentary. By examining the combination of contexts, it is hoped to reveal more clearly the issues and influences that school leaders face as they perform their work, the nature of the context within which these issues and influences arise, the strategies school leaders adopt to deal with the complexities of their work and the reasons behind these strategies, and the implications of the specific needs, concerns, challenges and problems faced by school leaders in distinctive contexts for policy and practice.

References

Chapman, C. and Harris, A. (2004). Improving schools in difficult and challenging contexts: Strategies for improvement. *Educational Research*, 46(3), 219–228.

Clarke, S. R. P. and O'Donoghue, T. A. (eds). (2013). *School-level leadership in post-conflict societies: The importance of context*. London: Routledge.

Clarke, S. and Wildy, H. (2004). Context counts: Viewing small school leadership from the inside out. *Journal of Educational Administration*, 42(5), 555–572.

Dimmock, C. (2005). The leadership of multi-ethnic schools: What we know and don't know about values-driven leadership. *Education Research and Perspectives*, 22(2), 80–96.

Gronn, P. and Ribbins, P. (1996). Leaders in context: Postpositivist approaches to understanding school leadership. *Educational Administration Quarterly*, 32(3), 452–473.

Sullivan, J. (2006). Faith schools: A culture within a culture in a changing world. In M. de Souza, G. Durka, K. Engebretson and A. McGready (eds). *International handbook of the religious, moral and spiritual dimensions in education* (pp. 937–947). Heidelberg: Springer.

Walker, A. (2004). *Priorities, strategies and challenges: Proactive leadership in multi-ethnic schools*. National College for School Leadership. Available at: www.ncsl.org.uk/publications-index.htm

2

THE CRUCIAL MATTER OF SCHOOL LEADERS TAKING COGNIZANCE OF EDUCATIONAL CONTEXTS

Tom O'Donoghue and Simon Clarke

Introduction

This chapter provides the broad background to the remaining chapters in the book, each of which deals with school leadership as it is understood and practised in a distinctive context. It opens by examining what is meant by context in relation to individual schools. It goes on to detail the thrust of the tradition in comparative education which stresses that the possibility of any set of educational ideas and practices proposed for any context being adopted successfully is maximised when attention is paid to the nature of that context. Consideration is then given to how those involved in educational leadership can benefit not only from taking into account each of these two matters, but also by deliberating on the extent to which other subdisciplines within educational studies have paid attention to them and the consequences that have followed. Overall, the chapter is aimed at impressing that much school leadership practice for the future could be unsuccessful if leaders are not sufficiently sensitive to context. This position provides the justification for considering the sorts of cases reported in the chapters that follow.

What is meant by context

In a relatively recent work addressing policy makers and policy analysts, Braun *et al.* (2011) recognise that educational policies are informed by various commitments, values and forms of experience, and that these should be made explicit in frameworks for policy enactment. They also hold very strongly to the importance of those using such frameworks taking cognizance of the reality that policies are 'enacted in material conditions, with varying resources' (Braun *et al.*, 2011, p. 588). They conceptualise this situation in terms of four sets of contexts: the 'situated contexts', the 'professional contexts', the 'material contexts' and the 'external contexts'. The argument is that while it is helpful to isolate each of these sets of contexts in order to facilitate policy analysis and to plan for policy enactment, it needs to be recognised that disaggregating them can sometimes be an artificial exercise since, in certain instances, they are interconnected and can overlap. One example they give on this is that while school intake can be presented as 'situated', intake in turn 'can shape professional factors such as values, teacher commitment and experiences, as well as 'policy management' (Braun *et al.*, 2011, p. 588). With this very much in mind, what is meant by each context is now outlined.

Situated contexts

It is somewhat unusual within studies of leadership in education for researchers to recognise that schools' histories and the associated matter of schools' reputations can be alive within the collective consciousness of schools and can have an influence on school leaders. This innovative view, however, is adopted by Braun *et al.* (2011, p. 588) in their explication of what they term situated contexts. This set of contexts, as they see it, consists of those aspects of context that are 'historically and locationally linked to the school, such as a school's setting, its history and intake'. Furthermore, as with the stress they place on the interrelationship between the four aspects of context, Braun *et al.* (2011) also stress interrelationships within the dimensions of each individual context. On this, they point out by way of an example in relation to situated contexts, that location and intake are interrelated. As they put it, while schools can become defined by their intake, they can also define themselves by it (Braun *et al.* 2011, p. 590).

Professional contexts

For Braun *et al.* (2011), the notion of professional contexts refers to somewhat less tangible context variables. They include 'values, teacher commitments and experiences, and "policy management" in schools' (Braun *et al.*, 2011, p. 591). They see that there is a necessity to ask if these have an influence on policy enactment and, if so, what is the nature of that influence. To adopt such an approach, they argue, is to go beyond the position of those who consider that it is sufficient to pay attention only to the head teacher, or to specific individuals, when emphasising broad professional contexts. Furthermore, they stress once again that there are interdependencies within the dimensions of this specific set of contexts. An example they give is that of strong interdependencies between professional values, intake, and what and how policies are pursued. To this they add that these relationships are not always smooth, with 'potential dissonances [existing] between embedded institutional values and national policy trends, such as an emphasis by government on uniform in schools' (Braun *et al.*, 2011, p. 592). They also remind us that we should not assume that context always refers to the whole school, since subject departments can sometimes operate as fairly autonomous units, as can individual teachers, including those employed part-time.

Material contexts

The third set of contexts identified by Braun *et al.* (2011, p. 592) is entitled 'material contexts'. This refers to such matters as staffing, budget, buildings, available technology and surrounding infrastructure. Each of these has the potential to have a major impact on policy enactment, including by school leaders, at the individual school level. For example, just on buildings alone, schools can differ greatly, even in the one location, in terms of their layout, quality and spaciousness. This can mean that schools located in close proximity to each other can vary significantly in terms of teachers' and students' experiences of schooling, and the nature of the school leadership that is adopted. Differences between locations can also have a similar result. For example, the quality of teachers that any particular school can employ may be influenced by variations in the cost of housing for them and the nature and extent of transport infrastructure.

Braun *et al.* (2011, p. 592) also point out that while school funding is primarily driven by student numbers, 'differences in school size, local authority subsidies and location, can mean considerable differences in overall budgets'. Again, this can have an impact on school leaders in relation to the type of leadership approach they adopt.

External contexts

The fourth set of contexts identified by Braun *et al.* (2011, p. 592) is entitled 'external contexts'. These are conceptualised as pressures and expectations (including on leaders at the school level) as a result of the influence of broader local and national policies. They include such matters as local authority support, inspectors' reports, league table positions, legal requirements and responsibilities. Also included within this set of contexts is the relationship that any particular school has with other schools.

The tradition within comparative education of paying attention to context

It is one thing to detail the nature of what constitutes educational contexts, it is another to consider why it is important for educationalists to pay attention to them. This section considers the matter by focusing on the thrust of the tradition in comparative education which places stress on the proposition that the possibility of any set of educational ideas and practices proposed for any context being adopted successfully is maximised when attention is paid to the nature of that context. Elsewhere we have elaborated on this proposition in detail (O'Donoghue and Clarke, 2010). In particular, we have highlighted the research of comparative educationalists that indicates how apparently well thought-out ideas on curriculum change and initiatives aimed at improving student learning have floundered because they have involved inappropriate transnational educational knowledge transfer. By such transfer is meant the process which involves the exchange of theories, models and methods for academic or practical purposes among countries.

For centuries different countries have tried to learn from each other in order to enhance their own knowledge base and practices. On this, Wolhuter *et al.* (2007) record how the Ottomans travelled to France in 1721 to visit the fortresses, factories and the workings of French society in general, and to report on how they might be applicable at home. Similarly, by the latter half of the same century industrialists in France, Germany and North America were copying and replicating the new technology spawned by the Industrial Revolution (Wolhuter *et al.*, 2007). Then, in the latter half of the nineteenth century, Japan embraced many aspects of Western culture and institutions. It was during the nineteenth century also, as nation states began to emerge in Western Europe and North America, and national systems of primary school education were created, that the practice of travelling abroad to see what could be learned that would help improve the quality of educational systems and educational leadership ideas and approaches at home, took off in earnest (Wolhuter *et al.*, 2007; Fraser and Brickman, 1968).

As we have pointed out elsewhere (O'Donoghue and Clarke, 2010), Americans, including Horace Mann and Henry Barnard, visited Europe in search of ways of improving American education. In Canada, Edgerton Ryerson founded a non-denominational public school system in the Canadian province of Ontario, based on the results of his studies of European and American education (Wolhuter *et al.*, 2007). The British were also active in studying their neighbours' schools, while the French sought to learn from the Prussian educational system. In fact, the fundamental law of the French system of primary schools in the early nineteenth century, the Guizot Law of 1833, was based on a report conducted by Victor Cousin (1792–1867) of his study tour on behalf of the French Ministry of Education (Wolhuter *et al.*, 2007).

As Crossley (1984) has pointed out, the European and American models of education were exported to colonial dependencies. The Japanese were also active borrowers in the field. As part of their effort to develop a modern state after the Meiji restoration (1868), they launched, in the words of Thut and Adams (1964), 'the greatest of all hunting expeditions' to reconstruct their educational system along Western lines. What eventuated was a combination of the French centralistic pattern of administration, American teaching methods and textbooks, and aspects of German idealism (Wolhuter *et al.*, 2007).

At the same time, some powerful cautionary voices were raised, especially at the turn of the twentieth century. Among the most famous of these was that of Sir Michael Sadler, British historian, educationalist and university administrator. Sadler was at pains to stress that national education systems could only be understood by first of all understanding the national contexts in which they functioned. This was the position expounded in his famous Guilford lecture of 1900 as a response to his central question – namely, 'How far can we learn anything of practical value from the study of foreign systems of education?'. The most oft-quoted section from this lecture is as follows:

> We cannot wander at pleasure among the educational systems of the world, like a child strolling through a garden, and pick off a flower from one bush

> and some leaves from another, and then expect that if we stick what we have gathered into the soil at home, we shall have a living plant. A national system of Education is a living thing, the outcome of forgotten struggles and difficulties, and 'of battles long ago'. It has in it some of the secret workings of national life.
>
> (Quoted in Higginson, 1979, p. 49)

The essence of Sadler's conclusion is that national contextual forces must be understood and that it could be futile to borrow an educational practice or innovation which had evolved in one national context and transplant it into a different societal context. To this, it is reasonable to add that the same can be said with regard to local contexts and that it is matter to which leaders at the individual school level need to be equally alert.

Sadler's position was very much central to the thinking of a group of later world-leading comparative educationalists, including Issac Kandel (1881–1965), Nicholas Hans (1888–1969) and Friedrich Schneider (1881–1969) (Wolhuter *et al.*, 2007), who concerned themselves with devising schemes of societal forces that shape education systems. At the most fundamental level, they stressed the vital importance of paying attention to such factors as geographical environment, the economy, culture, religion and social differentiation. Nevertheless, notwithstanding the influence of their work on academics, policy makers in many contexts were either oblivious to their insights, or chose to ignore them, as the process of transnational knowledge transfer continued into the twentieth century, and not only at the level of national policies, but also at the individual school level.

The folly of the latter approach was particularly evident in the 1950s, 1960s and 1970s, when the predominant model being adopted for such transfer between industrialised nations and developing nations was one of imitation and intervention; of attempting to solve problems in non-Western countries by utilising Western knowledge (Kumar, 1979; Useem and Useem, 1980). Elsewhere, we have outlined in some detail a range of examples from a variety of South Pacific Island nations which are illustrative of this (O'Donoghue and Clarke, 2010). These include the failure of projects for the development of social studies curricula for nine nations because they were incompatible with contextual assumptions about learning (LeSourd, 1990; Thaman, 1991), the failure of curricula designed by overseas 'experts' emphasising teaching for understanding rather than rote learning and pupil participation rather than lecture methods, because of the fact that teachers and school leaders were not engaged in efforts aimed at discovering their views on what was needed by way of preparation to facilitate successful implementation, and teachers' and school leaders' resistance to embracing new approaches to teaching because external examinations continued to dominate the educational system and they felt that any change might jeopardise pupils' chances of getting high scores (Mangubhai, 1984; Thomas, 1984).

Among other unsuccessful projects was a mathematics programme that introduced 'the new maths' through pupil-centred, individual discovery methods, but was erroneously based on a premise that Melanesian children progress at roughly the same rate from cognitive to symbolic thinking as do Western children (McLaughlin, 1990, p. 26). A 'very well-designed and trialled (Jones, 1974, p. 47) primary science programme for Melanesian schools also failed, this time because there was a lack of equivalence between students' conceptualisations and the concepts to which the programme had been aiming. Another failure was a 'General Teaching Programme' which attempted to provide an integrated multi-subject approach in the first two grades of high school in Papua New Guinea by, in Beeby's (1966) terms, demanding 'stage of meaning' thinking and practices from school leaders and teachers who were only in 'the stage of formalism' (O'Donoghue and Clarke, 2010, p. 146).

Nevertheless, during the 1970s, with the emergence of dependency theory, the rise of Third World consciousness and the increasing cultural awareness of some Western social scientists (Lee *et al.*, 1988), heed began to be taken again of the wisdom of the likes of Sadler, Kandel, Hans and Schneider. The failure of many ambitious educational innovations, like those mentioned above, made donors, lenders, recipients and borrowers considerably aware of the complexity and context-dependence of educational change (O'Donoghue and Clarke, 2010, p. 11). A new group of academics, this time from the fields of curriculum studies and educational administration, also voiced the issue using a set of metaphors similar to those of Sadler, yet more in keeping with the tone of the age. Prominent among these was Hargreaves (1993, p. 149), who argued as follows on why educational innovations frequently fail quite disastrously:

> in grafting new ideas onto schools, we do it with so little knowledge about the nature of the everyday world of teachers, pupils and schools that our attempted grafts (and various forms of major and minor surgery) merely arouse the 'anti-bodies' of the host which undermine our attempts to play doctor to an educational patient.

He went on to argue that it is 'only when we understand the precise nature of the host body that we can design our innovatory grafts with any confidence that they will prove to be acceptable' (1993). This was an echoing of Fullan's (1982) argument that to introduce change that promises more success and less failure, the world of the people most closely involved in implementation must be understood. Concurrently, policy makers were advocating the adoption of flexible, iterative and incremental strategies (O'Donoghue and Clarke, 2010, p. 12). In particular, they argued that there is a vital need to pay attention to culture, to adopt participatory, bottom-up processes, and to take notice of the views of all stakeholders in educational planning and evaluation (Little, 1988; Rondinelli *et al.*, 1990). In a similar vein, Carron and Chau (1996) argued that one of the foremost reasons for suboptimal implementation of new educational projects is that planners do not consult sufficiently with those who have to implement their plans.

While the matter will be taken up in more detail in the next section, here it is apposite to point out that the emerging area of educational leadership (Townsend and MacBeath, 2011) also benefited from the new-found interest in stressing the vital importance of not trying to impose uncritically on national systems, teachers and leaders at the school level, sets of preordained models of educational thought and action without considering the cultural context. Among the areas that began to be highlighted is that different cultures have different approaches to leadership and that these have strong cultural foundations. Increasingly, also the argument was put forward that educational leaders need to be aware of the possible inappropriateness of uncritically adopting for their own context curriculum and pedagogical proposals deemed eminently suited for another context.

Finally, it might be concluded that by the turn of the twenty-first century, primarily as a result of the influence of comparative educationalists, the point of no return had been reached with regard to universal embracement of the argument running through this section of the chapter so far. This, however, is not so. On the contrary, some of the developments of the past two decades, which have involved greater centralisation of many aspects of education, including in relation to the curriculum, have led to calls once again for the invention and discovery of sure-fired prescriptive models in all aspects of education which would lead to easily generalisable solutions in each of them. Associated with this is the expectation that leaders at the school level should be 'trained' appropriately in order to ensure the successful implementation of these solutions. Accordingly, it is valuable at this point to consider how certain developments within other branches of educational studies are also persuasive in their emphases on why those involved in educational leadership, including leaders at the individual school level, should heed those who stress the importance of paying attention to context.

Why educational leaders need to take cognizance of context

The one academic discipline more than any other that has been associated with the promotion of the notion that sure-fired prescriptive models for education can be developed, and that is looked upon to do so, especially in relation to pedagogy, is psychology. This, however, is to overlook the still compelling argument made by William James back in the 1890s, when, regarding the function of the study of psychology for educationalists, he stated that one makes a great mistake to think that it can provide definite programmes, schemes and methods of instruction for specific classroom contexts. Rather, he went on:

> Psychology is a science, and teaching is an art. An intermediary inventive mind must make the application, by using its originality. The science of logic never made a man reason rightly, the science of ethics never made a man behave rightly. The most such sciences can do is to help us catch ourselves up, check ourselves, if we start to reason or behave wrongly; and to criticise

> ourselves more articulately if we make mistakes. A science only lays down lines within which the rules of the art must fall, laws which the follower of the art must not transgress; but what particular thing he shall positively do within those lines is left exclusively to his own genius . . . and so while everywhere the teaching must agree with the psychology, it may not necessarily be the only kind of teaching that would so agree; for many diverse methods of teaching may equally well agree with the psychological laws.
>
> (James, 1958, p. 15)

For many decades this position was overlooked as educationalists sought, in relation to a variety of areas, to identify 'best practice', find 'the one best way' to proceed, and seek to 'train' leaders at the individual school level to make sure their teaching staff acted accordingly (O'Donoghue and Clarke, 2010, p. 73). Eisner (1983) was one of the key players to question this view. Like James, he highlighted the importance of considering context. His argument was that 'because of the changing uniqueness of the practical situations that make up the educational domain, only a portion of professional practice can be usefully treated in the manner of a prescriptive science' (O'Donoghue and Clarke, 2010, p. 73). The gap between 'general prescriptive frameworks and successful practice is', he held, 'dependent more on the reflective intuition, the craft, and the art of the professional practitioner than on any particular prescriptive theory, method, or model' (O'Donoghue and Clarke, 2010, p. 73). The implication for leaders at the school level is that they should be cognizant of this view and be guided by it in mentoring teachers.

A little later, psychologists themselves entered the debate, with some powerful voices pointing out that many of the findings presented in psychology textbooks around the world are based on research undertaken within a particular context – namely, that of American psychology undergraduates. On this, Sears (1986) questioned the unwarranted influence of studies in social psychology based on a narrow data base generated in the laboratory with college sophomores as participants. More recently, Henrich *et al.* (2010) took up the same point, criticising the quest in psychological research for generalisations about human nature, and the neglect of the actual diversity of humankind. Watkins (2000), in relation to educational psychology and classroom practices, had offered particularly enlightening insights on this. He pointed out that most of the related major theories in the field are based on the values of Western culture and on an individualistic, independent conception of the person (O'Donoghue and Clarke, 2010, p. 12). This, he concluded, does not mean we should assume that such literature is inappropriate for other cultures, but rather that we should find out through research how to demonstrate its appropriateness. To illustrate his position he provided examples in relation to Confucian-tradition learners. Regarding memorising, for example, he stated that the repetition involved is important for them in deepening understanding by discovering new meaning. He also pointed out that whereas Western teachers expect classroom questions to be asked by students during the process of learning 'to fill in gaps in their knowledge, or to aid understanding of the reasoning involved' (Watkins, 2000, p. 171), Chinese students ask questions after they have learnt independently of the teacher since they consider that questions should be based on knowledge (O'Donoghue and Clarke, 2010, p. 13). Finally, he pointed out that while there is a belief among many teachers from a Western tradition that children learn through being creative, Chinese teachers see creativity as a slow process that depends on solid basic knowledge (Watkins, 2000).

Members of a second body of educationalists – namely, curriculum theorists, were also prompted to promote the crucial importance of leaders at the policy level, the school level and the classroom level taking cognizance of the importance of context, because of a homogenising tendency. In this case, the reaction was to developments aimed at seeking 'same-size-fits-all' technological solutions to curriculum planning. These developments were stimulated by the publication, dissemination, popularisation and, above all else, simplification, of Tyler's (1949) rational curriculum model for curriculum design and development. Among those to initially contest this approach was Taba (1962), who maintained that teachers and their school-based leaders need to 'diagnose the level of thinking of their students before embarking on any curriculum activity' (Marsh, 1992, p. 79). This sort of contestation took off in earnest in the 1970s, with the advent of the school-based curriculum development movement, especially in Britain and Australia, and was extended to contextual considerations beyond the pupil alone. Among the leaders in this movement were Reynolds and Skilbeck (1976), with one of their major contributions being the highlighting of the importance of 'situational analysis'.

The reference to 'situation' in 'situational analysis' refers to 'the initial state in which the learner finds himself/herself' (Marsh, 1992). The point is that it would be folly to enact any set of curriculum proposals without analysing what this state is. Also, while proponents recognise that many educationalists are able to do this intuitively and quickly, they argue that it is worthwhile addressing it systematically by using a framework in which they distinguish between external factors to a school and internal factors to a school. The framework usually offered (Marsh, 1992, p. 79) is as follows.

(a) Analysis of external factors to the school

- Changes and trends in society which indicate tasks for schools – e.g. industrial development, political directives, cultural movements, ideological shifts.
- Expectations and requirements of parents and employers.
- Community assumptions and values, including patterns of adult–child relations.
- The changing nature of the subject disciplines.
- The potential contribution of teacher support systems including teacher centres, colleges of education and universities.
- Actual and anticipated flow of resources in the school.

(b) Analysis of internal factors to the school

- Pupils, their aptitudes, abilities, attitudes, values and defined educational needs.
- Teachers, their values, attitudes, skills, knowledge, experience and special strengths and weaknesses.
- School ethos and political structure, common assumptions and expectations including traditions and power distribution.
- Material resources including plant, equipment and learning materials.
- Perceived and felt problems and shortcomings in existing curriculum.

Similar frameworks were devised by English and Kaufman (1975) and Soliman *et al.* (1981). The overall thrust of all of them is the same. The important point is that which was made by Marsh and Stafford (1988, p. 107) that they need to be used by school-based leaders to collect lots of data so that 'those involved in site-specific curriculum planning can be alerted to how their plans, cherished hopes and strategies' can not only be facilitated, but also thwarted, by the school context.

This approach continues to be advocated. For example, Woolfolk and Margetts (2007, p. 458) state as follows:

> to plan creatively, and effectively, teachers need to have wide-ranging knowledge about their students, their interests and abilities; the subjects being taught; alternative ways to teach and assess understanding; working with groups; the expectations and limitations of the school and community; how to apply and adapt materials, texts and multimedia; and how to pull all this knowledge together into meaningful activities and experiences.

At the same time, some of the developments of the past decade, including moves towards greater centralisation of the curriculum, have somewhat disempowered teachers in this regard and have tended to create the impression that they cannot be entrusted with real curriculum decision-making power. This provides challenges for leaders at the school level; as Smith and Lovat (2003, p. 95) put it over ten years ago, notwithstanding increasing control from educational systems, they need to be able to help their staff take account of the importance of context and 'create decision-making space so that they can exercise autonomy and critical professional judgment in, at least, their own classrooms'.

The third body of educationalists to be considered here are those who study educational leadership itself. This is a group whose members are also demonstrating a recognition of the importance of attending to context if one is to maximise the possibility of successfully enacting educational policies and associated practices. As early as 1996, Gronn and Ribbins (1996) posited clearly that the approach to educational leadership in any particular circumstance needs to take that circumstance into account. Dimmock and Walker (1997) were quick to respond. Drawing their examples primarily from Confucian-based learning settings, they highlighted the Eurocentric nature of much research, writing and practices in relation to leadership in schools. Overall, they succeeded in illustrating persuasively that different cultures have different approaches to leadership and that these have solid cultural foundations.

Developing his work in the field, Dimmock (2005) eventually came to the forefront among those mounting arguments that while many were writing about the appropriateness and virtues of particular approaches to leadership, very little attention was being paid to the specific contexts within which it was being exercised. By now others were also responding to the challenge. Clarke and Wildy (2004), for example, reported investigations into the ways leadership was understood and practised in the distinctive environment of the small, remote school, Walker (2004) provided insights from his study of the idiosyncratic characteristics of leadership in multi-ethnic schools, and Fitzgerald (2003a, 2003b, 2004) drew attention to how educational leadership might be practised differently by females, by indigenous leaders and by female indigenous leaders.

Not long afterwards, Shah (2006) and Sullivan (2006) opened up another avenue for research by focusing on leadership in the context of faith-based schools. Shah (2005), in fact, was concerned specifically with illustrating how learners from diverse philosophical and ethnic backgrounds conceive of, and perceive, educational leadership, and also with illustrating that how they receive it is bound to interact with their learning experience and performance. She addressed this by presenting philosophical and theoretical underpinnings of leadership from an Islamic perspective, and exploring the implications for the British context, where Muslims are in a minority. In a later work (Shah, 2008) she highlighted how the student population across much of the world is increasingly reflective of diverse cultures, religions and ethnicities. This rich diversity, she argued, could become a challenge for educational leaders, teachers and policy-makers in the absence of an understanding of the diverse sources of knowledge that people draw on for directing their beliefs and daily practices.

Shah's (2008) conclusion is that educational leaders need to be cognizant of the need to draw on diverse ethnic knowledge sources to inform and enrich approaches towards managing diversity. A similar position was taken by Jansen (2007) in relationship to providing leadership in societies in transition, including democratising societies. To this body of work has been added that of Moos (2011) on transnational and local conditions and expectations on school leaders and our own contributions on the importance of educational leaders at the school level working in post-conflict societies paying attention to the contexts in which they work (Clarke and O'Donoghue, 2013).

Conclusion

The central argument of this chapter was well summed up by Bridges (2007) when he questioned some of the assumptions of the 'evidence-based practice' movement. In particular he called into question the view that generalisations derived from large population studies can lead to recommendations at the national level for implementation at the local level. He went on:

> you cannot logically derive lessons from a single specific instance from such generalizations. They always have to be linked to consideration of local conditions which might well point to a different recommendation . . . a teacher or school may test out different teaching strategies in their own environment and find out 'what works' for them. The fact that this enquiry was small scale and local does not invalidate it as a reliable basis for local practice even if it might be regarded as an unreliable basis for national policy without some further work.
>
> (Bridges, 2007, p. 2)

Thus, Bridges concluded, one cannot treat local and national decisions as if they have exactly the same requirements.

This brings us back to where we started at the beginning of the chapter, and particularly to the work of Braun *et al.* (2011, p. 585), who argue that it is important to take context seriously. They hold that policies are intimately shaped and influenced by school-specific factors, even though in much central policy-making the associated constraints, pressures and enablers of policy enactment tend to be neglected. Instead, policy-makers 'tend to assume "best possible" environments for implementation: ideal buildings, students and teachers and even resources' (Braun *et al.*, 2011, p. 585). To this they add three further points. First, while one should always try to capture the full range of contextual factors in any situation, such a list can never be exhaustive. Consequently, any framework one uses to this end should be seen 'as a heuristic device that is intended to stimulate interest and to ask questions about the circumstances of policy enactment in "real" schools, rather than cover all possibilities' (Braun *et al.*, p. 595). Second, and related to the latter point, context is 'dynamic and shifting, both within and outside of schools' (Braun *et al.*, p. 595), with possible changes taking place in staff and student profiles, including attitudes. The third point of Braun *et al.* (2011) is that while it is crucial to pay attention to Thrupp and Lupton's (2006, p. 312) argument that 'there still tends to be much more focus on schools' differential internal organisation and practice . . . than on diverse "external" contexts', one should also never lose sight of paying attention to 'the most "material" of contexts – the buildings and budgets, available technologies and local infrastructures' (Braun *et al.* 2011, p. 595). It is such thinking that influenced our decision to seek out the set of case studies presented in the remaining chapters on leadership at the individual school level in a wide variety of contexts in order to illustrate the nature of such contexts, and portray the range and complexity of challenges they pose for those who are ascribed school-level leadership roles, or who might want to take them on.

References

Beeby. C.E. (1966). *The quality of education in developing countries*. Cambridge, MA: Harvard University Press.

Braun, A., Ball, S. J., Maguire, M. and Hoskins, K. (2011). Taking context seriously: explaining policy enactments in the secondary school. *Discourse: Studies in the Cultural Politics of Education*, 32(4), 585–596.

Bridges, D. (2007). Evidence-based reform in education: A response to Robert Slavin. European Educational Research Association Annual Conference, Ghent. 19 September.

Carron, G. and Chau, T. N. (1996). *The quality of primary schools in different development contexts.* Paris: International Institute for Educational Planning, UNESCO Publishing.

Clarke, S. and O'Donoghue, T. A. (eds). (2013). *School-level leadership in post-conflict societies: The importance of context.* London: Routledge.

Clarke, S. and Wildy, H. (2004). Context counts: viewing small school leadership from the inside out. *Journal of Educational Administration*, 42(5), 555–572.

Crossley, M. (1984). Strategies for curriculum change and the question of international transfer. *Journal of Curriculum Studies*, 16, 75–88.

Dimmock, C. (2005). The leadership of multi-ethnic schools what we know and don't know about values-driven leadership. *Educational Research and Perspectives*, 32(2), 80–96.

Dimmock, C. and Walker, A. (1997). Comparative educational administration: developing a cross-cultural conceptual framework. *Educational Administration Quarterly*, 34(4), 558–595.

Eisner, E. (1983). *Cognition and curriculum: A basis for deciding what to teach.* New York: Longman.

English, F. W. and Kaufman, R.A. (1975). *Needs assessment: A focus for curriculum development.* Alexandria, VA: Association for Curriculum Development.

Fitzgerald, T. (2003a). Interrogating orthodox voices: Gender, ethnicity and educational leadership. *School Leadership and Management*, 23(4), 431–444.

Fitzgerald, T. (2003b). Changing the deafening silence of indigenous women's voices in educational leadership. *Journal of Educational Administration*, 41(1), 9–23.

Fitzgerald, T. (2004). Powerful voices and powerful stories: reflections on the challenges and dynamics of intercultural research. *Journal of Intercultural Studies*, 25(3), 233–245.

Fraser, S. E. and Brickman. W. W. (eds). (1968). *A history of international and comparative education: Nineteenth century documents.* Glenview, IL: Scott, Foreman.

Fullan, M. (1982). *The meaning of educational change.* New York: Teachers College, Columbia University.

Gronn, P. and Ribbins, P. (1996) Leaders in context: Postpositivist approaches to understanding school leadership. *Educational Administration Quarterly*, 32(3), 452–473.

Hargreaves, D. (1993). Whatever happened to symbolic interactionism? In M. Hammersley (ed.). *Controversies in classroom research* (pp.135–152). Buckingham: Open University Press.

Henrich, J., Heine, S. J. and Norenzayan, A. (2010). Most people are not weird. *Nature*, 466(7302), 29–30.

Higginson, J. H. (1979). *Selections from Michael Sadler: Studies in world citizenship.* Liverpool: Dejall and Meyorre International Publishers.

James, W. (1958). *Talks to teachers on psychology: And to students on some of life's ideals.* New York: W. W. Norton.

Jansen, J. (2007). The leadership of transition: correction, conciliation and change in South African education. *Journal of Educational Change*, 8(2), 91–103.

Jones, J. (1974). Quantitative concepts, vernaculars and education in Papua New Guinea. ERU Report 19. Waigani: Educational Research Unit, University of Papua New Guinea.

Kumar, K. (1979). *Bonds without bondage: Explorations in transcultural interactions.* Honolulu: University Press of Hawaii.

Lee, J. J., Adams, D., and Cornbleth, C. (1988). Transnational transfer of curriculum knowledge: a Korean case study. *Journal of Curriculum Studies*, 20, 233–46.

LeSourd, S. J. (1990). Curriculum development and cultural context. *The Educational Forum*, 54, 205–16.

Little, A. (1988). *Learning from developing countries.* London: University of London, Institute of Education.

McLaughlin, D. (1990). Teaching the teachers of teachers: Tertiary teacher education. *British Educational Research Journal,* in Papua New Guinea. Unpublished Ph.D. thesis, Institute of Education, University of London.

Mangubhai, F. (1984). Fiji. In R. M. Thomas and T. N. Postlethwaite (eds). *Schooling in the Pacific Islands: Colonies in transition* (pp. 167–202). London: Pergamon Press.

Marsh, C. (1992). *Key concepts for understanding curriculum.* London: The Falmer Press.

Marsh, C. and Stafford, K. (1988). *Curriculum: Practices and issues.* Sydney: McGraw-Hill.

Moos, L. (2011). Transnational and local conditions and expectations on school leaders. In T. Townsend and J. MacBeath, J. (eds). (pp. 65–80). *International handbook of leadership for learning: Part 1 and Part 2.* Dordrecht: Springer.

O'Donoghue, T. A. and Clarke, S. (2010). *Leading learning: Process, themes and issues in international perspective.* London: Routledge.

Reynolds, D. and Skilbeck, M. (1976). *Culture in the classroom.* London: Open Books.

Rondinelli, D., Middleton, J. and Verspoor, A. (1990). *Planning education reforms in developing countries: The contingency approach.* London: Duke University.

Sears, D. O. (1986). College sophomores in the laboratory: Influences of a narrow data base on social psychology's view of human nature. *Journal of Personality and Social Psychology,* 51(3), 515–530

Shah, S. (2006). Educational leadership: An Islamic perspective. *British Educational ReSCHOOL search Journal,* 32(3), 363–385.

Shah, S. (2008). Leading multi-ethnic schools: Adjustments in concepts and practices for engaging with diversity. *British Journal of Sociology of Education,* 29(5), 523–536.

Smith, D. and Lovat, T. J. (2003). *Curriculum: Action on reflection.* Tuggerah, New South Wales: Social Science Press.

Soliman, I., Dawes, L., Gough, J. and Maxwell, T. (1981). *A model for school-based curriculum development.* Canberra: Curriculum Development Centre.

Sullivan, J. (2006). Faith schools: A culture within a culture in a changing world. In M. de Souza, G. Durka, K. Engebretson and A. McGready (eds). *International handbook of the religious, moral and spiritual dimensions in education* (pp. 937–947). Heidelberg: Springer.

Taba, H. (1962). *Curriculum development: Theory and practice.* New York: Harcourt, Brace & World.

Thaman, K. H. (1991). Towards a culture-sensitive model of curriculum development for the Pacific countries. *Directions: Journal of Educational Studies,* 13, 1–13.

Thomas, R. M. (1984). American Samoa and Western Samoa. In R. M. Thomas and T. N. Postlethwaite (eds). *Schooling in the Pacific Islands: Colonies in transition* (67–110). London: Pergamon Press.

Thrupp, M. and Lupton, R. (2006). Taking school contexts more seriously: The social justice challenge. *British Journal of Educational Studies,* 54, 308–328.

Thut, I. N. and Adams, D. (1964). *Educational patterns in contemporary society.* Tokyo: McGraw-Hill, Kogakusha.

Townsend, T. and MacBeath, J. (2011). *International handbook of leadership for learning: Part 1 and Part 2.* Dordrecht: Springer.

Tyler, R. (1949). *Basic principles of curriculum and instruction.* Chicago: University of Chicago Press.

Useem, J. and Useem, R. H. (1980). *Generating fresh research perspectives and study designs for transnational exchange among the highly educated.* DAAD Research and Exchange. Proceedings of the German-American Conference at the Wissenschaftszentrum, Bonn, November.

Walker, A. (2004). Priorities, strategies and challenges. Proactive leadership in multi-ethnic schools. *National College for School Leadership*. Available at: www.ncsl.org.uk/publications-index.htm

Watkins, D. (2000). Learning and teaching: A cross-cultural perspective. *School Leadership and Management*, 20(2), 161–173.

Wolhuter, C. C., Lemmer, E. M. and de Wet (eds). (2007). *Comparative education: Education systems and contemporary issues*. Pretoria: Van Schaik.

Woolfolk, A. and Margets, K. (2007). *Educational psychology*. Sydney: Pearson Education Australia.

3

LEADING HIGH POVERTY URBAN SCHOOLS

Bruce G. Barnett and Howard Stevenson

Introduction

Gradually, the world's population is becoming more urbanised. In 2010, half of the world's 7.1 billion people lived in cities, with over half of these city dwellers residing in communities of 100,000 to 500,000 people (World Health Organization, 2014). In fact, the term 'urbanisation' has become part of our lexicon, acknowledging the transition from a rural agriculturally based economy to an urban service, technology and industry-based economy. The continuing influx of people to urban centres has had a significant impact on the social, economic, political and educational context. As a result, urban school settings have the following distinctive characteristics when compared with rural and suburban school systems, as noted by the National Center for Education Statistics (1996) and Chung (2005):

- Urban schools have higher student enrolments, absenteeism, weapons possession and teen pregnancies.
- Urban schools have more teachers and instructors teaching out of their content area(s).
- Urban students are less likely to live in two-parent households.
- Urban students are more likely to feel unsafe in school, less likely to do homework and watch more television.
- Urban students change schools more frequently.
- Urban teachers have fewer resources to work with and less control over the curriculum.

Given the rising urbanisation of communities around the world, the purpose of this chapter is to examine the realities that confront principals who are leading urban schools. Many of the examples supporting our ideas are taken from research conducted by members of the International School Leadership Development Network (ISLDN), a joint collaboration between two educational leadership professional organisations, the British Educational Leadership Management and Administration Society (BELMAS) and the University Council for Educational Administration (UCEA). ISLDN researchers from around the world are conducting studies of leaders who are committed to: (a) providing social justice for under-represented and marginalised students and (b) working in high-need schools located in high poverty communities with poor student performance.

We begin the chapter by reviewing the societal- and school-level contextual factors that define and have an impact on urban schools before highlighting the specific challenges these factors create for urban school principals. Next, leadership strategies used by urban principals to combat these challenges are described, including the rationale for their decisions. We conclude by describing conceptualisations of effective urban school leadership emerging from the ISLDN research. Our framework presents a revised way of thinking about macro and micro contexts that have emerged from the research undertaken in the ISLDN collaboration. Our hope is that this framework adds to the important debate about the relationship between context and leadership practice, and the need to recognise the diverse and complex ways in which a range of local contextual factors play out in different ways in individual schools.

The context of urban schools

The editors of this volume describe 'context' as a multi-faceted construct, consisting of external (macro) factors and internal (micro) elements that have an impact on school leaders' decisions. We use the contextual typology described by Walker and his colleagues (2012) in considering these macro and micro features. In their review of literature on school leadership, they refer to three contextual levels: (a) *societal* – culture, administrative systems, political ideology, (b) *school* – location, level, teaching staff, resources, community stakeholders, and (c) *personal* – age, gender, experience, and knowledge of the principal. For our purposes, we focus on the first two contextual levels affecting urban schools: societal (macro) and school (micro) contexts.

Societal-level context

A variety of factors outside the local school community have an impact on urban schools. These macro-level factors can be long-standing cultural values, social and economic trends, and government policies. These are now examined below.

Cultural values

Societal norms and values affect urban schools and their leaders. In certain Asian cultures, for example, Confucian values of respecting authority, avoiding conflict, seeking harmony and saving face are prominent (Walker *et al.*, 2012). To maintain harmony and avoid conflict, principals are less inclined to observe classroom teaching practices or to suggest instructional improvements for teachers (Lee and Hallinger, 2012; Pan, 2012). In addition, Arab societies tend not to accept women in formal leadership roles; therefore, female principals evaluating male teachers find it difficult to provide them with constructive feedback. Furthermore, powerful families (i.e. hamullas) in the community can overrule principals' decisions about teachers' performance reviews and/or dismissal, pressuring principals to compromise their values and decisions when working with underperforming teachers (Arar, 2014).

Social and economic trends

Lee and Hallinger's (2012) study of principals in different societies underscores important ways in which national-level context influences principals' time use and responsibilities. Their analysis revealed:

- Principals working in countries with high power differentials between roles allocated less time to curriculum and instructional development than school leaders in societies with lower power differentials.
- Principals in less hierarchical societies spent more time with community members and parents than those in more hierarchical societies.
- Principals from developed countries spent more time at school, but less time dealing with curriculum and instruction, than school leaders from developing countries.

Governmental policies

Urban school leaders at the campus and district/provincial levels are greatly affected by the educational policies enacted by state and federal government agencies (Haberman, n.d.; Klar and Brewer, 2013). Because urban schools have a history of struggling to improve student achievement and graduation rates, they have become prime targets for policy-makers (Halford, 1996). On one hand, policy-makers identify shortcomings in the system, which are compromising the quality of education that students receive. For instance, the Ministry of Education and Science in the Republic of Georgia has acknowledged the problems associated with a centralised governance system, outdated textbooks and programmes, inadequate teacher preparation, inefficient funding for schools, and corruption and nepotism (Sharvashidze and Bryant, 2014). Furthermore, in Costa Rica, policy-makers have identified the key challenges facing the country, including 'achieving universal preschool and secondary education, improving the quality of the educational system, reducing failure and improving efficiency, focusing on critical moments of transitions across grade levels, and expanding investment in education from 4.8 per cent to 6 per cent' (Slater *et al.*, 2014, p. 111).

On the other hand, once problems are identified, governments are prone to enact policies and provide resources to address shortcomings. For instance, because education in India has tended to be elitist and ignored females, policy-makers passed the National Policy on Education in 1996, which ensured educational opportunities to all Indian citizens regardless of gender or social class. The law implemented a quota system to allow educationally and socially disadvantaged castes access to a university education and established incentives (e.g. giving bicycles to girls to travel to school, offering child daycare to allow young female sibling caretakers to attend school) to increase females' access and retention in schools (Richardson and Sauers, 2014). In addition, Mexican principals have used government-financed textbooks, extended-day programmes, and programmes to reduce school violence, to stimulate new teaching practices in reforming their schools (Rincones, 2012).

Another mounting problem in urban settings is the rapid increase in the student population, oftentimes resulting in large numbers of new students attending schools. In the United States, for example, Latina/o students constitute the fastest growing school-aged population in the country, and are represented in significant numbers in certain geographical regions (e.g. 50 per cent of school-aged children in Texas) (U.S. Census Bureau, 2010). In addition, during the 1950s, when many Mainland Chinese families moved to Hong Kong, the government responded by building numerous 'rooftop' schools on the top of existing buildings in public housing projects (Chung and Ngan, 2002). This temporary solution was replaced with another government initiative to work with non-profit religious and charitable organisations and the private sector to finance schools (Sweeting, 1995). By the mid-1960s, the government funded the majority of operating costs for these new 'subsidised' or 'aided' schools (Walker, 2004).

Another political strategy for resourcing schools is identifiable in the United Kingdom, beginning with the Locally Managed Schools movement in the 1980s (Higham *et al.*, 2009). More recently, the formation of Academy Schools and Free Schools has allowed private corporations to own and operate schools that were previously part of the Local Government Authority (Gunter, 2011). As a result, school leaders are becoming chief executive officers leading publically financed independent schools (Gunter and Fitzgerald, 2013). A growing concern is that urban schools with their myriad challenges will be ignored by private enterprise as being too financially risky, widening the gap between the types of resources and services afforded to children living in high poverty communities.

School-level context

The school context consists of the features of the surrounding community as well as the school's infrastructure, principals, teachers and student population.

Community context

Urban communities reflect a complex array of demographic features:

- High levels of ethnic minorities, immigrants, mobility, homeless families, children in foster care, incarcerated students and drug abuse.

- High rates of poverty.
- High proportion of students of colour (Duke 2008, 2012b; Picus *et al.*, 2005).

These community features are also reflected in the ISLDN research sites with median family incomes well below the national average (Medina *et al.*, 2014), high unemployment rates (Slater *et al.*, 2014), declining enrolments (Slater *et al.*, 2014) and increasing numbers of ethnic minorities and immigrants moving into the community (Szeto, 2014). Often, to maintain adequate student enrolment, urban principals must overcome the school's history of failure by convincing parents that the school will meet their expectations (Gurr *et al.*, 2014; Qian, 2013; Slater *et al.*, 2014; Szeto, 2014). These schools tend to be situated in communities with high crime rates and with families that have been dislocated because of natural disasters, political unrest and inability to pay the rent (Rincones, 2012; Sharvashidze and Bryant, 2014; Slater *et al.*, 2014).

School context

The resources and infrastructure, leadership and teaching staff, and students in urban schools are quite different from those in suburban and rural schools. For example, the working conditions in schools affect recruiting and the hiring of urban school teachers. Teachers in high poverty urban schools tend to have fewer instructional resources at their disposal and have less control over the curriculum than teachers in high poverty rural schools (Chung, 2005; National Center for Education Statistics, 1996). Similarly, the educational infrastructure of urban education can be problematic, as evidenced by highly politicised school boards, cumbersome central office bureaucracies, incoherent instructional practices, inadequate data management systems and resources, and decaying buildings (Haberman, n.d.; Jacob, 2007; National Center for Education Statistics (NCES), 2006). As a result, teachers teaching outside their licensure area, high absenteeism, low morale and constant turnover are common occurrences (Barnett and Stevenson, 2015; Duke 2008, 2012b; Picus *et al.*, 2005).

Finally, leadership turnover, especially of superintendents and principals, creates instability and inconsistent programme implementation (Haberman, n.d.). Filling principal vacancies in urban schools is difficult; there are substantially fewer applications for these positions than in suburban and rural schools (The New Teacher Project, 2006). Compounding this recruitment problem, many principal vacancies occur just before the beginning of the school year, making it difficult to recruit and select high-quality candidates. Districts also report not having adequate pools of qualified assistant principals capable of filling principal vacancies (The New Teacher Project, 2006).

The ISLDN studies capture the realities of urban school teachers, which are particularly evident in developing countries. For example, in the Republic of Georgia, schools may be staffed with teachers who have completed formal training and are certified by the ministry; however, other teachers may be hired locally, having no formal preparation for the job (Sharvashidze and Bryant, 2014). This situation results in a bifurcated teaching staff, one that is committed to the future educational advancement of students, the other far less so. In addition, these teachers are paid low wages and receive no health insurance or retirement packages.

Finally, demographic trends of urban school students reveal:

- Large percentages do not reach expected levels of achievement.
- High numbers of truancies, suspensions and dropouts.
- Low attendance and graduation rates.
- High numbers of minorities and English Language Learners (Barnett and Stevenson, 2015).

Furthermore, ethnic and language differences among the student population can strain the instructional resources of the school. In some of the urban schools we studied, up to 100 per cent of the students were from economically disadvantaged and Latina/o families, 75 per cent were at risk of dropping out of school and almost 50 per cent had limited English proficiency skills (Medina *et al.*, 2014). Immigration rates, even in developed countries like Hong Kong, were up to 70 per cent of the school's population (Szeto, 2014). Students in Costa Rican schools were in the lowest quartile of academic performance (Slater *et al.*, 2014).

The challenges facing urban schools

As suggested above, the contextual factors influencing urban schools and communities pose monumental problems for system- and campus-level leaders. Taken together, these challenges can be cultural, social or structural (Barnett and Stevenson, 2015). A major cultural challenge is when educators believe that urban students are incapable of learning academic content and social skills (referred to as 'deficit thinking') because of their social circumstances and family upbringing. They sense parents are less likely to support the school's efforts to educate their children, and are not motivated to provide assistance at home (O'Conner and Fernandez, 2006). Many of these beliefs are rooted in negative stereotypes about race and class, leading teachers and administrators to perceive that these students have learning deficiencies as well as behavioural and emotional problems. The ISLDN studies revealed the resistance principals experienced from teachers unwilling to try new ideas or work with low-performing students (Norberg *et al.*, 2014).

Urban schools and communities also are confronted with myriad social challenges that affect parents' abilities to support their families and students' motivation to attend school. Resource needs are extremely critical given the high levels of poverty, mobility, homelessness, drug abuse and English Language Learners (Duke 2008, 2012b; Picus *et al.*, 2005). These social issues translate into problems for many students, including health problems, teenage pregnancy, dropouts, absenteeism, disciplinary problems and unemployment (Ahram *et al.*, n.d.; National Center for Education Statistics, 1996, 2006).

Finally, an under-resourced and fragile infrastructure accounts for structural challenges in urban schools. Many urban systems have dilapidated and unsafe buildings, inefficient data-management systems, soaring bureaucracies and inadequate resources for school improvement, professional development and personnel management (Haberman, n.d.; Jacob, 2007; NCES, 2006). Consequently, recruiting and retaining quality teachers is a constant challenge. They may be asked to teach courses outside their certification areas, morale can suffer and turnover rates can run high. Similar challenges occur with administrators. Flaws in matching candidates to desired criteria and lack of staff to manage principal recruitment and selection compromise hiring decisions (The New Teacher Project, 2006). These high turnover rates of teachers and administrators can have serious effects on student performance. Studies indicate that when principals leave, student achievement suffers for the next two years (Miller, 2013) and when teacher turnover occurs, especially in schools with low-performing African American students, performance in language arts and maths decreases (Ronfeldt *et al.*, 2011).

Strategies used by urban principals

An empirical literature base is emerging that captures the strategies urban principals are using to combat issues associated with the challenging macro and micro contexts of their schools. Two specific literature sources inform our discussion: (1) school turnaround leadership and (2) ISLDN studies. We conclude the section by summarising the rationale underlying the actions of urban school leaders working in these contexts.

Turnaround schools

In the 1990s, efforts to improve high-need, low-performing schools fuelled the school turnaround movement (Duke, 2012b). There are few empirical studies of turnaround leadership; however, preliminary results demonstrate what these leaders are doing to improve their schools' performance. Summarised below are the initial and ongoing strategies they use in dealing with teachers and the programmes and procedures they establish. We conclude by describing the effects leaders who participate in turnaround leadership preparation programmes are having on their schools.

Approaches with teachers

Often turnaround school leaders have been given a mandate to alter the performance of teachers and students as quickly as possible, being urged to achieve 'quick and dramatic' results (Duke, 2012b, p. 9). In their desire for immediate impact, these school leaders often take a very direct or authoritarian approach by challenging the status quo, demanding teachers embrace the school's new direction, and forcing recalcitrant teachers to leave the school (Hollar, 2004). Evidence also shows that as positive results occur, school leaders relinquish this direct leadership style, becoming more democratic and collaborative with their staff (Ylimaki *et al.*, 2014). Examples of increasing teachers' decision-making include encouraging teacher-directed professional development, establishing teacher-led committees, allowing teachers to set their own improvement goals, increasing teachers' responsibility for data analysis and curriculum alignment, and scheduling common planning time for teachers (Duke, 2008, 2012a, 2012b; Halford, 1996).

Turnaround leaders also work diligently with teachers to:

- Increase their problem-solving capacities (Chenoweth and Theokas, 2013).
- Develop their commitment to instructional improvement (Herman *et al.*, 2008).
- Examine their beliefs about teaching and learning, increase instructional time for low-performing students, employ new grouping approaches for students, create orderly learning environments, and use different data sources for monitoring student progress (Duke, 2004).
- Redesign the school organisation around learning, collaboration and capacity building (Ylimaki *et al.*, 2014).
- Support, retain and develop effective instructors (Duke, 2014; Klar and Brewer, 2013).

Programmes and procedures

In addition to working directly with teachers to alter their attitudes and teaching strategies, turnaround principals promote new programmes and procedures. One of the driving philosophies of turnaround principals is the notion of 'quick wins' by accomplishing tangible improvements early in the process (Herman *et al.*, 2008). In some cases, they look outside the school by restructuring school governance to foster greater local community involvement and ownership (Halford, 1996), increasing parental involvement and choice (Duke, 2012a, 2012b), and working with local faith-based organisation leaders to promote programmes (Klar and Brewer, 2013). In other cases, they implement procedures and processes aimed at increasing classroom processes and effectiveness. Examples include reducing class size (Halford, 1996), maximising instructional time (Chenoweth and Theokas, 2013), creating clear and consistent daily schedules (Duke, 2008), extending the school day (Duke, 2012b), instituting cross-grade ability grouping (Duke, 2012a), implementing single-gender programmes (Klar and Brewer, 2013), eliminating 'pull-out' programmes in favour of 'push-in' programmes (Duke, 2012a), developing new approaches to school discipline (Duke, 2008) and targeting interventions on low-achieving students (Duke, 2008). Finally, they institute and support instructional interventions, such as targeted literacy and numeracy programmes (Duke, 2008), interim and benchmark testing (Duke, 2012b), Advancement Via Individual Determination (AVID) programmes (Klar and Brewer, 2013), culturally responsive teaching practices (Ylimaki *et al.*, 2014) and STEM and project-based learning (Duke, 2014).

Turnaround leadership preparation and effects

Recently, a variety of leadership development programmes in the United States has surfaced to support aspiring and practising school leaders to work in high-need, low-performing schools. For example, the Virginia School Turnaround Specialist Program (VSTSP) has been operating for a decade, offering professional learning experiences and coaching for Virginia principals leading high-need schools (Duke, 2012b). In addition, the Florida Turnaround Leaders Program (FTLP) identifies teacher leaders with the potential to become turnaround specialists by assigning four-person teams to work in a low-performing school for six months followed by a one-semester internship in an under-achieving school (Duke, 2014). Furthermore, the Texas Education Agency (2013) established the Texas Turnaround Leadership Academy (TTLA) to build the capacities of schools and districts to identify qualified turnaround specialists, establish improvement strategies for underperforming campuses, and collaborate with other schools engaged in turnaround initiatives. Finally, the state of Arizona has funded the Turnaround Leadership Development Project (TLDP) to encourage school-based teams to improve student performance in underperforming and culturally diverse schools (Ylimaki *et al.*, 2014).

Although few turnaround schools receiving school improvement grants from the U.S. Department of Education demonstrate substantial gains in reading and maths (Brinson *et al.*, 2008; Klein, 2012), emerging evidence suggests that those principals and teachers participating in professional development programmes are having a positive effect on their schools. For instance, 60 per cent of schools where principals participated in the Virginia STSP demonstrated at least a 10 per cent increase in reading proficiency and over 50 per cent demonstrated at least a 10 per cent improvement in maths performance (Harriman, 2008). In addition, a recent study conducted with teams participating in the Arizona TLDP revealed promising findings (Ylimaki *et al.*, 2014). Along with discovering that campuses receiving district-level support implemented TLDP content more quickly, they found that teams involved in the project increased their capacity to overcome deficit thinking and increase collaboration, their schools' state assessment and letter grades improved, and professional learning communities evolved to develop culturally responsive organisational capacity and school improvement.

ISLDN studies

The studies of social justice leaders in high-need schools conducted by ISLDN researchers confirm and expand the findings from research conducted on turnaround school leaders. We discovered four trends in how these leaders strive to combat the educational, social and political challenges they encounter. First, many school leaders sought to alter the school's vision and culture. Examples include clarifying and communicating desired values and performance expectations (Gu and Johansson, 2012; Hipp and Baran, 2013), developing integrated intervention plans using comprehensive data collection and decision-making processes (Drysdale *et al.*, 2012) and being organised and planning thoughtfully (Notman, 2012). As was discovered with turnaround leaders, teachers who were unable or unwilling to meet new performance expectations were relocated to other schools (Wildy and Clarke, 2012).

Second, gaining an understanding of the factors affecting the community context, especially the values and assets of parents and community organisations, was an important aspect of these principals' actions. They were well aware of the chronic problems facing families living in poverty, such as lack of food and healthcare services (Gurr *et al.*, 2014; Medina *et al.*, 2014; Richardson and Sauers, 2014). Attempting to overcome these challenges, principals utilised school resources to purchase food for students, worked with local agencies to provide medical, social and educational services, organised multicultural activities for parents and community members, and provided job training for disabled adults (Richardson and Sauers, 2014; Szeto, 2014; Wildy and Clarke, 2012). To gain greater parental involvement, some schools established formal agreements with parents, requiring them to monitor their children's homework assignments, attend conferences with teachers and provide transportation (Hipp and Baran, 2013). Communities gained a renewed sense of hope and commitment when leaders revitalised the school grounds (Sharvashidze and Bryant, 2014) and acknowledged how the school was overcoming previous failures and inefficiencies (Drysdale *et al.*, 2012; Qian, 2013). In extreme cases, principals and teachers were forced to deal with periodic traumatic events that disrupted their local communities, such as illnesses (e.g. the SARS crisis), student suicides or natural disasters (Notman, 2012; Szeto, 2014).

Third, principals sought to utilise teachers' expertise and to develop their capacity (Gurr *et al.*, 2014). This occurred by ensuring that leadership team meetings allowed opportunities for professional learning and sharing as well as conducting leadership development sessions for teachers and staff members (Drysdale *et al.*, 2012). Other principals recognised the value of engaging teachers in decision making by involving them in determining areas for improvement, planning and implementing goals, and reviewing progress (Hipp and Baran, 2013). One Australian principal noted that when he commenced his tenure, about 30 per cent of teachers were assuming responsibilities outside the classroom, but it grew to nearly 80 per cent (Gurr *et al.*, 2014). In understanding the importance of relationship building, another Australian principal commented: 'I am best at getting along with people. I think my greatest success here has been to build good relationships among teachers, throughout the community, and between all the students' (Wildy and Clarke, 2012, p. 26).

Finally, our case studies revealed concentrated efforts by principals to improve and monitor the teaching and learning process in their schools (Gu and Johansson, 2012; Hipp and Baran, 2013; Notman, 2012). Not only did they strive to retain talented teachers, but they also engaged teachers in redesigning classroom assignments across the entire curriculum (Gurr *et al.*, 2014; Szeto, 2014). In some instances, they utilised externally mandated resources to stimulate reform in their schools (Rincones, 2012). Despite resistance from teachers to these new reforms, principals realised these governmental resources allowed them to provide instructional support beyond what their local communities could afford. In other cases, they took advantage of local needs and interests in designing the curriculum. For example, a Costa Rican principal developed art, music and computer video-game programs to have students see the school as a place where their talents and interests could be applied (Slater *et al.*, 2014). In a similar vein, an Australian principal used the students' and community's love of art by displaying murals and pictures around the school, designing maths lessons to incorporate artistic drawings, and creating an art gallery to display students' work (Wildy and Clarke, 2012).

Rationale

The studies conducted by the ISLDN teams reveal the underlying motivation and rationale leaders employ in working in such challenging circumstances. These fall into four categories: (1) student-centred; (2) community-centered; (3) political astuteness, and (4) life experiences.

Student-centred

First, and most significantly, principals had an unwavering commitment to provide better life chances for the students who enter their schools' doors. They strove to give a voice to students by treating them as individuals, ignoring their past mistakes and providing them with learning opportunities they had not previously experienced (Richardson and Sauers, 2014; Slater *et al.*, 2014). Their compassion for students is evident in these comments from around the world:

> I think about equality, opportunities, human rights, dignity for all, and trying to level the playing field. I think one cannot help but live here in India and not question, why me? Why do I have these opportunities in life? Why not this other person? (Indian principal).
>
> (Richardson and Sauers, 2014, p. 107)

> I came at being a social justice leader as I did as a Mum . . . I run the school as I run my family . . . I believe in the young people . . . they come first . . . They are not scared of me . . . they are scared of me disapproving of what they have done. [However,] I am not a Mum to the adults . . . I am a hard-nosed professional (English principal).
>
> (Slater *et al.*, 2014, p. 114)

> Every person has a value, not only to themselves but to the world. You never know which student might be that one student that ends up making a difference. Taking the time to figure out those individual needs and taking the time to get to know how to fulfill those needs makes a tremendous

difference. It is important that we maximise our resources. Our resources are our kids (Swedish principal).

(Norberg *et al.*, 2014, p. 103)

But a kid who's damaged, who's been sexually abused, who's been removed from his parents, where his father has walked out of his life, where he has witnessed a lot of violence, physical and verbal, where he is anxious and depressed – no amount of very effective teaching will bring that child to a point where they can socialise and engage in purposeful engagement in society. They need therapy, and it's not available (New Zealand principal).

(Notman, 2012, p. 5)

Community-centred

Principals worked tirelessly to learn more about the values and challenges of the parents and citizens in their communities. They were highly visible in order to better understand the physical, economic, social and cultural aspects of the environment. This first-hand knowledge allowed them to reconnect with communities that may have lost confidence in the school, seek additional resources to address the community's needs, and advocate community values within the school environment and curriculum. They viewed community values and culture as an asset, rather than a liability to the school. Their advocacy for communities is succinctly expressed by two of these principals:

Expectations have to be high for everyone, but accountability needs to be realistic. I cannot spend my money just on teachers, I have to spend it on social support, enforcement officers, personal tutors and the like (English principal).

(Slater *et al.*, 2014, p. 114)

As a principal, I feel the pain and the struggles that the families are going through. So, when the parent calls you and says "My car is broken in the driveway, I need to get my child to school," I'll put them in my car and I'm going to bring them to school. Some parents do not have money to have their children's uniform, some do not have money for electricity and their children cannot do homework (American principal).

(Medina *et al.*, 2014, p. 95)

Political astuteness

These school leaders were aware of the restrictions and problems associated with external state and federal policies; however, they were quite adept at using policy to their advantage, realising how these types of resources supported their efforts beyond what was available at the local level. For instance, many Mexican principals took advantage of government reforms, including competency-based teaching practices, extended-day programmes, site-based/community participatory decision making, and programmes to reduce school violence (Rincones, 2012). Not only were principals aware that school improvement takes time and there will be setbacks, but they also recognised that they need to gain confidence from system leaders to enact their programmes (Gurr *et al.*, 2014). Some of their responses underscore the importance of being politically aware and active:

> I belong to the union myself; however, that does not give me any privileges for not wanting to do my job. It is necessary to know the laws that apply to the worker in education and counter their arguments in an informed way. Teachers take advantage of that. I did not let that happen (Mexican principal).
>
> (Rincones, 2012, p. 13)

> First, I would tell the world to tell the new government of Georgia to finish the good beginnings of the previous government and provide internet to the villages like Karajala. They already have a new, well-equipped school building, but have no access to internet, to be integrated to the rest of Georgia and the world through the social networks and/or other internet facilities (Republic of Georgia principal).
>
> (Sharvashidze and Bryant, 2014, p. 99)

Life experiences

Finally, principals' commitment to leading urban school reform was based on a host of life experiences. Becoming a relentless advocate for students and communities with many social, medical and emotional needs is not something that can be easily taught to school leaders. Clearly, the demands of the principalship have increased in recent years and perseverance, tenacity, self-belief and moral purpose are needed to maintain the school's direction (Fenwick, 2000; Hall *et al.*, 2003; Stevenson, 2006). The ISLDN research suggested that such significant life experiences as their religious upbringing and having experienced disadvantaged conditions had strong effects on principals' tenacity and devotion to their teachers, students and communities. The words of three of them highlight the important life experiences that shaped their commitment to underprivileged youth:

> Growing up in an at-risk home, but hanging around with a friend who had money and a father who exposed me to other areas, other than I was exposed to when I was growing up, helped me to broaden my vocabulary and allowed me to learn new things. I can pay attention to those kids with the same background as I had and say to them that regardless of where you come from, you actually have the ability to be anything that you want (Swedish principal).
>
> (Norberg *et al.*, 2014, p. 104)

> As a Latina leader, I work for restorative justice because we had a difficult road growing up and in our education. We will never forget the struggles we had within our families (American principal).
>
> (Medina *et al.*, 2014, p. 95)

> Like most values, it is established through your parents. I had a tremendous example through my father, mother, grandfather, and immediate family about how to treat people. For example, racism was inexcusable (American principal).
>
> (Norberg *et al.*, 2014, p. 103)

Conceptualisations of effective urban school leadership

The research we have presented from the broad range of projects conducted in the ISLDN initiative highlights the complex and nuanced ways in which contexts shape the experiences and practices of school leaders. This is clearly an iterative relationship whereby school leaders make a difference in their context, but they too are shaped by their context. Powerful factors, working at different levels, can both help and hinder school leaders who seek to pursue socially just objectives in areas of high need. In order to better understand how particular factors can shape leadership practices in different ways colleagues in the ISLDN have developed a model depicting how macro and micro factors have an impact on school leadership. The model presented here remains a 'work in progress'. It seeks to build on previous iterations (Angelle *et al.*, forthcoming; Barnett and Stevenson, 2015; Dimmock *et al.*, 2005) and is likely to be developed further as the project's growing evidence base allows the framework to be refined and finessed.

The framework can be presented visually in the following figure:

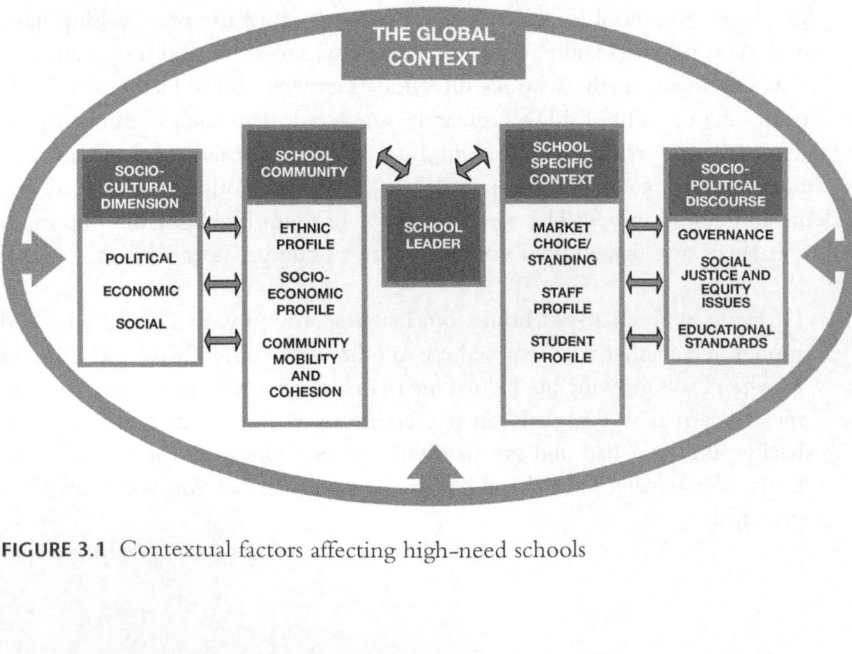

FIGURE 3.1 Contextual factors affecting high-need schools

The framework captures the actions and practices of school leaders as being nested within a set of micro and macro factors, although we do not see a neat and tidy distinction between these descriptors. While the notion of levels or tiers can be superficially attractive, it is important to see the layers of the framework as porous. For our purposes, we have chosen to work from the outside in, deliberately seeking to demonstrate how the wider contextual factors shape leadership practices. We begin by acknowledging the importance of the global context. Global institutions and global discourses frame education as never before. Globalisation, based as it is on a rapidly spreading 'fast capitalism' (Gee and Lankshear, 1995) generates intense pressures on schooling, and it is important to recognise how these play out in very common ways across extremely diverse contexts. However, the homogenising pressures of globalisation are tempered by other factors that operate at the national level – powerful differences exist at the level of the nation state. Globalising influences may have diminished the power of the nation state, but the nation state remains a powerful shaper of contexts (Rizvi and Lingard, 2010).

Within the framework, we distinguish at this level between a range of social cultural dimensions that act as descriptors of distinguishing national features, and a set of socio-political discourses that frame the debates within which national policies are developed. To illustrate the importance of these factors with a single example of each highlights how they can shape school leadership contexts in very different ways. For instance, the framework identifies a country's economic profile as a central socio-cultural dimension. Clearly, an important issue here is the level of national income, but other factors are also important. Is the economy growing or declining? If there is decline, is this short term or long term? Such factors inevitably shape contexts because not only do levels (and the distribution) of national income have an impact on levels of need, but they also shape the extent to which resources might be brought to bear on social problems.

Several ISLDN projects have illustrated graphically how school leadership contexts have been shaped decisively by the aftershocks of the economic crisis and the austerity policies that followed in its wake (Angelle, 2012; Potter, 2012). An illustration of how socio-political discourses vary across nation states can be seen by examining how national governments approach issues of social justice and equity. The language of social justice can often be described as a global discourse in which all are committed to the principle. However, the precise nature of this looks different in different contexts and is perhaps best illustrated by approaches to inequality.

It is very apparent that attitudes to inequality can vary significantly between countries and this clearly has implications for shaping the policy contexts in which school leaders operate. In recent years the social democratic welfarism associated with Nordic and Scandinavian countries has been challenged, but as the ISLDN studies illustrate, the commitments to social solidarity remain relatively strong (Norberg *et al.*, 2014; Risku, 2012). This can be contrasted with more market-driven societies in which school leaders are urged to 'close the gap' by politicians who preside over ever-widening gaps in their own society. In our view, it is impossible to understand how school leaders in challenging urban contexts do their work, without understanding how that work is shaped by these factors. Equally important, it is necessary to recognise how these factors are framed differently in different contexts.

As at the macro-level, so too is there a corresponding set of factors that help us to understand the parameters in which school leaders function. Research presented in this chapter points to the importance of recognising the profile of a school's local community, and how this is formed in terms of class and ethnicity factors. Some of the studies also point to a specific set of issues relating to 'turbulent' communities, whereby population movements within the community are significant. Such factors not only present very significant challenges, but they also determine particular types of responses by school leaders. However, the studies considered in this chapter highlight that it is not enough to look at the community in which a school is located. Rather, it is necessary to look at the school as a community. For example, in some cases the student profile in a school may not reflect that of the school's immediate local community. This is most likely in contexts where so-called 'choice' policies create situations where a school's intake is increasingly stratified along class and racial lines. Our argument in this chapter is that these factors have a powerful impact on the choices and actions that school leaders can make and take when they seek to lead in challenging urban contexts. A school leader in a poor, but stable local community without competition from neighbouring schools, can act in quite different ways to a school leader in a poor and unsettled local community in which neighbouring schools seek to select and reject the students they either want or do not want.

The framework therefore acts as heuristic device to help us better understand the factors that shape the actions and practices of school leaders. There can be no question that leaders have significant agency in their work, and that their actions are capable of making a real difference to the life chances of individual students. However, it is important to develop a much more comprehensive and nuanced analysis of how contextual factors at both the macro and micro levels shape leadership behaviours. Such a framework not only helps us understand how contextual factors can both help and hinder school leaders in their work, but also begins to explain the important and significant differences we see between how school leadership is practised in different national contexts.

References

Ahram, R., Stembridge, A., Fergus, E. and Noguera, P. (n.d.). Framing urban school challenges: The problems to examine when implementing response to intervention. *RTI Action Network*. Washington, DC: National Center for Learning Disabilities.

Angelle, P. (2012). ISLDN project on social justice leadership: USA case study findings. Paper presented at the University Council for Educational Administration Convention, Denver, CO.

Angelle, P., Morrison, M. and Stevenson, H. (forthcoming). 'Doing' social justice leadership: Connecting the macro and micro contexts of schooling. In D. Armstrong and J. Ryan (eds). *Working (with/out) the system: Educational leadership, micropolitics and social justice*. Charlotte, NC: Information Age Publishing.

Arar, K. (2014). Principals' and teachers' perceptions of teacher evaluation and their implications in Arab schools in Israel. In A. J. Bowers, A. R. Shoho and B. G. Barnett (eds). *Using data in schools to inform leadership and decision making* (pp. 181–203). Charlotte, NC: Information Age Publishing.

Barnett B. and Stevenson, H. (2015). International perspectives in urban educational leadership: Social justice leadership and high-need schools. In M. Khalifa, N. W. Arnold, A. F. Osanloo and C. M. Grant (eds). *Handbook of urban educational leadership* (pp. 518–531). Lanham, MD: Rowman & Littlefield.

Brinson, D., Kowal, J. and Hassel, B. C. (2008). *School turnarounds: Actions and results.* New York: Public Impact Center on Innovation and Improvement, Academic Development Institute.

Chenoweth, K. and Theokas, C. (2013). How high-poverty schools are getting it done. *Educational Leadership,* 70(7), 56–59.

Chung, C. and Ngan, M. Y. (2002). From rooftop to millennium: The development of primary schools in Hong Kong since 1945. *New Horizons in Education*, 46, 24–32.

Chung, D. (2005). *Analysis of urban schools.* Retrieved from: http://sitemaker.umich.edu/chung.356/urban_education_

Dimmock, C., Stevenson, H., Bignold, B., Shah, S. and Middlewood, D. (2005). *Effective leadership in multi-ethnic schools: Part 2: School community perspectives and their leadership implications.* University of Leicester, Centre for Educational Leadership and Management. Nottingham: National College for School Leadership.

Drysdale, L., Gurr, D. and Villalobos, M. H. (2012). Leading the formation and transformation of Hume Secondary College. Paper presented at the annual convention of the University Council for Educational Administration, Denver, CO.

Duke, D. L. (2004). The turnaround principal: High-stakes leadership. *Principal,* 84(1), 12–23.

Duke, D. L. (2008). *The little school system that could: Transforming a city school district.* Albany, NY: State University of New York Press.

Duke, D. L. (2012a). Raising test scores was the easy part: A case study of the third year of school turnaround. Paper presented at the annual convention of the University Council for Educational Administration, Denver, CO.

Duke, D. L. (2012b). Tinkering and turnarounds: Understanding the contemporary campaign to improve low-performing schools. *Journal of Education for Students Placed at Risk,* 17, 9–24.

Duke, D. L. (2014). A bold approach to developing leaders for low-performing schools. *Management in Education,* 28(3), 80–85.

Fenwick, L. T. (2000). *The principal shortage: Who will lead?* Cambridge, MA: Harvard Principals' Center.

Gee, J. P. and Lankshear, C. (1995). The new work order: Critical language awareness and 'fast capitalism' texts. *Discourse: Studies in the Cultural Politics of Education,* 16(1), 5–19.

Gu, Q. and Johansson, O. (2012). Sustaining school performance: School contexts matter. Paper presented at the annual convention of the University Council for Educational Administration, Denver, CO.

Gunter, H. M. (2011). *The state and education policy: The Academies Programme.* London: Continuum.

Gunter, H. M. and Fitzgerald, T. (2013). New public management and the modernisation of education systems 1. *Journal of Educational Administration and History,* 45(3), 213–219.

Gurr, D., Drysdale, L., Clarke, S. and Wildy, H. (2014). High-need schools in Australia: The leadership of two principals. *Management in Education,* 28(3), 86–90.

Haberman, M. (n.d.). *Urban education – Students and structure, special challenges, characteristics of successful urban programs.* Retrieved from: http://education.stateuniversity.com/pages/2524/Urban-Education.html

Halford, J. M. (1996, Summer). Policies of promise. *ASCD Information Brief*, 5, 1–6.

Hall, G. E., Berg, J. H. and Barnett, B. (2003). Beginning principal studies in America: What have we studied what have we learned. Paper presented at the annual meeting of the American Educational Research Association, Chicago.

Harriman, D. (2008). *University of Virginia school turnaround report*. Retrieved from: www.darden.virginia.edu/web/uploadedFiles/Darden/Darden_Curry_PLE/UVA_School_Turnaround/UVASTSPAnnualReport2008_Excerpts.pdf

Herman, R., Dawson, P., Dee, T., Greene, J., Maynard, R. and Redding, S. (2008). *Turning around chronically low-performing schools*. Washington, DC: Institute for Education Sciences, US Department of Education.

Higham, R., Hopkins, D. and Mathews, P. (2009). *System leadership in practice*. Maidenhead: Open University Press/McGraw-Hill.

Hipp, K.K. and Baran, M.L. (2013). Leadership for new schools: A glimmer of hope in urban schools. Paper presented at the annual meeting of the American Educational Research Association, San Francisco, CA.

Hollar, C. (2004). The principal as CEO. *Principal*, 84(1), 42–44.

Jacob, B.A. (2007). The challenge of staffing urban schools with effective teachers. *The Future of Children*, 17(1), 129–153.

Klar, H. W. and Brewer, C. A. (2013). Successful leadership in high-needs schools: An examination of core leadership practices enacted in challenging contexts. *Educational Administration Quarterly*, 49(5), 768–808.

Klein, A. (2012). Turnaround momentum still fragile. *Education Week*, 31(28), 18–21.

Lee, M. and Hallinger, P. (2012). National contexts influencing principals' time use and allocation: Economic development, societal culture, and educational system. *School Effectiveness and School Improvement*, 23(4), 461–482.

Medina, V., Martinez, G., Murakami, E. T., Rodriguez, M. and Hernandez, F. (2014). Principals' perceptions from within: Leadership in high-need schools in the USA. *Management in Education*, 28(3), 91–96.

Miller, A. (2013). Principal turnover and student achievement. *Economics of Education Review*, 36, 60–72.

National Center for Education Statistics (1996). *Urban Schools: The challenge of location and poverty*. Washington, DC: United States Department of Education.

National Center for Education Statistics (NCES) (2006). *Characteristics of schools, districts, teachers, principals, and school libraries in the United States, 2003–04, schools and staffing report*. Washington, DC: United States Department of Education.

New Teacher Project, The (2006). *Improved principal hiring: The New Teacher Project's findings and recommendations for urban schools*. Brooklyn, NY: Author.

Norberg, K., Arlestig, H. and Angelle, P. S. (2014). Global conversations about social justice: The Swedish-US example. *Management in Education*, 28(3), 101–105.

Notman, R. (2012). ISLDN project on high-need schools: New Zealand case study findings. Paper presented at the annual convention of the University Council for Educational Administration, Denver, CO.

O'Conner, C. and Fernandez, S. D. (2006). Race, class, and disproportionality: Reevaluating the relationship between poverty and school education placement. *Educational Researcher*, 35(6), 6–11.

Pan, H. W. (2012). *Instructional leadership in East Asian schools*. Presentation at the Asia Pacific Centre for Leadership and Change Asia Leadership Roundtable, Ho Chi Minh City, Vietnam.

Picus, L. O., Marion, S. F., Calvo, N. and Glenn, W. J. (2005). Understanding the relationship between student achievement and the quality of educational facilities: Evidence from Wyoming. *Peabody Journal of Education*, 80(3), 71–95.

Potter, I. (2012). ISLDN project on social justice leadership: England case study findings. Paper presented at the University Council for Educational Administration Convention, Denver, CO.

Qian, H. (2013). 'Ordinary' schools in Shanghai: How principals make a difference. Paper presented at the annual conference of the British Educational Leadership, Management and Administration Society, Edinburgh, Scotland.

Richardson, J. W. and Sauers, N. J. (2014). Social justice in India: Perspectives from school leaders in diverse contexts. *Management in Education*, 28(3), 106–109.

Rincones, R. (2012). International perspectives on 'high need schools': Implications for leadership preparation and development. Paper presented at the annual convention of the University Council for Educational Administration, Denver, CO.

Risku, M. (2012). ISLDN project on social justice leadership: Finland case study findings. Paper presented at the University Council for Educational Administration Convention, Denver, CO.

Rizvi, F. and Lingard, B. (2010). *Globalizing education policy*. London: Routledge.

Ronfeldt, M., Lankford, H., Loeb, S. and Wyckoff, J. (2011). *How teacher turnover harms student achievement*. Cambridge, MA: National Bureau of Economic Research.

Sharvashidze, N. and Bryant, M. (2014). A high-need Azeri school: A Georgian perspective. *Management in Education*, 28(3), 97–100.

Slater, C., Potter, I., Torres, N. and Briceno, F. (2014). Understanding social justice leadership: An international exploration of the perspectives of two leaders in Costa Rica and England. *Management in Education*, 28(3), 110–115.

Stevenson, H. (2006). Moving towards, into and through principalship: Developing a framework for researching the career trajectories of school leaders. *Journal of Educational Administration*, 44(4), 408–420.

Sweeting, A. (1995). Educational policy in a time of transition: The case of Hong Kong. *Research Papers in Education*, 10(1), 101–129.

Szeto, E. (2014). From recipient to contributor: The story of a social justice leader in a Hong Kong primary school. *Management in Education*, 28(3), 116–119.

Texas Education Agency (2013). *Texas Turnaround Leadership Academy*. Retrieved from: www.texasturnaround.net/about-us.html

U.S. Census Bureau (2010). *The Hispanic population: 2010*. Retrieved from: www.census.gov/prod/cen2010/briefs/c2010br-04.pdf

Walker, A. (2004). Constitution and culture: Exploring the deep leadership structures of Hong Kong schools. *Discourse: Studies in the Cultural Politics of Education*, 25(1), 75–94.

Walker, A., Hu, R. and Qian, H. Y. (2012). Principal leadership in China: An initial review. *School Effectiveness and School Improvement*, 23(4), 369–399.

Wildy, H. and Clarke, S. (2012). At the edge of the silent centre: An Australian principal's reflections on leading an isolated school. Paper presented at the annual convention of the University Council for Educational Administration, Denver, CO.

World Health Organization (2014). *Urban population growth*. Retrieved from: www.who.int/gho/urban_health/situation_trends/urban_population_growth_text/en/

Ylimaki, R. M., Brunderman, L., Bennett, J. V. and Dugan, T. (2014). Developing Arizona turnaround leaders to build high-capacity schools in the midst of accountability pressures and changing demographics. *Leadership and Policy in Schools*, 13(1), 28–60.

4

SMALL RURAL SCHOOL LEADERSHIP

Creating opportunity through collaboration

Karen Starr

Introduction

Leading a small rural school presents specific challenges for principals: there are fewer people to perform as many tasks as exist in larger schools; teaching consumes a greater percentage of leaders' time in multigrade, mixed-ability classes; there is often limited or no access to resources that are taken for granted elsewhere; and there is no dilution of stakeholder expectations regarding school improvement, policy accountability or student achievement outcomes. Small rural school leadership is complex, diverse and labour-intensive and the exigencies of life in small rural communities create unconventional leadership circumstances. Daunting as this may sound, many principals revel in small rural school settings, achieving success and professional enjoyment due in large part to the ways in which they address these particular challenges. They have recast contextual challenges as opportunities, which is the focus of this chapter.

Definitions

There are contested views about what constitutes a small school and what constitutes rurality, with various agencies and levels of the Australian government using differing definitions and criteria (Coladarci, 2007; HREOC, 2000). For the purposes of this chapter, definitions from the Department of Education and Early Childhood Development in Victoria, Australia, have been adopted. 'Rural' schools are those 70 kilometres or more from Melbourne, the state capital, or 25 kilometres from a regional centre with a population of 10,000 or more. 'Small' schools have an enrolment of no more than 100 students.

There are also contested views and perceptions about 'leadership' (Starr, 2014). Here, it is acknowledged that school leadership is distributed and enacted by many people and at all levels within and outside small rural schools. However, the study reported in this chapter focused specifically on the principalship.

The research

The findings discussed in this chapter arose from a three-year professional learning and research programme for principals of small rural schools funded by the Department of Education and Early Childhood Development in Victoria, Australia. The programme focused on the development of teamwork, leadership capacity-building, and cross-school, school-community alliances to bring about change for the benefit of schools, students and school leadership. Up to 90 principals participated each year in a series of residential forums, supported by recently retired small rural school principals who acted as 'critical friends' or mentors, collaborating with tertiary personnel and an advocacy team for rural education, with financial, collegial and professional support and assistance from the Department of Education and Early Childhood Development (Starr, 2009a, 2009b). A dearth of information on the subject of small rural school leadership in Victoria in the context of globalisation provided a compelling research void that required redress.

The research was an exercise in grounded theory building (Glaser and Strauss, 1967). In this approach, theory is not derived deductively but emerges from the data through an inductive process whereby emerging research insights are analysed and continually tested, producing further evidence and new theoretical insights. The research is data-driven rather than theory-driven. This iterative process of developing claims and interpretations determines its own end point when new data does not reveal any further insights but confirms theoretical elements that have already been identified (Punch, 1998).

Grounded theory is responsive to research situations and the people in it, supporting examination of individual standpoint, complex contexts, while considering the inextricability of macro, meso and micro connections, influences and consequences simultaneously (Corbin and Strauss, 2008). Real-life experience is taken as a starting point that connects individual agents to the structural, the social and the historical. In other words, large-scale social structures affect tangible realities that are inseparable from contextualised practice or from the historicity of the period (Ball, 1994). In this case, micro-level experience in the small rural school is where the effects of local, systemic, national and global, political, economic and social decisions and events have an impact in ways that differ from effects in other contexts. N-Vivo qualitative data software aggregated emergent themes, with initial data informing subsequent questions and forum discussions. Research data were shared with participants to confirm key findings and interpretations (Starr and White, 2009).

The context: globalisation and education policy

For more than three decades Australian educational provision and administration have changed continually through economic structural reforms at state and federal levels in response to globalisation. Resultant reforms have altered the purposes, nature and scope of government departments/agencies, as public policy and government procedures align more closely with the free market and neoliberal policy foundations (Apple, 2006). Education is bound up with the nation state's economic exigencies emanating from capitalist modes of production, and their maintenance and protection in globalising deregulated markets. Valorised are the precepts of individualism, consumer choice, competition, deregulation, local autonomy, the devolution of authority and the rolled-back state (small government), and individualised responsibility for risk and life chances, especially through health and education (Levin and Belfield, 2006). In collusion with these dominant discourses are those supporting a new public administration based on corporate management: centralised regulation, compliance, accountability and risk aversion, fiscal constraint and the imperative of value-for-money, with emphases on quality assurance, continuous improvement and outcomes gauged via performance indicators, professional standards, standardised testing and benchmarking (Ball, 2006; Duignan, 2006; Starr, 2012). Waves of restructuring and reform have fundamentally reconfigured the dominant discourses and philosophical, organisational or budgetary bases of public sector agencies, including schools. In Australian education these have focused on strengthened national productivity, international economic competitiveness in trade, workforce capacity and innovation, and internationally recognised educational achievement.

Like many other places in the world, Australia's neoliberal and neoconservative education policy agenda has been justified and legitimised through political discourses highlighting educational 'crises', inefficiency in the public sector, and the need for parental choice and voice in education to drive school improvement and innovation (Dale, 1989; Shapiro, 1990; Pusey, 1991). Crises within the political economy have been parried downwards through the state to the institutional level. Hence as Bottery (2004, p. 34) claims, globalisation encompasses the 'processes which affect nation states and produce policy mediations, which in turn have a direct impact on the management and principalship of educational institutions'.

Educational leadership has, therefore, become the focal point for educational policy reforms. It is the means by and through which governments and schooling jurisdictions aim to implement educational reforms, school improvement, higher student learning outcomes and improved 'standards'. To enhance leaders' capacity to deliver on macro- (national) and meso- (state) policy agendas in education, the Commonwealth and the Australian states have introduced leadership standards and capability statements to guide the work, professional learning and development of school leaders. These documents emphasise school improvement through the attainment of superior student achievement results and leadership capacity building with a focus on distributed leadership and shared-responsibility in schools (Starr, 2014). Comparative league tables based on standardised student testing and public examination results are published nationally on the *My School* website, providing institutional competitive incentive, consumer transparency for the exercise of choice and ensuring principals' accountability in instructional leadership.

Globalisation and small rural communities

Small rural communities are experiencing various forms of social and economic decline, especially with deregulated markets and Australia's northern neighbours supplying abundant low-cost labour and production. Global economic competition has encouraged long-standing rural industries to relocate commercial activities offshore or close altogether. Many small rural communities have been divested of private enterprises and public services, including the closure of institutions such as banks, commercial enterprises, industries and schools. Adding to this, climatic events such as drought, bushfires and floods have been widespread and are occurring more regularly (Flannery, 2005), taking a toll on economic activity and livelihoods, especially in agricultural communities. These phenomena have exacerbated rural unemployment and population migration to cities and mining areas for work, with concomitant effects on the viability and survival of local rural businesses and public services, including schools. Meanwhile, many small rural schools located closer to larger regional centres or the outer metropolitan suburbs have noticed a shift in enrolment trends as lower income or welfare-dependent families relocate to acquire affordable accommodation. Against this background, the following is a discussion of the major themes that emerged from the research programme about leading small rural schools in Victoria.

Major leadership challenges in small rural schools

Many leadership challenges were common to all principals in small rural schools. These challenges were manifest in diverse ways but are recursively linked and interconnected (Starr and White, 2008, 2009).

The changing nature of the principalship

Recent policy reforms exhort that educational institutions must become more autonomous, self-reliant and responsible; raise standards and improve student outcomes, especially measurable outcomes, while adapting to greater cost efficiencies/cutbacks and market competition. 'Doing more with less' is the new 'bottom line', but demands go beyond the 'core business' of teaching and learning to include numerous elements that were once alien to the educational environment (Gard, 2013). In a dynamic policy environment, principals have to be agile, adaptable and flexible to cope with continual change and uncertainty. The ability to save time and labour through technology and governmental pressures for economic growth, increased productivity and continuous improvement through education policy have resulted in the intensification and unremitting nature of educational work, a major feature of which is 'function creep', in order to ensure that a rising number of requirements are met.

All principals commented on the increasing amount of mandatory accountability, compliance and administrative work arriving from district, state and federal governments, and the negative impact this 'administrivia' was having on teaching, learning and the social life of schools. Principals explained that the situation was continually getting worse and described their working lives in terms of being 'always busy', 'never stopping', 'running the whole day' with work that is 'never-ending'. These administrative burdens are unrelated to school-based priorities, take considerable time to execute and are professionally 'invisible' and unrewarding, with principals referring to such increasing external impositions as the 'bane of my life', 'the worst part of the job' and 'soul destroying' in a context of cost-cutting and resource 'efficiencies'. Ironically, they say, this means they cannot perform all tasks to the best of their ability due to time constraints, despite widespread policy discourses promoting 'excellence'. The only way they can cope is to put in increasingly longer hours on the job. Principals in all schools might have similar complaints (Buckingham, 2003; Gronn, 2003; Wildy and Louden, 2000), but the problem is exacerbated in small rural schools where principals' work involves activities conducted by other professionals in metropolitan schools. Work intensification also steals time from family life.

Given pressures to 'perform' and being compared with other schools add to concerns about spending quality time with students and teachers. One principal said: 'I think it's a really big task to have quality results in both areas [teaching and administration]. . . . Something has to give at some point.' Unwanted policy and procedural interventions were seen as isolating and adding to stress, while also detracting potential aspirants to the principalship. Also, new tasks such as having to formally apply for competitive funding for specific needs were mentioned. Resources are declining so they are now competitive. Previously, schools received resources for specific needs and purposes as a matter of course, but they are now dependent on the preparation of successful funding submissions. One area of competitive funding concerns additional resources for students with special needs. 'Special needs' are now more tightly defined, so fewer students qualify for extra assistance. 'Targeted' funding is a controversial change, while securing resources for addressing educational needs is viewed as being totally dependent on a principal's ability to prepare strong, convincing funding submissions.

A surprising perception was that principals felt their work in schools was supported insufficiently by the education bureaucracy at state and/or district level. 'The system' was reported as being 'a nuisance' and of having 'no idea what we do because they've never done it', with these sentiments being intertwined with principals' concerns about incessant waves of policy reforms. Principals' comments indicated a sense of being dislocated and marginalised from debates about education policy and direction. The majority view was that a division exists – with policy makers 'on the inside' having very little understanding about small rural school life and their leadership challenges.

Revealing comments included: 'the lack of understanding from the hierarchy . . . would be from my Deputy Regional director upwards'; 'It's no good taking problems to the District Office . . . if you complain or ask for help, you're considered to be a nuisance or ineffective'; 'Everything they want us to do just gets in the way of what you're really here for – the kids.' Added to the view that no one really knows what small rural school principals do is the perception that systemic praise, acknowledgement or reward for their work is rare. On this, one principal said: 'You're doing a fantastic job and you never stop, but you have no point of reference and no one's telling you you're doing a great job, so you always feel inadequate.'

Small rural school principals are concerned about having to implement policy they perceive to be irrelevant or inappropriate to the needs of their schools. Overlaying all this is not only physical isolation, but also a sense of psychological alienation from the new policy hegemony. Principals of small rural schools believe that their working conditions have deteriorated and that they have subsequently been relegated to a lower positioning within the education employment hierarchy.

Governance

School governance was commonly raised as an important issue in small rural locations. School councils oversee the work of all schools, yet it can be difficult to generate sufficient interest for involvement in small communities. Not only is it difficult to attract the interest of parent and community volunteers in the first place, but small rural schools often have difficulty in maintaining the required number of school councillors. School councils are drawn from the immediate community, which in rural areas does not leave much room for choice. In some cases, principals reported having councils that renewed their membership too infrequently, which hindered school change and fresh ideas. School councils have to oversee a very tight global budget that usually requires top-up through fundraising or sponsorship efforts, but shortfalls are reported as being difficult to avoid in some hard-strapped rural contexts. Principals also reported problems when micro-political local gossip that spilled over into school governance agendas. In the words of one principal, 'Local issues spill over into the school all the time. Everyone knows everyone else and if there's any local conflict, it will be evident in the school as well.'

School closures

Small rural school viability is an issue of negative economies of scale, with a far greater cost per student for schooling provision in small rural locations (Picard, 2003). Schools receive recurrent funding and staffing levels based on per capita formulae, meaning that annual budgets, the number of teachers employed and the educational programme may change noticeably as enrolments fluctuate even slightly. Cash flow problems were reported to occur regularly, with government grants sometimes arriving too late to cover many operational costs. There are widespread concerns about budget shortfalls, with necessary maintenance work being put off and expenditure on resources or new initiatives being delayed. Higher poverty rates and lower incomes limit community fundraising possibilities.

School enrolment viability was a constant source of stress for many respondents, a situation also reported elsewhere (Eastley, 2004; Goode, 2007). If schools become too small, they will be closed. Accordingly, several respondents worried that their school's longevity was under threat. Viability is about meeting enrolment targets and attracting students, although many schools faced continual enrolment decline with population growth trends showing no immediate solution to this problem.

There have been more school closures over the past three decades than ever before in Australia, and communities that lose their schools struggle to survive (Eastley, 2004). If a rural school closes, children are forced to travel long distances to alternative schools. A significant complication in closures and amalgamations is that a school principal loses his/her job, adding a personal dimension to the issue of diminishing community assets.

Educational equity

Allied with the above-mentioned concerns were associated worries about equal opportunities, social justice and equity policies for students of small rural schools. Principals say that previously overt policy goals for educational equity have slipped off the policy agenda or have become too bureaucractised in their execution (such as the new competitive special needs funding arrangements and tightened eligibility criteria mentioned above). They perceive discourses concerning competitive individualism and efficiency have overturned the previous social democratic, welfarist consensus about equality in educational provision and outcomes. There is a prevailing sense that policy morality has disappeared along with previous policy and resourcing measures, with deleterious effects at the micro-school level. Underlying this is the view that fundamental, incontrovertible values about equity should underpin education policy and the work of schools, yet these have been abandoned, disadvantaging students in small rural schools.

The principals' comments suggested a struggle between school-based crusaders for better social outcomes and 'making a difference' against negative macro policy forces that generate resource reductions, feelings of loss through the diminution of social principles and values, and a devaluing of education as a fundamental right for all. Parodying Orwell (1965), there was a strong sense that 'all schools are equal but some are more equal than others'. One principal summed up many of the above dilemmas in this way:

> You have to constantly be on the front foot. . . . You try and keep up with what the Department wants, you have to watch your numbers [enrolments], you have to keep an ear to the ground to know what's happening in the community that might spill over into the school, and you have to watch how staff in the school are faring with pressures to do as much as a large school does. It's a juggling act that's a lot about survival.

Such key challenges are affecting how small rural principals operate, but several significant and effective school leadership trends are emerging in response.

Emerging trends and responses

Even though principals may feel marginalised systemically, the research revealed the opposite effects in local contexts. Numerous creative initiatives to leadership challenges emerged, with many common themes running among them. In response to rural challenges, school communities are moving beyond traditional pathways to deliver educational benefits.

There is a trend towards collaborative governing councils that oversee education and other social services within a whole district. These volunteers are concerned about developing and preserving broad coverage of educational provision from pre-school to post-school education, alongside other social service provisions within their geographical location. The groups have not replaced individual school councils but are evolving as an adjunct to them, and may, in time, replace them. These larger, combined governance structures assist in overcoming the usual limitations of smallness, rurality and resource scarcity. Collaborations with other professionals such as health workers were reported. School principals are pivotal players in these groups, with their involvement taking school leadership into the realms of community leadership.

There is an inextricable link between regional economic development and education provision in rural locations. Some councils and principals are highly entrepreneurial, bringing in involvement of local government and businesses. The support resulting from such efforts includes educational collaborations across districts, sponsorships and donations, capital works and maintenance projects, facilities sharing and usage, short-term resource exchanges, the sharing of expertise, and lobbying for greater state and federal government support, a topic returned to later in this chapter. The school's educational capacity is built alongside community development and governing councils can be very instrumental and helpful in this regard.

Combined leadership among principals, school councils and education department officers facilitates future scenario planning, the sharing of expertise and strategic plans to affect community educational provision, including making decisions about what is educationally viable and what is not. Combined governance is about enhancing the services and provisions of entire regions by taking a prospective view of educational and other human services needs across whole districts (Country Education Project, 2007), with school planning spanning all school years and beyond, including co-located preschooling and health provisions. These emergent rural community development plans require the services of community builders and 'boundary-crossers' (Centre for Research and Learning in Regional Australia, 2001). One principal explained as follows:

> Small places like ours need people who put in, otherwise small towns die. . . . It's surprising how much a group can do – and if you can't do it, someone will know someone who can and rope them in. . . . We've looked at

education from birth right through so no kid loses out from living out here – that's the main goal . . . and it's the same for health services.

School leaders reported collaborations across schools to deliver teaching, learning, leadership and management requirements, with such partnerships expanding and being viewed as increasingly essential. Collective activities prompted by the requirements of structural reforms and problems of limited resources are aided by new technologies and a sense of community 'self-help'. Collaborations included sharing the costs of peripatetic specialist teachers, arranging collaborative professional development activities for teachers, and organising cross-school drama and arts events, school camps, excursions and field trips. There are student and teacher exchanges, volunteers are used and new flexible configurations of school timetables are implemented to enable all these activities. Combined regional planning occurs to ensure consistency in curriculum provision, especially in LOTE (languages other than English). Small rural schools share expertise, ideas and resources, including equipment and instructional materials.

Although schools are one of the few sources of employment in small rural locations, when availability becomes an issue, schools cooperate to attract recruits to multi-school positions from elsewhere in the state. Retirees with all manner of skills and experiences are used to mentor, train and fill in. Pragmatism is at the basis of collaborative arrangements.

Principals work closely with teachers to form leadership teams in planning learning activities and in implementing new curricula, enacting pastoral care duties and other programme coordination exercises. They work with parents on extra-curricular provision, on teacher aide assistance, and to maintain schools and their grounds, among many other things. Principals work with municipal councils to develop strategy, to maintain budgets and expenditure, to attract funds, to marshal community support and to solve higher order management problems in schools and broader educational issues across the district. Principals work with members of their local rural communities who are more engaged with the school as a community hub. The small rural principal has no option but to collaborate with many stakeholders to execute their jobs effectively. Working together is vital as schools determine how they can cover the range of teaching, leadership, administration and professional learning programmes collectively, thereby reducing the workload and resources outlaid by any single school. The same can be said of school councils.

These sorts of activities strike a chord with the levels of clustering identified by VicHealth, the state's government health department, that identifies 'levels of clustering' thus: *Networking*: exchanging information for mutual benefit, requiring little time or trust between participants. *Coordination*: which goes beyond networking to include transformative practices towards a common purpose, such as coordinating a district event. *Cooperation*: which goes further still to include the sharing of resources, requiring more time, and a higher level of trust and sharing. *Collaboration* (highest level of clustering): extends all the above and includes enhancing the capacity of other partners for mutual benefit and towards a common purpose. This requires partners to give up a part of their 'turf' to another partner to create an improved or more seamless approach. In the schooling context, giving up a part of one's turf may mean relinquishing an activity being done well and passing control to another school in order to focus on a leadership strength within and on behalf of the cluster.

The research project reported here identified all the levels of clustering described above, with many examples of the higher level collaborative clustering and collaboration. High-level collaborations include non-school players: government (municipal, state and Commonwealth); business (chambers of commerce, local businesses); community services (such as youth, sporting, health, community groups, service clubs and neighbourhood centres); as well as other education providers (from preschool, vocational education, tertiary institutions). School involvement in community-building activities also accentuates a two-way dependency, with schools being consumers of goods and services while providing local employment and the provision of physical resources such as meeting places, sports venues for the integration of many community activities.

Also evidenced were a large number of cross-disciplinary cultural, community-building or environmental projects in the curriculum of small rural schools. For example, a common goal is for schools to engage with an emerging ecological and tourism economy, harnessing human and natural capital. In these ways, there is a recursive positive relationship between small rural schools, their communities, local cultures and the environment.

One cluster of schools established a combined administrative bureau, hiring multi-skilled personnel to manage communications, finances, maintenance works, co-operative purchasing, and to service co-operating governing councils, and this led to the systemic roll-out of LABs (Local Administrative Bureaus). The LABs also co-ordinate funding grant applications, sponsorships and donations, hire out school facilities and facilitate equipment exchanges, saving costs and time.

Several clusters of principals participating in the leadership professional development programme made use of university expertise to devise, collate and analyse their own statistical and qualitative research data. Principals are using evidence-based information to attract funds and resources, or as the basis for collaborative curriculum developments. Many rural schools made special arrangements to attract university student teachers during their compulsory trainee teaching rounds. Also evidenced were teacher exchanges (with the flexible school timetabling arrangements enabling such exercises) and collaborative efforts to attract enrolments through promotions and public relations exercises.

Educational capacity is being built alongside community development so that sustainability replaces fear about school closures. Local people already feel their communities are under-serviced, and are the hardest hit by climatic events and the retreat of social institutions and local industries, but they still want excellent education provision. The collective resistance of rural communities, fighting to keep their local services including resistance against efficiencies and economies of scale, is viewed as a necessity.

Concluding remarks

Much was learned through the research programme being reported here about the very particular experience of small rural school leaders, especially about how they lead, learn and work when remoteness and the shortcomings of multifunctional, demanding and boundary-crossing jobs have to be negotiated constantly. The main concerns of school leaders in small rural schools are:

- Their ability to cope with the leadership and management aspects of their jobs, which are continually changing and expanding, while having responsibility for their own teaching, student welfare and community involvement.
- Constraints due to the multiple nature of their role.
- Making time and mustering support to create significant school change.
- Overcoming feelings of isolation and removal from usual avenues of support.
- Catering for students with special learning needs.
- Equity and social justice policies remaining overt in rural education.
- Perceptions of being marginalised from major educational decision making.
- The viability and survival of their small rural schools.

(Starr and White, 2008)

The most obvious conclusion to be derived from the research is that context matters. Principals of small rural schools face distinctive challenges such that what works in large cities does not necessarily work in small rural schools. Principals highlighted how 'one-size-fits-all' education policies and practices often disadvantage them, while there is also a general lack of policy or provision relating specifically to small rural schools. Resultant challenges generate new distinctive rural leadership responses and collaboratively derived outcomes. The tenacity, ingenuity, supreme commitment and unlikely but critical relationships derived from small rural school leadership lead to an understanding of why such contexts yield different leadership responses than may be witnessed in other educational settings.

Rural decline, alongside structural reforms and connective technologies, is creating innovative school leadership practices with the involvement of community players. So as to best service their schools and help themselves, small rural principals are turning to each other and their communities for support and collaboration in conducting various necessary and innovative activities to effect positive results. There are many activities afoot for overcoming the problems of smallness and rurality.

Small rural schools are enhanced by strong community linkages and attendant shared school-community, boundary-crossing leadership practices. These have arisen through informal, locally derived and pragmatic means. For more than a decade official policy rhetoric and research suggests that distributed leadership forms are endorsed as the most appropriate for schools (Department of Education, 2007; Hay Group, 2006; Starr, 2014). In the small rural communities in this research, however, leadership distribution was seen to go beyond the boundaries of the school. Many people play an important part in running small rural schools in which leadership is increasingly viewed as a collective community responsibility in the context of diminishing and more tightly controlled resources. Para-professionals and willing contributors assume greater significance by assisting with all manner of necessary activities to get things done. School leadership is not only distributed within and across schools, but within and across communities. Also witnessed were a variety of formal and informal leaders and leadership styles that contributed to the effectiveness of collaborations within and across schools. Small rural principals, however, must have the ability to communicate ideas and goals to provide links between people, organisations and projects to create change and renewal towards collective goals. These individuals enhance school-community programmes and collaborations. Without community support and cooperation, many fruitful projects, programmes and activities would not happen in small rural schools.

Quite simply, collaborative enterprises across small rural schools make significant sense in addressing the pressing challenges confronting their principals. In order for education and other social services to survive and thrive, local rural people are making the best of their new circumstances and the challenges they bring. The principals involved in this research are adamant that essential collaborative arrangements should be supported actively and systemically with formal recognition and funding. These fruitful partnerships are proving to be of benefit for communities, schools, students and small rural principals. Small rural principals understand that performing in their jobs is not just about what they do, but how they do it (Barley and Beesley, 2007).

Finally, small rural school principals had many suggestions for positive change for small rural schools, including the need for:

- research into the needs of small rural schools;
- policy specifically relating to the needs of small rural schools;
- contextualised resourcing;
- research into alternative governance models for clusters of schools;
- teacher education and educational leadership courses focusing specifically on small rural schools;
- schemes to attract new recruits such as compulsory teaching practice for student teachers in small and rural schools;
- professional learning on meeting the needs of multi-age and diverse classes, cross-disciplinary teaching, team teaching, multi-skilling, special education and community liaison skills.

These suggestions are helpful starting points for policy makers, educational researchers and teacher educators.

References

Apple, M. (2006). Producing inequalities: Neo-liberalism, neo-conservatism, and the politics of educational reform. In H. Lauder, P. Brown, J. Dillabough, and A. H. Halsey (eds). *Education, globalization & social change* (pp. 468–489). Oxford: Oxford University Press.

Ball, S. (1994). *Education reform: A critical and post-structural approach*. Buckingham: Open University Press.

Ball, S. (2006). Performativity and fabrication in the education economy: Towards the performative society. In H. Lauder, P. Brown, J. Dillabough, and A. H. Halsey (eds). *Education, globalization & social change* (pp. 692–701). Oxford: Oxford University Press.

Barley, Z. A. and Beesley, A. D. (2007). Rural school success: What can we learn? *Journal of Research in Rural Education*, 22(1). Retrieved 25 April 2014 from: http://jrre.psu.edu/articles/22–3.pdf

Bottery, M. (2004). *The challenges of educational principalship*. London: Paul Chapman Publishing.

Buckingham, D. (2003). The rural principalship: For better or worse. In Australian Primary Principals Association *Gold Matters*, 4(2), March 2003. Retrieved 25 April 2014 from: www.appa.asn.au/uploads/gold

Centre for Research and Learning in Regional Australia. (2001). *Building dynamic learning communities: Ten regional case studies*. Launceston, Tasmania: University of Tasmania.

Coladarci, T. (2007). Improving the yield of rural education research: An editor's swan song. In *Journal of Research in Rural Education*, 22(3). Retrieved 23 February 2008, from: http://jrre.psu.edu/articles/22–3.pdf

Corbin, J. and Strauss, A. (2008). *Basics of qualitative research* (3rd edn). Thousand Oaks, CA: Sage.

Country Education Project. (2007). *P-12 Education research project, summary report, May 2007*. Wangaratta, Victoria: Country Education Project.

Dale, R. (1989). *The state and education policy*. Milton Keynes: Open University Press.

Department of Education (2007). *The developmental learning framework for principals*. Melbourne: Office of School Education, Victoria.

Duignan, P. (2006). *Educational principalship: Key challenges and ethical tensions*. Port Melbourne; Cambridge University Press.

Eastley, T. (2004). *Rural schools closing a sign of the times*. Transcript from AM, Australian Broadcasting Corporation, Radio National, 07.10. Retrieved 3 July 2007 from: www.anc.net.au/am/content/2004/s1264658.htm

Flannery, T. (2005). *The weather makers: The history & future of climate change*. Melbourne, Victoria: Text Publishing.

Gard, M. (2013). Non-core demands overload teachers. *The Sydney Morning Herald*, 3 June.

Glaser, B. G. and Strauss, A. L. (1967). *The discovery of grounded theory: Strategies for qualitative research*. New York: Aldine.

Goode, A. (2007). *Totalitarian cuts to education to hit rural schools hard*. Retrieved 4 August 2007 from: www.theadvertiser.news.com.au/?from=ni_story

Gronn, P. (2003). *The new work of educational principals*. London: Paul Chapman Publishing.

Hay Group (2006). Distributed leadership: The five pillars of distributed leadership in schools. National College of School Leadership: Nottingham, UK.

Human Rights and Equal Opportunity Commission (HREOC). (2000). *National inquiry into rural and remote education*. Canberra: Commonwealth of Australia.

Levin, H. M. and Belfield, C. R. (2006). The market place in education. In H. Lauder, P. Brown, J. Dillabough and A. H. Halsey (eds). *Education, globalization and social change* (pp. 620–641). Oxford: Oxford University Press.

Orwell, G. (1965). *Animal farm: A fairy story*. Harmondsworth, Middlesex: Penguin.

Picard, C. J. (2003). Small school districts and economies of scale. Paper presented to the State Board of Elementary and Secondary Education, Louisiana Department of Education Strategic Planning Study Group Committee.

Punch, K. E. (1998). *Introduction to social research: Quantitative and qualitative approaches*. London: Sage.

Pusey, M. (1991). *Economic rationalism in Canberra: A nation-building state changes its mind*. Cambridge: Cambridge University Press.

Shapiro, S. (1990). *Between capitalism and democracy*. New York: Bergin and Garvey.

Starr, K. (2009a). Leadership and learning across small rural schools. In Starr, K. and White, S. (eds). *Willing to lead: Leading across effective small schools*. Melbourne, Victoria: Dept of Education and Early Childhood Development, 13–22.

Starr, K. (2009b). Mentoring in LAESS: the perspectives of 'critical friends'. In Starr, K. and White, S. (eds). *Willing to lead: Leading across effective small schools*. Melbourne, Victoria: Dept of Education and Early Childhood Development: Melbourne, 69–74.

Starr, K. (2012). *Above and beyond the bottom line: The extraordinary evolution of education business management*. Camberwell, Victoria: ACER Press.

Starr, K. (2014). Interrogating conceptions of leadership: School principals, policy and paradox. *School Leadership and Management*, 34(3), 224–236.

Starr, K. and White, S. (2008). The Small Rural School Principalship: Key Challenges and Cross-School Responses. *Journal for Research in Rural Education*, 23(5), 1–12.

Starr, K. and White, S. (eds). (2009). *Willing to lead: Leading across effective small schools*. Melbourne, Victoria: DEECD. Available at: www.eduweb.vic.gov.au/edulibrary/public/staffdev/schlead/Willing_to_Lead/Willing_to_Lead_-_Leading_Across_Effective_Schools.pdf

Wildy, H. and Louden, W. (2000). School restructuring and the dilemmas of principals' work. *Educational Administration and Management*, 28(2), 173–184.

5

LEADING PRIMARY SCHOOLS IN POST-CONFLICT RWANDA

Some current concerns of the practitioners

Gilbert Karareba, Simon Clarke and Tom O'Donoghue

Introduction

Much has been written about the role of school leadership in promoting students' learning and school success (Leithwood *et al.*, 2008; Marks and Printy, 2003; Watson, 2009). However, while the importance of school leadership in this respect is known, there have been few empirical studies undertaken on the status of this leadership in post-conflict societies (Clarke and O'Donoghue, 2013). This suggests that there are limited examples of school leadership in post-conflict societies that can be used to develop theoretical models for informing leadership development in such complex situations. The study reported in this chapter, which aimed to generate an understanding of the issues which are of current concern to primary school leaders in post-conflict Rwanda and the strategies adopted by them in order to deal with those issues, is offered as one contribution to filling the gap existing in this area of educational leadership at the school level in post-conflict societies.

Since Rwanda is not only a post-conflict country, but also a developing country, the study also contributes to understanding school leadership in developing countries. Thus, it can be seen as a response to Oplatka's (2004, p. 428) call for empirical exploration of school leadership in developing countries when he noted that 'educational reforms and policies draw almost exclusively on perspectives of educational leadership taken from Western literature and practice, thereby giving an impression that Western models of principalship are universal'. Oplatka (2004) went on to say that cultural context and politics may affect school leadership and management in developing countries. Thus, any research aimed at deepening our understanding of how cultural context and politics inform leadership theory and practice is of paramount importance.

This chapter is in four parts. First, the Rwandan context is outlined. Second, an overview of the literature on education in post-conflict societies is provided. The findings of the study on the issues which are of current concern to primary school leaders in Rwanda and the strategies adopted by them in order to deal with those issues are then presented. Finally, concluding remarks are made to re-emphasise key elements of the narrative on primary school leadership in post-conflict Rwanda and to suggest how primary school leadership may be improved.

The Rwandan context

Rwanda, known poetically as the 'Land of a Thousand Hills', is a landlocked republic in east-central Africa. Its neighbouring countries include Burundi, Uganda, Democratic Republic of the Congo (DRC) and Tanzania. The country has a small surface area, 26,338 square kilometres, which accommodates 10,515,973 people (National Institute of Statistics of Rwanda, 2014). This places the nation among the most densely populated countries in Africa. The Rwandan population is composed of three ethnic groups sharing the same indigenous language, culture and habitat (Kiwuwa, 2012). These groups include the Hutu, the Tutsi and the Twa (Kiwuwa, 2012). The nation was also colonised by two European countries – namely Germany from 1900 until 1916, and Belgium from 1917 up until 1962.

Rwanda's recent political history has been dominated by the 1994 genocide. The genocide claimed the lives of more than 800,000 people, mostly Tutsis but also moderate Hutus, in only one hundred days (Moghalu, 2005). The origin and causes of this genocide are too complex to be discussed in this chapter. What tends to be widely agreed upon by many 'seasoned' scholars, however, is that the genocide emanated from the ethnicisation of political power whereby ethnicity was used by politicians to justify formal political power as well as social and economic privileges (Buckley-Zistel, 2009). This situation resulted in ethnic conflict that led to the four-year civil war between the then incumbent government and the Rwanda Patriotic Front (RPF)'s armed forces. The latter launched an armed attack from Uganda in 1990 and was composed mainly of descendants of Tutsis who had fled Rwanda to neighbouring countries in the late 1950s (Moghalu, 2005). The civil war culminated eventually in the genocide of 1994, the year in which the RPF won the war and started to reconstruct the country.

The effect of the genocide on children's schooling was devastating. Indeed, education came to a standstill during this time. The following comment by Obura and Bird (2009) illustrates the devastation that the war and genocide had on the lives of Rwandans generally and on children's education specifically:

> Over two million people, one-third of the entire population, fled to neighbouring countries. One million more were internally displaced. Women headed 60 per cent of the families. Tens of thousands of unaccompanied children were in temporary centres six months later; 100,000 children lost their parents or were separated from them; 80 per cent of Rwandan children

> experienced death in their immediate family; 90 per cent saw dead bodies of victims or body parts; 70 per cent witnessed atrocities; 200 children under 14 years old were still being held in one of the country's major prisons in 1998, suspected of involvement in the genocide; and the number of women and girls raped remains uncounted.
>
> (p. 8)

In addition, the educational infrastructure was destroyed, and 75 per cent of teachers were either killed or imprisoned for alleged participation in the genocide (Cole and Barsalou, 2006).

Twenty years after the war and genocide in Rwanda, it is pertinent to ask the following questions: is the current primary school leadership in the country shaped and/or influenced by the legacy of war and genocide as was obviously the case in the immediate aftermath of the conflict?; is the current picture of primary school leadership shaped solely by endemic manifestations of political and economic underdevelopment characterising many post-colonial and developing countries?; or is the current primary school leadership shaped by both the conflict legacy and post-colonial and developing country status of the country? These questions are attended to in the study reported later in this chapter.

The above questions were posed in relation to primary school leadership against a background of Rwanda's international reputation for having made a noticeable recovery from the genocide. According to the World Bank (2014), the average growth in Gross Domestic Product (GDP) between 2001 and 2012 was 8.1 per cent per year. The same source indicates that the rate of poverty decreased from 59 per cent in 2001 to 45 per cent in 2011. In addition, Rwanda has been ranked recently as the second easiest place for doing business in Sub-Saharan Africa (World Bank, 2014). Furthermore, the country has reduced corruption quite significantly as evidenced by the fact that between 2008 and 2013, its ranking rose from 102 to 49 in Transparency International's Corruption perceptions Index (Transparency International, 2014). The empowerment of women is also being promoted as evidenced by the highest number (64 per cent) of female parliamentarians in the world (*The Guardian*, 2014a). Public health, educational access and tourism have also improved in recent years (*The Guardian*, 2014a).

Notwithstanding the above gains, Rwanda remains one of the world's poorest countries with 63 per cent of the population continuing to live on less than the equivalent of $US1.25 a day and 82 per cent on less than $US2 (*The Guardian*, 2014a). In a similar vein, although the 2013 Human Development Report recognises the significant progress Rwanda has made in terms of human development, it ranks the country 167 out of 187 countries and territories, and locates it in the low human development category (UNDP, 2013). Additionally, there are very high urban versus rural imbalances within the economy, with the rural population being the most affected by poverty. This urban/rural gap is telling since 83 per cent of the population live in rural areas where subsistence agriculture is practised on small, often fragmented, parcels of land (National Institute of Statistics of Rwanda, 2014; *The Guardian*, 2014a). With scant natural resources, the country's economy remains agrarian, and economic development depends largely on modernising and intensifying agriculture.

Education in post-conflict societies

There seems to be a number of education-related problems common to post-conflict settings. These include the lack of domestic revenue to run pre-crisis educational programmes, the destruction of educational infrastructure and buildings, the lack of qualified teachers, poor record keeping, corruption, a lack of transparency in educational institutions, poor coordination and planning and a substantial number of war-affected children and youth (Buckland, 2006). There are also challenges that seem to be specific to particular post-conflict societies, especially where ethnic identity or religion was integral to the initial war. These challenges may relate to curriculum reform, the high politicisation of education, the teaching of history and the selection of the language of instruction. Such problems have characterised the education systems in post-conflict Bosnia and Herzegovina (Kreso, 2008; Torsti, 2009; Weinstein *et al.*, 2007; World Bank, 2005) and Timor-Leste (Boughton, 2011; World Bank, 2005).

Thus far, there has been a scarcity of research into how the above challenges affect leadership at the school level in post-conflict societies. More importantly, the strategies school leaders adopt to deal with the challenges they face have been neglected. Likewise, Clarke and O'Donoghue (2013) observe that very little empirical research has been undertaken at an international level into how school leaders in (post-) conflict settings conceptualise their work. The lack of attention to school leadership in such environments is partly attributable to the neglect by scholars of the importance of considering context and its influence on leadership practices, especially at the individual school level. As Vroom and Jago (2007, p. 22) have argued, 'the field of leadership has identified more closely with the field of individual differences and has largely ignored the way the behaviour of leaders is influenced by the situations they encounter'. To put it another way, leadership is context-bound (Clarke and Wildy, 2004).

Even though the literature specifically connected with school leadership in post-conflict societies is scarce, some work has been undertaken that focuses on the relationship between education and conflict. Indeed, this is an emerging and pressing area of enquiry (Paulson and Rappleye, 2007; Smith, 2005) which bears various names, such as 'education and fragility' and 'education and insecurity' (Mosselson *et al.*, 2009; Paulson, 2011). Scholars and practitioners in the area have also highlighted the role of education in contributing to, and fuelling, violent conflict (Bush and Saltarelli, 2000; Hilker, 2011; King, 2005) as well as the importance of the quality of education for peace building, reconciliation and post-conflict reconstruction and development (Acedo, 2011; Hodgkin, 2006; Paulson, 2011). At the same time, some scholars argue that work being undertaken in the field lacks rigorous research-based insights, being based simply on evidence that emerged from the delivery and evaluation of educational programmes in societies ruined by conflict (Paulson, 2011). Consequently, there is a call for more critically informed and policy relevant research in this emerging area of inquiry (Novelli and Lopez Cardozo, 2008).

The study

The study reported in this chapter was aimed at developing an understanding of the issues which are of current concern to Rwandan primary school leaders and at investigating the strategies adopted by them in order to deal with those issues. The study was interpretive in nature. It employed qualitative methods of data collection comprising semi-structured interviews and informal observations. Participants consisted of head teachers, deputy head teachers and representatives of parent–teacher associations (PTA) from primary schools within the Nine Year Basic Education (NYBE) schools. NYBE schools accommodate primary schools offering a six-year primary school education and lower secondary schools offering a three-year lower secondary school education (Ministry of Education, 2013). There are also some primary schools which do not have the lower secondary school level. Unlike NYBE schools, which have a head teacher and a deputy head teacher, primary schools without the lower secondary school level are usually led by one head teacher (Republic of Rwanda, 2012). The rationale for selecting primary schools within the NYBE schools arose out of the need to incorporate deputy head teachers and parents in the study. This is because most insights into school leadership to date have tended to come from the principal (head teacher), with other school leaders at the school level being neglected in school leadership research (Day *et al.*, 2010).

As the focus of the study was on primary school leadership, interviews concentrated mainly on primary school education. The findings of the study are presented under the following headings. First, the issues that are of current concern to primary school leaders are delineated. Second, there is a discussion of the strategies school leaders adopt to deal with the challenges. Third, the leadership style that seems to have been adopted by many school leaders is examined. The nature of the context within which school leadership is exercised is depicted throughout the exposition on the issues, on strategies and on leadership styles of primary school leaders.

Issues of current concern to school leaders

The issues faced by those school leaders interviewed include conflict prevention, the lack of teacher professionalism and motivation, student drop-out and absenteeism, and the lack of parental involvement in the education of their children. Each of these issues is now discussed.

Issues associated with conflict prevention

In one of the six schools selected, there had been a situation occurring between two primary school children in 2012 that related to identity. Children A and B were friends and were from the same ethnic group, but B was also a friend of another child, C. After simply seeing B and C walking together, A kept asking B whether C shared the same ethnic group with them. Such a question can be sensitive since it used to be asked during the genocide by militias on road blocks when they were trying to single out who to kill. The school leader interviewed stated that child A reported the incident to him. When asked whom he thought had given the children identity/ethnicity-related information, the school leader stated that although primary school children were born after the genocide, they were still exposed to influences from neighbours and friends of their families. He put it this way: 'Based on the conversation I had with the parent of this child [child A], I can say that kids learn ethnicity outside their nuclear families. There are adult persons who tell kids about it.' Another school leader in the same school mentioned that children were getting ethnicity-related information from both their nuclear families and the wider community.

Discussions about ethnicity are not common, at least in public places, since the identification of Rwandans as Hutus, Tutsis or Twas was outlawed officially by the government as part of the promotion of unity and reconciliation (Fussel, 2001; Power, 2013). In addition, despite the fact that ethnicity is not discussed publicly, there have been cases of genocide ideology entering Rwandan schools in recent years (*The New Times*, 2013a). It seems, therefore, that the problem of ethnicity in schools is one that needs to be considered seriously because, historically, it was one of the contributing factors to the conflict which culminated in the 1994 genocide (Hilker, 2011; Walker-Keleher, 2006).

Lack of teacher professionalism and motivation

Some of the school-based realities depicted by school leaders interviewed suggest a lack of teacher professionalism in their schools. This lack of professionalism was manifested in the absence of the use of participatory teaching methods, teachers' absenteeism and teachers being late for work. These matters, however, can only be understood if cognizance is taken of the contextual complexity characterising primary school education and the teaching profession in Rwanda. Indeed, as discussed below, contextual barriers to teacher professionalism exist, some of which are, unfortunately, beyond the control of school leaders and teachers.

For the sake of clarification, it is appropriate to define teacher professionalism. Here, it refers to the improvement of quality and standards of practice. It entails constantly improving teaching practice through teachers' commitment, expertise and knowledge (Hargreaves, 2000; Helsby, 1999). Owing to the very limited opportunities for in-service teacher professional development in Rwanda, primary school teachers' use of participatory teaching methods is rare. The absence of such opportunities is a barrier to teacher professionalism. This observation resonates with

Al-Hinai's (2007) theoretical linkage between professionalism and professional learning, according to which 'professionalism requires professional knowledge, competence and expertise, which in turn require further development through continuous professional education' (p. 43).

The dearth of in-service professional learning opportunities has meant that most teachers at the primary school level continue to teach using colonially inherited teacher-centred pedagogy, with little interactive participation occurring in classrooms, despite the government's desire to develop the critical thinking of students. Not surprisingly, the school leaders interviewed were perplexed that their teachers were still teaching the way they had been taught. The following statement on this illustrates the concern of one deputy head teacher of a school located in a rural area:

> I encourage my teachers to use active teaching methods to enable students to discover new things themselves. However, teachers rarely use active learning strategies. They often use expository teaching methodology because they say it helps them cover all the content and finish the programme on time.

In a similar vein, another educational leader at the level of the district expressed his concern that professional development for teachers is centralised at the Rwandan Education Board level and that only very few teachers are able to benefit from these learning opportunities. He put it this way:

> We need teacher professional development programs for our teachers. Teachers teach like they used to teach 20 years ago, and the world has changed. Many teachers do not receive training. In-service teacher training is centralised in the Rwandan Education Board (REB), and sometimes REB requests the district to send one or two teachers in REB-organised training. Two teachers in the whole district is a very small number.

In the light of the above circumstances, school leaders are faced with challenges of supporting teachers to implement student-centred and critical thinking approaches to teaching and learning.

Equally, teachers are very reluctant to use participatory teaching methods when approaching specific topics in the classroom. This reluctance is especially true in relation to teaching genocide-related issues. While the development of critical thinking of students is instrumental to the examination of what led to the 1994 genocide, many primary school teachers provide little opportunity for student debate and discussion on ethnicity.

It will be recalled that there is a relationship between ethnicity and the genocide of 1994 in Rwanda. On this, one of the school leaders interviewed highlighted that teachers do not allow for open discussion on ethnic groups (Hutu, Tutsi and Twa) in the classroom:

> Teachers may explain what genocide is, but they teach with reservation the Rwandan genocide. Children may ask who is *Hutu*, *Tutsi* or *Twa*, but teachers do not like such discussions/questions on *Hutu*, *Tutsi*, *Twa* . . . Teachers choose to read what is written, and rarely welcome discussion about ethnic groups. They even fear teaching the lesson on the Rwandan genocide.

This quote serves to illustrate the fact that besides experiencing difficulties in applying learner-centred pedagogy, teachers also tend to avoid implementing it in their teaching of controversial topics. In a similar vein, it appears that the adoption of the lecture method is a strategy teachers adopt to both prevent the emergence of discussion that may give rise to genocide ideology in classrooms and/or to protect themselves from any prosecution for inculcating genocide ideology in students. They tend to watch their words and behaviour in the classroom because, in recent years, some dozens of head teachers, teachers and students have been suspended, sacked and/or sent to prison for alleged transmission of genocide ideology (International Planned Parenthood Federation, 2007).

In addition to the scarcity of professional development opportunities for teachers, the development of teacher professionalism is also inhibited by such factors as teachers' lack of motivation. This is a substantial concern for school leaders. In rural areas, those interviewed revealed that poor and unattractive working and living conditions, and very low teacher salaries are the chief factors contributing to teachers' dissatisfaction with their jobs. Moreover, teachers working in urban schools earn up to three times as much as their colleagues in rural schools. This inequity has resulted from relatively affluent parents in urban areas being able to supplement local school budgets and teacher salaries. This is a matter that also needs to be taken seriously by the current government, not least because pre-genocide educational inequality was a contributing factor to the 1994 genocide (Hilker, 2010).

Teachers' incompetency in English, the new language of instruction, also hampers leadership for teacher professionalism and motivation. After almost a century of teaching in French as part of the Belgian colonial legacy, English replaced it and became the medium of instruction throughout the Rwandan education system. Despite the recent introduction of school-based mentoring to address teachers' deficiencies in the English language, school leaders highlighted that primary school teachers are facing very serious problems associated with the non-mastery of the language since most teachers grew up in the French-language dominated school system.

Student drop-out and absenteeism

Despite Rwanda's impressive progress in attaining the highest primary school enrolment rates in Africa (UNICEF-Rwanda, n. d.), student attrition remains a problem for school leaders in many of the primary schools in the research. While a large number of children enter the first grade of primary school, many leave school before completing the full cycle. Poverty was mentioned by many school leaders as being the chief cause of student drop-out and absenteeism. Some school leaders in rural areas pointed out that children from poor households tend to leave schools to work temporarily in order to obtain money to purchase basic school materials. On this, one deputy head teacher commented:

> Because parents are very poor in this region some students abandon school for work to be able to purchase basic school materials. When you ask them the reasons for their absence once they come back to school, they tell you that they were looking for money to purchase notebooks and uniform as their parents do not have the money to do it. Others tell you that they were absent because they were working for money to spend on a haircut.

This deputy head teacher added that students from poor families tend to wear torn and/or dirty clothes, not to wear shoes and to possess fewer than the required notebooks.

While the above commentary indicates that some students do return to school after a certain period of absence, school leaders highlighted that many of them do not come back. A parent chairing the school board at one school stated that after the end of the 2013 school year there were more than 20 cases of students who had left the school for good. This parent went on to say that these students were involved in such casual activities as transporting sugar cane to the market and being employed as domestic workers. In addition, two schools located near mining excavations tended to have many of the children dropping out being involved in activities associated with mineral extraction.

Another contributing factor to student attrition, which is less apparent at the primary school level, is pregnancy. While only one primary school student in one of the six schools selected had dropped out due to pregnancy, the district education officer reported that teenage pregnancy is a common cause of attrition for girls at the post-primary school level (i.e. years 7, 8 and 9 of the Nine Year Basic Education scheme). These childhood pregnancies can be considered as a violation of children's rights since students in years 7, 8, and 9 are usually aged between 13 and 15. At the national level, the Gender-Based Violence in Schools report has indicated that 522 students aged between 10 and 18 years became pregnant and stopped attending school in 2012 (*The New Times*, 2013b). This age group of 10–18 years would also have included primary school students since their age normally ranges between seven and twelve.

It is important to mention at this juncture that those students who dropped out in the schools investigated were not genocide orphans. While it has been reported that 15 per cent of children affected by the genocide were unlikely to finish grade three or four six years after it occurred (Akresh and de Walque, 2008), the school leaders interviewed suggested this is not now the case twenty years hence. Rather, school leaders mentioned that those students dropping out are mainly non-genocide orphans, children from poor families and children witnessing conflict in their nuclear families. However, it can be argued that the legacies of war and genocide have had (and are continuing to have) an impact on the work of school leaders, especially at the secondary school and university levels. There remain cases of young genocide survivors who are still traumatised as a result of painful legacies of the past. In addition, there exist young people born as a result of rape at that time (*The Guardian*, 2014b); rape was widespread during the genocide and children born from rape have faced (and are still facing) extraordinary challenges related to rejection and acceptance by their mothers (*The Guardian*, 2014b). Many of these young people also live in poverty as they do not qualify for government assistance to the same extent as do genocide orphans (*The Guardian*, 2014b).

Lack of parental involvement in education

School leaders also highlighted the lack of parental involvement in education as a substantive concern. School leaders in the rural areas pointed out that the lack of parents' interest in the education of their children is evidenced by the fact that some, because of their ignorance, are deliberately not giving sufficient school materials to their children. Furthermore, in rural settings, parents' reluctance to contribute money for the teacher allowance was also mentioned as an indicator of parents' lack of interest in the education of their children. On this, school leaders stated that parents in the rural areas believe that using their financial means to supplement teacher salaries is contrary to the State Education Act, which stipulates that primary education is free and compulsory. Leaders also expressed a belief that poverty and ignorance about the purpose and importance of education are prime causes of parental apathy.

In urban areas, poverty as a contributing factor to the reticence of parents to be involved in education was not highlighted quite as much by school leaders. Rather, they seem to hold that parents believe that, so long as the financial means are available, education is the business of the teachers and the school. The following observation captures this concern:

> The most difficult problem I have relates to parents. Parents in this city contribute financially to the education of their children, but in spite of this contribution they throw kids to us. They rarely come to school, and many do not follow what happens here. They are not available, they are not available.

The unavailability of parents to talk to teachers is a serious challenge for school leaders and teachers, who are required to provide academic support for children who often stay at home alone. On this, one head teacher in an urban school declared:

> We have students who appear to live alone. We have a child who has reached primary 6 after repeating previous grades many times. This child told me he stays alone in the house. He lives only with one parent who works during the night. It means the child reaches home from school when his parent

> leaves home for work. This problem is very challenging to us. We have many cases similar to this. You understand we deal with such problems and parents do not help us. Even our good performance comes from the effort of our teachers, not parents.

This quote is illustrative of a belief among school leaders in urban areas that the reluctance of parents to be involved in the education of their children can be attributed to daily commitments that render many of them too busy to participate in school activities.

The above challenges affecting school leaders in post-conflict Rwanda should not be overstated. Indeed, overemphasising the concerns of school leadership may obscure tangible milestones achieved in primary school education and the strategies the Rwandan government has adopted to deal with the challenges facing basic education. While it is true that school leaders encounter the complex problems already highlighted, significant progress has been made in Rwanda in terms of primary school enrolment, increasing girls' access to education, textbook delivery, the introduction of free Nine Year Basic Education (which is now evolving towards free Twelve Year Basic Education), and the creation of new teacher training colleges and colleges of education to produce enough qualified teachers for primary and lower secondary education. These developments constitute just some of the progress that has been made in education. At the more micro level, school leaders are also adopting strategies to deal with the challenges encountered, a matter that is the next concern of this chapter.

Strategies for dealing with the concerns

Conflict prevention

In order to prevent the reoccurrence of violent conflict, there seems to be a concerted effort at the primary school level to create a socially cohesive and conflict free society. When participants in the study were asked to identify the strategies their schools were using to prevent large-scale violence, most of them mentioned engaging in dialogue on Rwandan history, unity and reconciliation. This dialogue takes place while engaging in compulsory extra-curricular activities in students' clubs.

Different types of students' clubs exist in primary schools. These range from environment clubs to English clubs. Conflict prevention dialogue occurs in specific anti-genocide clubs, unity and reconciliation clubs, and patriotism clubs. In most cases, these anti-violence clubs are led by a committee of students and are advised by one or two teachers. Additionally, in most schools only Primary Four to Six students are allowed to be members of these anti-genocide clubs since they are relatively senior and are deemed to be able to understand the complex and tragic situations experienced by Rwandan society in the past. Furthermore, school leaders highlighted that clubs do not segregate students along any lines since members of these clubs emanate from the three ethnic groups making up the Rwandan population.

In addition to promoting dialogue in clubs, some of the schools selected contribute to conflict prevention by commemorating the genocide at the school level and by visiting genocide memorial sites. During genocide commemoration, the clubs are involved in preparing and organising genocide commemoration events, and students, regardless of their ethnic background, compose songs and poems to present during the event. Also, as part of this commemoration, schools invite local leaders to give talks to children about such topics as patriotism, unity and reconciliation, and the origins and causes of the Rwandan genocide. Moreover, two of the six schools investigated take both student leaders in the clubs and other students' representatives to genocide memorial sites. At the memorial sites, school leaders reported, students are briefed about issues surrounding the Rwandan genocide and come back to school to share their new knowledge with fellow students.

Peer-to-peer learning strategies

Head teachers from three urban schools in the study were part of a club comprising other head teachers. This club of head teachers meets regularly and visits schools led by club members to share ideas, experiences and good practice. School visits are often undertaken when a club member is experiencing an especially tough problem in his or her school, with the aim of helping individuals to deal with the problem encountered. The following comment from a head teacher captures what is sometimes done during school visits and the perceived value of the club for its members:

> We advise each other on different issues. In this club, we visit schools we lead. A head teacher can tell us that the personnel at his/her school are rebelling or that there is something wrong at his/her school. We visit this school and observe how things are done. We observe students gathering in the morning; we enter classes; we look at the level of hygiene, and so on. We then meet teachers and discuss together important issues. I have seen this is a good practice, and it would be good if other head teachers form such clubs.

The same head teacher recommended that other head teachers form peer-to-peer learning clubs because of the critical role of the head teacher in promoting school success. She put it this way:

> I strongly recommend that head teachers make such clubs because I have realised that the head teacher plays a big role in the improvement and development of the school. I used not to agree with this, but I am convinced now that the role of the principal is critical.

Apart from intervening when there is a pressing challenge in a club member's school, the members also coach new head teachers on how school issues may be dealt with.

The coaching offered by peers is especially important since most head teachers in Rwanda have not received formal or specific preparation to manage schools. For example, one head teacher stated that she learnt managerial and leadership strategies from her peers prior to receiving formal professional development, which came one year after appointment:

> I studied education, but not school leadership and management. So I faced leadership related challenges when I was appointed head teacher. Managing teachers, students, and parents was not easy for me. I approached experienced head teachers and we implemented what we call 'peer learning'.

She concluded by saying, 'these head teachers gave me advice while I was waiting for the Ministry of Education training'.

Dealing with teachers' lack of motivation

The ways in which school leaders dealt with teachers' lack of motivation varied from one situation to another. While some school leaders empathised with teachers and showed them compassion and care, others did not. One male deputy head teacher commented: 'I tell my teachers that the doors are open and that they can go and look for a better job if they are not happy with their salary.'

Similarly, another male head teacher tried to integrate spirituality in the workplace by referring to accountability to God and to society while trying to counteract teachers' anti-professional behaviours arising from lack of motivation:

> I tell teachers that they are answerable to the nation and to society, and that they are failing the nation and society whenever they do not perform their duties well. I also tell them that God will ask them what they will have done during their teaching career. On this, I advise them to leave the system if they do not want to face God's judgment. I therefore tell them that it is better to leave the teaching career instead of rendering bad service deliberately.

Unlike the above school leaders, there was one head teacher who, in keeping with her caring character, stated that she tried to create an atmosphere of caring and respect to raise the commitment of her teachers:

> I try to be humble and respect my teachers. I also acknowledge and praise their teaching efforts and try to support them. I know it is human to make mistakes, and I discuss their problems with them without being intimidating.

In doing so, she sought to deal with teachers' lack of motivation by placing respect, care and support at the heart of her relationship with teachers.

It should also be pointed out that some school leaders stated that addressing teachers' lack of motivation is beyond their competency inasmuch as it is caused mainly by poor teacher pay and poor living conditions. On this, they said that addressing teachers' lack of motivation is the responsibility of the State, which should increase teachers' salaries to improve their standard of living. Some progress has been made in this respect, with the government establishing the teachers' Savings and Credit Cooperative (SACCO), to boost teacher motivation and retention (Umwalimu SACCO, 2012). Although criticised by some school leaders interviewed, this cooperative is expected to improve teachers' economic conditions through granting them low-interest loans.

Dealing with drop-out and the lack of parental involvement

The strategies adopted by school leaders to deal with student attrition and parents' lack of involvement in education varied from discussing the issues with parents to reporting them to local administrative bodies. The school–local-administration collaboration was especially apparent when parents resisted sending their children to school, or when they were complicit in a student dropping out. Local administration authorities in Rwanda fine parents who jeopardise the government's aim to increase access to education. At the same time, some parental behaviours, such as not attending school meetings, tend to be ignored.

The above strategies cannot be considered as definitive answers to the challenges faced by school leaders in post-conflict Rwanda. This is because the problems discussed above are akin to those that Heifetz and Linsky (2002) portray as 'adaptive problems', or the kinds of problems for which we do not have ready answers and which take time to deal with. On a related matter, the leadership style that tends to be adopted by most school leaders seems to be inadequate for tackling adaptive problems. This leadership style and its ineffectiveness in handling such adaptive challenges are discussed below.

A glimpse of the leadership styles of school leaders

With only a few exceptions, a 'managerial' leadership style seemed to be predominant among the school leaders of the schools selected. This style becomes particularly apparent when the head teachers' daily work is analysed. Most head teachers spend much time performing activities that are managerial in nature. Such activities include inspection of teachers in classrooms, ensuring attendance of teachers at work, ensuring students' attendance, managing students' discipline in and outside classrooms, coordinating activities pertaining to the construction of new classrooms and the rehabilitation of old ones, purchasing teaching materials, managing school finance and resources, and attending meetings at the sector and/or district level. In addition, the predominance of managerial leadership is evidenced by the absence of a vision and strategic plans in some of the schools investigated.

Managerial leadership was also apparent in head teachers' bureaucratic compliance with prescribed government policies and district guidelines. Despite the decentralisation of the education sector since 2006, schools are still required to comply with education policies, curriculum and examination policies designed by higher levels within the bureaucratic hierarchy. In a similar vein, schools are required to incorporate in their performance contracts the annual education-related targets of the district. On this, one head teacher commented that he was going to include the purchase of a fire extinguisher in his school's performance contract although there was very little chance of the school's building catching fire. Indeed, this school does not have electricity or any other source of power that could cause a fire.

Another head teacher stated that performance contracts ought to flow from school to district, rather than the other way round. He put it this way:

> the district ought to formulate education targets based on schools' needs because schools know better what kids really need. But this is not the case. We first have to know the priorities of the district in education and then incorporate those priorities in our performance contracts and indicate our contribution to achieving them.

It can be argued that the managerial style of leadership is not sufficient for sorting out the adaptive problems facing schools. Few would dispute that such problems as the lack of teacher professionalism and motivation, the lack of parental involvement in education, the problems associated with endemic student attrition, and the challenges of conflict prevention do not have quick and known solutions. As mentioned earlier, these problems are adaptive in nature, and thus they require more adaptive approaches to leadership than managerial leadership to tackle them. As such, they contrast with technical problems which have known solutions and can be dealt with by applying authoritative expertise and maintaining the school's current values and ways of performing activities (Linsky and Lawrence, 2011). This maintenance of current organisational arrangements and the lack of engagement with change and innovation make managerial leadership appropriate for resolving technical problems.

In spite of the adaptive problems being faced by schools, there is very little evidence of adaptive leadership being exercised by school leaders. Adaptive leadership calls for the adoption and adaptation of more than one leadership style to deal with adaptive challenges. It does not relate to a style/theory of leadership on its own. Rather, it is the 'practice of mobilising people to tackle tough challenges and thrive' (Heifetz *et al.*, 2009, p. 14). On this, it would be desirable for school leaders in Rwanda to mobilise other members of the school's staff, parents and the local community to deal with the complex circumstances which schools face. This move requires them to learn about and implement adaptive change, which entails change in their beliefs, values and ways of doing things (Heifetz *et al.*, 2009; Linsky and Lawrence, 2011). Furthermore, as emotional labour is increasingly involved in school leadership, especially as it relates to the challenges posed by post-genocide circumstances, it would also be desirable for school leaders' emotional intelligence to be developed in order to handle relationships effectively and display empathy (Karareba and Clarke, 2011).

Conclusion

This chapter has focused on the issues faced by Rwandan primary school leaders and the strategies they adopt while dealing with those issues. The nature of the context within which school leadership takes place has also been depicted in the exposition on the challenges faced by primary school leaders and the strategies they employ to solve those problems encountered.

Although the civil war and genocide ended twenty years ago, some of the current school leadership challenges can be attributed directly to the legacies of the conflict. In particular, the issue relating to conflict prevention is specifically attributable to the conflict and its causes in Rwanda. The inability of school leaders to support teachers in their teaching of genocide-related and other controversial issues and teachers' reluctance to use 'participative' teaching methods while teaching genocide-related topics indicate how school leadership is constrained by the legacy of conflict.

However, not all the concerns emphasised by primary school leaders can be seen as related to post-conflict recovery. On this, twenty years after the end of atrocities the issues of student drop-out, low teacher salaries and the lack of parental involvement in education can be better understood against the context of poverty and a poor domestic revenue/economy characterising low income and developing countries, including Rwanda.

Some tasks need to be performed to improve current primary school leadership. Given that teachers have a prominent and direct influence on students' learning (Leithwood *et al.*, 2008), the enhancement of teacher professionalism and motivation is urgently needed. Specifically, professional development programmes for teachers on ways of teaching controversial and genocide-related topics are required. In addition, the ways in which parental involvement in education can be promoted need to be identified. The issue of student attrition also needs to be addressed if Rwanda is to continue on track for meeting education-related Millennium Development targets.

Finally, the challenging circumstances within which schools operate in post-conflict Rwanda require the preparation and development of capable, responsible and resilient school leaders who are crucial for exercising adaptive leadership. This requirement also calls for further research into the realities of school leadership as understood and practised in post-conflict societies. Such research can help inform leadership development and support programmes in post-conflict contexts, which meet school leaders' real, rather than imagined, needs (Harber and Dadey, 1993).

References

Acedo, C. (2011). Education and conflict: From emergency response to reconstruction and peacebuilding. *Prospects*, 41, 181–183.

Akresh, R. and D. de Walque (2008). Armed conflict and schooling: Evidence from the 1994 Rwandan genocide. HiCN Working Papers, 47. Retrieved from: www.hicn.org/papers/wp47.pdf

Al-Hinai, A. M. (2007). The interplay between culture, teacher professionalism and teachers' professional development at times of change. In T. Townsend and R. Bates (eds). *Handbook of Teacher Education: Globalization, Standards and Professionalism in Times of Change* (pp. 41–52). Dordrecht, the Netherlands: Springer.

Boughton, B. (2011). Timor-Leste: Building a post-conflict education system. In C. Brock and L. Pe Symaco (eds). *Education in South-East Asia* (pp. 177–196). Oxford: Symposium Books.

Buckland, P. (2006). Post-conflict education: Time for a reality check? Forced Immigration Review, 7–8. Retrieved from: www.fmreview.org/sites/fmr/files/FMRdownloads/en/FMRpdfs/EducationSupplement/03.pdf. 25/2/2013

Buckley-Zistel, S. (2009). Nation, narration, unification? The politics of history teaching after the Rwandan genocide. *Journal of Genocide Research*, 11(1), 31–53.

Bush, K. D. and Saltarelli, D. (2000). The two faces of education in ethnic conflict: Towards a peacebuilding education for children. Florence: UNICEF.

Clarke, S. and O'Donoghue, T. A. (eds). (2013). *School-level Leadership in Post-conflict Societies: The Importance of Context*. London: Routledge.

Clarke, S. and Wildy, H. (2004). Context counts: Viewing small school leadership from the inside out. *Journal of Educational Administration*, 42(5), 555–572.

Cole, E. A. and Barsalou, J. (2006). Unite or divide? The challenges of teaching history in societies emerging from violent conflict. Washington, DC: United States Institute of Peace.

Day, C., Harris, A. and Hadfield, M. (2010). Grounding knowledge of schools in stakeholder realities: A multi-perspective study of effective school leaders. *School Leadership* and *Management: Formerly School Organisation*, 21(1), 19–42.

Fussel, J. (2001, November). Group classification on national ID cards as a factor in genocide and ethnic cleansing. Paper presented at the Seminar Series of the Yale University Genocide Studies Program, Prevent Genocide International. Retrieved from: www.preventgenocide.org/prevent/removing-facilitating-factors/IDcards/index.htm#0

Guardian, The (2014a, July 7). Rwanda: A puzzling tale of growth and political repression-get the data. Retrieved from: www.theguardian.com/global-development/datablog/2014/apr/03/rwanda-genocide-growth-political-repression-data

Guardian, The (2014b, June 20). Rwanda 20 years on: The tragic testimony of the children of rape. Retrieved from: www.theguardian.com/world/2014/jun/08/rwanda-20-years-genocide-rape-children

Harber, C. and Dadey, A. (1993). The job of the headteacher in Africa: research and reality. *International Journal of Educational Development*, 13(2), 147–160.

Hargreaves, A. (2000). Four ages of professionalism and professional learning. *Teachers and Teaching: History and Practice*, 6(2), 151–182.

Heifetz, R. and Linsky, M. (2002). *Leadership on the Line*. Boston, MA: Harvard Business School Press.

Heifetz, R., Grashow, A. and Linsky, M. (2009). *The Practice of Adaptive Leadership: Tools and Tactics for Changing Your Organization and the World*. Boston, MA: Harvard Business Press.

Helsby, G. (1999). *Changing Teachers' Work: The 'Reform' of Secondary Schooling*. Buckingham: Open University Press.

Hilker, L. M. (2011). The role of education in driving conflict and building peace: The case of Rwanda. *Prospects*, 41, 267–282.

Hodgkin, M. (2006). Reconciliation in Rwanda: Education, history and the state. *Journal of International Affairs*, 60(1), 199–210.

International Planned Parenthood Federation. (2007). Suspension au Rwanda d' enseignants accusés de prôner le genocide. Retrieved from: www.panapress.com/Suspension-au-Rwanda-d-enseignants-accuses-de-proner-le-genocide–12–654538–58-lang1-index.html

Karareba, G. and Clarke, S. (2011). Acknowledging emotional intelligence in the preparation and selection of school principals. *Leading and Managing*, 17(1), 84–99.

King, E. (2005). Educating for conflict or peace: Challenges and dilemmas in post-conflict Rwanda. *International Journal*, 60(4), 904–918.

Kiwuwa, D. E. (2012). *Ethnic Politics and Democratic Transition in Rwanda*. London, New York: Routledge.

Kreso, A. P. (2008). The war and post-war impact on the educational system of Bosnia and Herzegovina. *International Review of Education*, 54, 353–374.

Leithwood, K., Harris, A. and Hopkins, D. (2008). Seven strong claims about successful school leadership. *School Leadership and Management*, 28(1), 27–42.

Linsky, M. and Lawrence, J. (2011). Adaptive challenges for school leadership. In H. O'Sullivan and J. W. Burnham (eds). *Leading and Managing Schools* (pp. 3–15). London: Sage Publications.

Marks, H. M. and Printy, S. M. (2003). Principal leadership and school performance: An integration of transformational and instructional leadership. *Educational Administration Quarterly*, 39(3), 370–397.

Ministry of Education. (2013). *2012 Education Statistics Year Book*. Kigali, Rwanda: Ministry of Education.

Moghalu, K. C. (2005). *Rwanda's Genocide: The Politics of Global Justice*. New York, Hampshire: Palgrave Macmillan.

Mosselson, J., Wheaton, W. and Frisoli, P. G. (2009). Education and fragility: A synthesis of the literature. *Journal of Education for International Development*, 4(1), 1–17.

National Institute of Statistics of Rwanda (2014). Rwanda Fourth Population and Housing Census, 2012. Kigali: National Institute of Statistics of Rwanda.

New Times, The (2013a, August 20). Genocide ideology steadily fading from schools. Retrieved from: www.newtimes.co.rw/section/Search/genocide%20ideology%20in%20schools

New Times, The (2013b, July 7). Teenage pregnancies denying girls opportunities. Retrieved from: www.newtimes.co.rw/section/Search/Teenage%20pregnancies%20denying%20girls%20opportunities

Novelli, M. and Lopez Cardizo, M. T. A. (2008). Conflict, education and the global south: New critical directions. *International Journal of Educational Development*, 28(4), 473–488.

Obura, A. and Bird, L. (2009). Education marginalisation in post-conflict settings: A comparison of government and donor responses in Burundi and Rwanda. Background paper prepared for the Education for All Global Monitoring Report 2010.

Oplatka, I. (2004). The principalship in developing countries: Context, characteristics and reality. *Comparative Education*, 40(3), 427–448.

Paulson, J. (ed.). (2011). *Education, Conflict and Development*. Oxford: Symposium Books.

Paulson, J. and Rappleye, J. (2007). Education and conflict: Essay review. *International Journal of Educational Development*, 27, 340–347.

Power, H. (2013). Unresolved identity conflicts as a barrier to reconciliation in Rwanda. *International public policy review*, 7(2), 1–9.

Republic of Rwanda. (2012). Law governing the organization and functioning of nursery, primary and secondary Education. In Official Gazette no. 31 of 30/7/2012. Retrieved from: www.primature.gov.rw/publications/official-gazettes.html

Smith, A. (2005). Education in the twenty-first century: Conflict, reconstruction and reconciliation. *Compare: A Journal of Comparative and International Education*, 35(4), 373–391.

Torsti, P. (2009). Segregated education and texts: A challenge to peace in Bosnia and Herzegovina. *International Journal on World Peace*, 26(2), 65–82.

Transparency International. (2014). Transparency international corruption perceptions index 2013. Berlin: *Transparency International.*

Umwalimu SACCO. (2012). Background. Retrieved from: www.umwalimusacco.co.rw/

UNDP (2013). The rise of the south: Human progress in a diverse world. New York: United Nations Development Programme.

UNICEF-Rwanda. (n.d.). Basic education. Retrieved from: www.unicef.org/rwanda/education.html

Vroom, H. V. and Jago, G. A. (2007). The role of the situation in leadership. *American Psychologist*, 62(1), 17–24.

Walker-Keleher, J. (2006). Reconceptualising the relationship between conflict and education: The case of Rwanda. *The Fletcher Journal of Human Security*, 21, 35–51.

Watson, L. (2009). Issues in reinventing school leadership: Reviewing the OECD report on improving school leadership from an Australian perspective. *Leading & Managing*, 15(1), 1–13.

Weinstein, M. H., Freedman, W. S. and Hughson, H. (2007). School voices: Challenges facing education systems after identity-based conflicts. *Education, Citizenship and Social Justice*, 2(1), 41–71.

World Bank. (2005). *Reshaping the Future: Education and Post-conflict Reconstruction*. Washington, DC: The World Bank.

World Bank. (2014). Rwanda overview. Retrieved from: www.worldbank.org/en/country/rwanda/overview#1

6

LEADING SCHOOLS IN TIMES OF CONFLICT

Between a rock and a hard place: a case study from the borderlands of Ireland

Anthony Kelly

Introduction

Schools along the Irish border operate on the cusp of two national education systems, two conflicting political affiliations, two opposing religious ideologies and, during the worst of the Troubles, two warring factions. While individual secondary schools have not formally operated in more than one national jurisdiction, their pupils frequently attend schools on one side of the border while living on the other, and in any case have been affected on a daily basis by the socioeconomic decline and political conflict going on around them. This chapter is essentially a case study of how school leadership is understood in this context, which includes the *internal* dimension of how the conflict impacts on students and on the curriculum; and the *external* dimension of how it influences parents and the local community. Some of the issues and challenges are distinctive, if sometimes subliminal, but generally the challenge is one of capability: a headship can only occur at a particular place at a particular time – we cannot choose when to live – and in conflict societies like Northern Ireland, schools deal on behalf of innocents with events that are outside their control.

The fashion in recent decades, particularly in the United Kingdom, has been for more leadership, so that the word itself has become imbued with a type of mysticism, as if the mere fact of having the commodity was enough to ensure its desired effect. Actually, in many cases, and particularly in conflicted societies, what is needed is not *more leadership*, but *better management*. The two are not mutually exclusive, but in practice there are probably as many typologies of leadership as there are actual management roles, and most have been constructed by 'consultants' with little practical experience and no demonstrable skill in the field, so that the academic study of leadership has become little more than a compendium of anecdote and folk wisdom designed to promote a marketable idea for lecture tours. There can be very few adjectives remaining that have not at some stage prefixed the word 'leadership', but there is little research evidence to quantify the effect on student or societal outcomes of all these so-called ground-breaking understandings. Certainly, we can reasonably assume that purposive leadership is probably better than distracted management, in the same way as an organised learning environment is probably better than a chaotic one, but it is difficult to find consistent evidence for the size of the effect on student learning or for the mechanisms by which its influence is exerted. Yet things are not all bleak for practitioners acting on the fault lines of society; several leadership models, like the Social Change model from the Higher Education Research Institute at UCLA, promote leadership as a social responsibility and as an activity which can enhance student self-awareness and citizenship (Dugan, 2006).

The education context: Northern Ireland[1]

The Northern Ireland (NI) state was created in 1921 following the partition of Ireland. Its first prime minister, James Craig, later Lord Craigavon, declared it to be 'a Protestant parliament and a Protestant state', although nearly half the population at the time was Roman Catholic (RC). NI had its own autonomous parliament and government until 1973 when it was abolished because the Conservative government in London, traditonally well-disposed towards the Unionist view, did not trust it to act impartially on behalf of all its citizens. NI remained under 'direct rule' from London until devolved government in the form of the NI Assembly and Executive returned in 1998 under the terms of the Good Friday (Belfast) Agreement. Today, the NI Executive has the power to legislate in areas, like education, not explicitly reserved for the UK parliament in London. It operates on a consociational/power-sharing principle whereby consensus among the parties is required to confirm decisions, and ministerial portfolios are allocated to the different political parties using the d'Hondt method.[2]

The Good Friday Agreement, so called because it was signed in Belfast on the Friday before Easter 1998, and the Northern Ireland (St Andrew's Agreement) Act of 2006, ended some four decades of civil war in NI (known as 'The Troubles') between 'nationalists' who are almost exclusively Roman Catholic, and 'unionists' who are almost exclusively Protestant. In the tribal nomenclature of NI, ultra-nationalists are known as 'republicans' and ultra-unionists as 'loyalists'. Historically, the middle-class unionist community was represented by the Ulster Unionist Party (UUP), the working-class loyalist community was represented mainly by the Democratic Unionist Party (DUP), middle-class nationalist voters by the Social Democratic and Labour Party (SDLP), and the working-class/small farming republican community by Sinn Féin (SF). Figure 6.1 shows how the more extreme political parties (DUP and SF) have squeezed out the more moderate centre-ground parties (UUP and SDLP) in NI since 1997, and Figure 6.2 shows how SF has prospered in the Republic of Ireland, especially in the border counties, so that the end of the conflict in NI has actually led to a more polarised political landscape. For comparison, Figure 6.3 shows the religious distribution within NI.

Primary schooling and secondary schooling are the responsibility of the Department of Education Northern Ireland (DENI), but at local level is

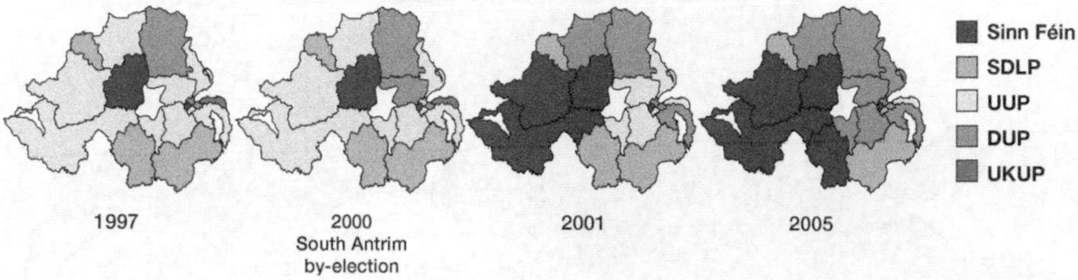

FIGURE 6.1 Voting patterns in general elections to the UK (London) parliament

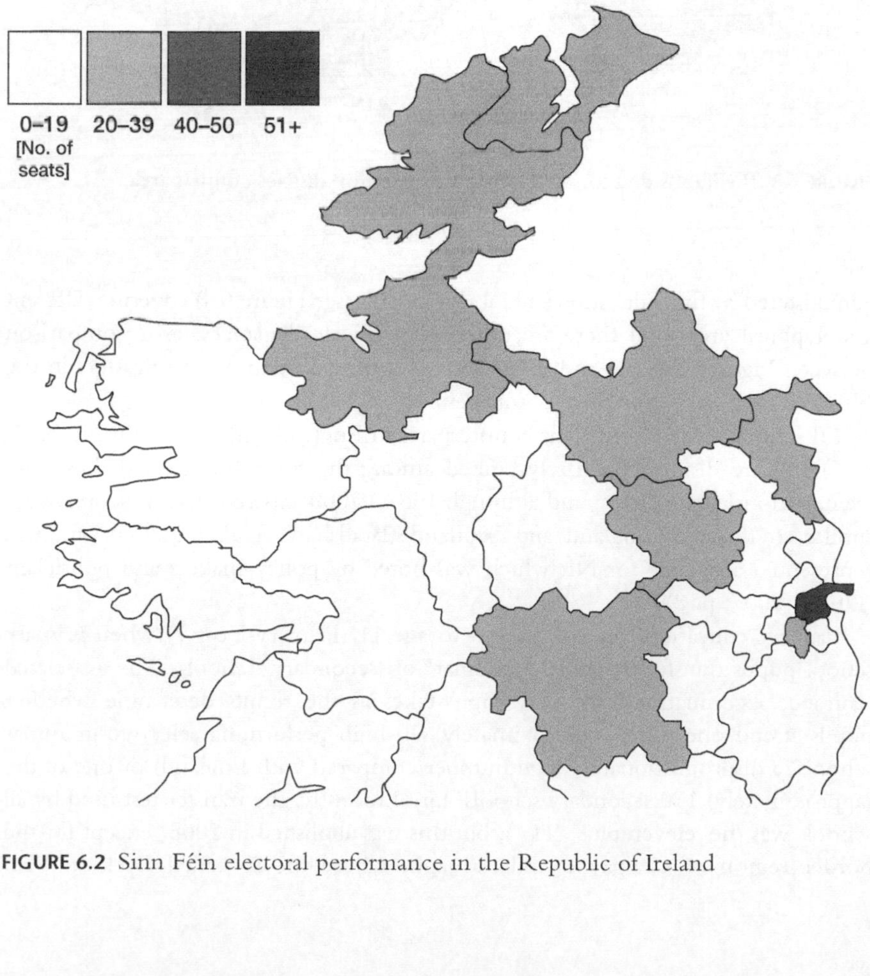

FIGURE 6.2 Sinn Féin electoral performance in the Republic of Ireland

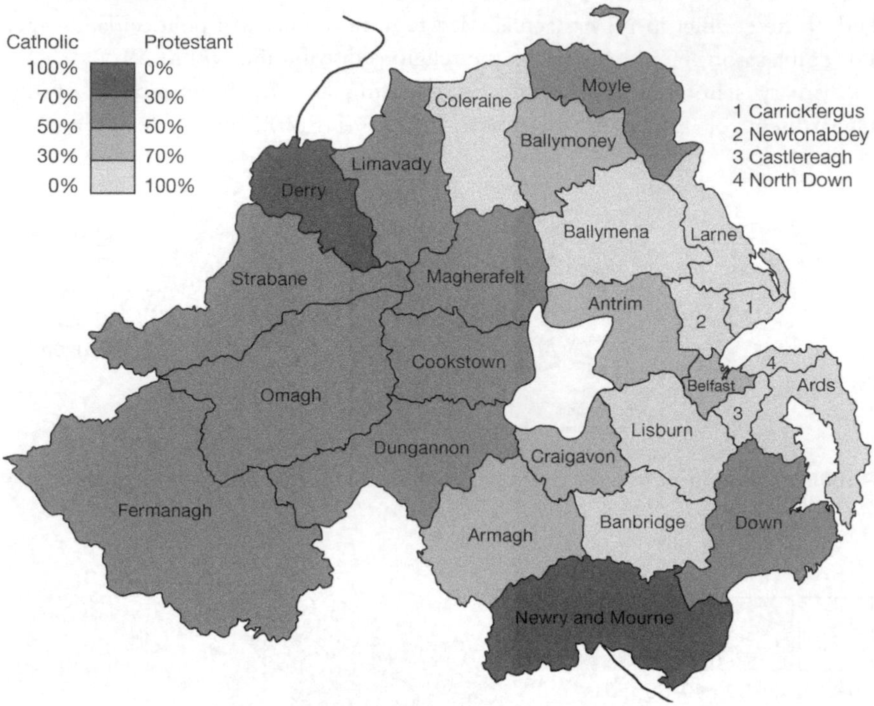

FIGURE 6.3 Religious division in Northern Ireland by district council area

administered by five Education and Library Boards (see Figure 6.4) covering different geographical areas and therefore different political allegiances, as a comparison between Figures 6.1, 6.3 and 6.4 reveals. To date, all education ministers in the NI Executive have come from Sinn Féin.

NI schools outperform their counterparts in England and Wales (DENI 2007, p. 7) and are disproportionately ranked among the top performers in UK state examination league tables, and although PISA[3] 2009 showed that its scores were similar to those of England and Scotland (Bradshaw *et al.*, 2010, p. xi), this represented a decline for NI, which was noted by policy-makers and politicians (DENI, 2007, p. 8).

Primary education lasts from age 4 to age 11 (Primary Year 7) when primary school pupils transfer to either 'grammar' or 'secondary' schools. The associated 'entrance examinations' are very high-stakes as the results determine whether pupils attend one of the (approximately) 70 high-performing selective grammar schools (a disproportionately high number compared with England) or one of the (approximately) 170 secondary schools. Until recently, the transfer test used by all schools was the 'eleven plus' (11+), but this was abolished in 2008[4] except for the border region of Craigavon and Armagh, where the so-called Dickson Plan remains in operation (SELB, 2011).[5] There is no coresponding 'selection' in the Republic of Ireland.

There is widespread agreement in NI that selection at age 11 puts too much pressure on pupils, but this is balanced by a general feeling that those who go to non-selective secondary schools in NI still receive a first-class education (Gallagher and Smith, 2003), and successive education ministers, all of whom have been SF, have chosen not to turn the system into a comprehensive one, although that is SF party policy.

It has recently become apparent that the new 'education poor' in NI are working-class Protestants/loyalists. Less than 20 per cent of low socioeconomic-status loyalist 16-year-olds obtain 5+ GCSE passes, which is 57 per cent lower than the top-scoring group, Roman Catholic girls. As the *Irish Times*[6] pointed out, the old system that discriminated against Catholics induced a reliance on a 'jobs for the boys' culture among Protestant working-class school-leavers. As a result, the RC community, which was forced to rely on educational achievement in order to progress, finds itself better prepared to benefit now from schooling in what is (wrongly) perceived as a zero-sum game where one group can win only at the expense of the other.

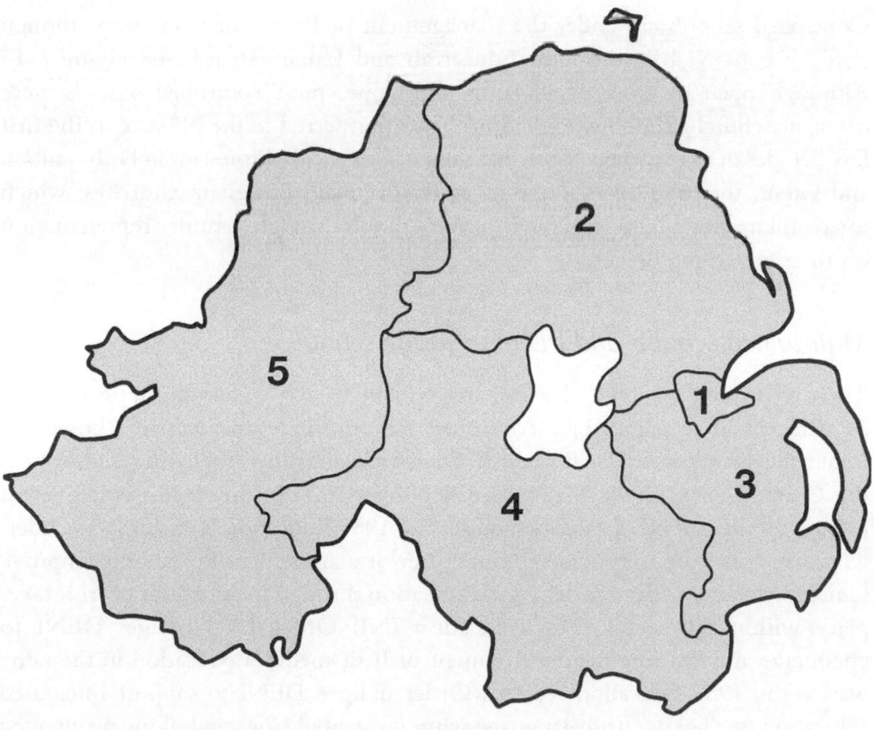

FIGURE 6.4 The five Education and Library Boards (1. Belfast; 2. North Eastern; 3. South Eastern; 4. Southern; 5. Western)

The percentage of pupils in selective education in NI is very high compared with England and Wales, which, according to its supporters is a factor in the State's success, though PISA 2009 reveals that NI has the largest achievement gap in the UK between those from well-off and those from poor backgrounds (Bradshaw *et al.*, 2010, p. xi). This, as the OECD (2004, p. 5) notes, probably means that 'students from disadvantaged backgrounds do not achieve their full potential'. In NI, 17 per cent of school pupils are entitled to free school meals (FSM) – 26 per cent in secondary and six per cent in grammar schools (DENI, 2011a, b) – and as in the rest of the UK, FSM entitlement is concentrated among lower-attaining pupils.

In addition to the division of schools by academic selection, there are divisions in the extent to which they are controlled by the state, which itself was established along ethno-religious lines. State or 'controlled' schools are in practice attended overwhelmingly by those from the Protestant community, and there is a separate publicly funded 'maintained' system for Roman Catholics. 'Integrated' schools, which attempt a balanced enrolment of pupils from both traditions, are becoming increasingly popular, notwithstanding the falling demographics, but the sector remains very small.

Controlled schools

Controlled schools are under the management of Boards of Governors, though staff are employed by the local Education and Library Board (see Figure 6.4). Although open to those of all faiths and none, most controlled schools were originally church schools whose control was transferred to the NI state in the first few decades of its existence. Since that state was explicitly Protestant in both outlook and intent, the 'transferors' were naturally the main Protestant churches, which today still maintain links with their former schools through statutory representation on their governing bodies.

Maintained schools and Irish-language schools

There are more than 500 Catholic-managed schools in NI educating approximately 51 per cent of all pupils. Like controlled schools, these 'maintained schools' are under the management of Boards of Governors, but the employing authority is the Council for Catholic Maintained Schools (CCMS), the largest employer of (8,500) teachers in NI. Established under the 1989 Education Reform (NI) Order, its primary aims are to provide an upper tier of management for schools, improve standards and plan effective delivery. Education through the medium of Irish takes place within this sector. The Education (NI) Order 1998 obliges DENI to encourage and facilitate the development of Irish-medium education in the same way as the 1989 Education Reform Order obliged DENI to support Integrated Education (see below). Irish-language schools can apply for stand-alone maintained status, or (where a free-standing school is not viable) for support as self-contained units within existing schools operating on the same site and under the management of the host (English-medium) school. There are 27 stand-alone 'Gaelscoileanna' (as Irish language schools are known), 12 Irish-medium units attached to English-medium host schools and two independent Gaelscoileanna. 'Comhairle na Gaelscolaíochta' (CnaG) is the representative body for Irish-medium Education in both parts of Ireland.

Some researchers like Wright and Scullion (2007) regard education through the medium of Irish as cross-cultural, but given that Gaelscoileanna are almost completely supported by parents from the nationalist tradition, they are not 'integrated' in any meaningful sense, though they do represent an accommodation within the NI state of 'the other' tradition, and testify to the growing cultural confidence of NI's Roman Catholic population.

Integrated schools

Although integrated education is expanding – there are approximately 40 primary and 20 second-level schools in the sector – NI remains a religiously segregated system, with in excess of 90 per cent of pupils attending either a maintained (Catholic) or a controlled (Protestant) school with their co-religionists (DENI, 2007). Fresh-start integrated schools – sometimes called 'grant maintained integrated schools' – were established by the voluntary efforts of parents (unsupported by the churches) under the 1989 Education Reform (NI) Order, which obliged DENI to facilitate and encourage the development of integrated education where there was parental demand (HMSO, 1989). Other Integrated schools, which were originally controlled (and therefore Protestant), but which opted through parental ballot to switch to the integrated sector, have since come on stream, and are called 'transformed' Integrated schools.

The voluntary Northern Ireland Council for Integrated Education (NICIE) develops and supports integrated education in Northern Ireland, but only through the medium of English. The Integrated Education Fund (IEF), the financial foundation for the development of integrated education established in 1992 by the EU Structural Fund, DENI, and the Nuffield and Joseph Rowntree foundations, offers bridging finance for start-up integrated schools before they secure full government funding, as well as supporting existing schools and those seeking to become integrated through 'transformation'. In some ways integrated schools were a forerunner of charter schools in the US and Free schools in England, and the absence of politico-religious support in the early days was not necessarily a bad thing since many advocates were in any case anxious not to be identified with any one particular political perspective.

School holidays in NI

School holidays in NI differ considerably from those of Great Britain (GB), but are similar to those in the Republic of Ireland (RoI), though they generally do not have full-week mid-term breaks. Summer vacation is longer than GB at 9–10 weeks, but shorter than the RoI's 12–13 weeks.

The education context: the Republic of Ireland

The Republic of Ireland (RoI) occupies about 80 per cent of the island of Ireland and has a population of 4.6 million. The RoI gained independence from the UK in 1922 while NI exercised its option to remain within the UK. RoI and NI had no official state formal relations until 1999 when the North–South Ministerial Council was created by the Good Friday Agreement. Ireland joined the European Union in 1973, along with the UK and Denmark, and remains one of the wealthiest countries in the world in terms of GDP per capita. The country underwent huge economic growth in the period 1995–2007 (the 'Celtic Tiger' era), but suffered a financial and banking crisis in 2008 as part of the global economic crash. Although the economy has not yet recovered to pre-crash levels, Ireland is still the seventh most developed country in the world according to the United Nations and performs well in terms of economic freedom and civil liberties. Ireland is a founding member of the Council of Europe and the OECD. Education is compulsory[7] in the Republic of Ireland from age 6 to 16, but in practice it lasts from age 4 to age 17 or 18. The general rule is that children start primary school in the September following their fourth birthday. Education is free at all levels (including university, through student service fees – currently €2500 – have recently been introduced following the financial crisis of 2008), and the RoI, like NI, has 100 per cent literacy. RoI has the youngest population in Europe with more than one-fifth of people under 14. The schooling system has 900,000 pupils across all phases.

Primary education

The primary education sector includes state-funded 'national' schools, state-funded special schools and private schools. All of these may be denominational, non-denominational, multi-denominational or Gaelscoileanna. For historical reasons, most primary schools are state-aided religious schools, of various denominations, and though state-funded, are owned by religious orders and parishes. All teachers' salaries are paid by the state; more specifically, by the Department of Education and Skills (DES), which is also responsible for their inspection.

Primary schooling has an eight-year cycle ('junior infants', 'senior infants' and Classes 1 through 6) after which pupils transfer to post-primary/secondary school, typically at the age of 12. The State's objectives for primary education are not typical of European countries in that they include the aim to 'enable the child to realise his or her potential as a unique individual', and to 'prepare for a continuum of learning'. The 1999 review of the primary curriculum was the first revision of the curriculum since 1971, so unlike the UK, which is seemingly in a constant state of policy hysteria, the system is very stable. It is divided into the following key areas: Irish and English languages; Mathematics; Science and the Environment; Arts, Music and Drama; Physical Education; and Social, Personal and Health Education. Church authorities – usually the RC Church, but not always – oversee the formulation and implementation of the religious curriculum in the schools they control. Unlike NI, there is no terminal examination at the end of primary schooling.[8]

'National' schools – the dominant type of primary school – date back to the introduction of state primary education under British rule in 1831. They are controlled by Boards of Management under diocesan (usually RC) patronage and typically include the local parish priest or clergyman as chairperson. Gaelscoileanna (the plural of Gaelscoil; literally 'Irish school') date from the 1980s as the Irish language increased in popularity among the middle classes. Approximately 10 per cent of pupils are educated in one of these (approximately 350) Gaelscoileanna wherein Irish is the working language. They are not under diocesan patronage and are not classified as religious/denominational, unlike Irish-language 'national' schools in Irish-language districts. Additionally, there are Irish language *pre-schools* called 'Naionrai'.

Multidenominational schools are a more recent innovation. Generally, they have been founded following parental demand and are under the nationwide patronage of a not-for-profit voluntary organisation, 'Educate Together'. They attract – and indeed their *raison d'être* is to attract – students from all religious and non-religious backgrounds. In total, there are more than 3,000 primary schools in the Republic of Ireland. Some 90 per cent are under RC church patronage, 6 per cent are under Church of Ireland (Anglican) patronage, 2 per cent are multidenominational, and the remaining 2 per cent are under Presbyterian, Quaker or non-Christian control.

Post-primary education

The post-primary sector comprises: secondary schools and community schools,[9] which are privately owned and managed by trustees from various religious communities; vocational schools and community colleges,[10] which are state-established and administered by one of sixteen local Education and Training Boards (ETB);[11] and a small number of comprehensive schools, which are managed by stand-alone Boards of Management.[12]

Gaelcholáistí (literally, 'Irish Colleges') are second-level schools outside Irish-speaking districts. Like Gaelscoileanna in the primary phase, the medium of instruction is Irish (and pupils progress to them from the Gaelscoileanna), with approximately 3 per cent of all second-level students attending these schools. So-called 'grind schools' are fee-paying commercial 'crammer' schools, the equivalent of private sixth form colleges in Britain. They operate outside the state sector and only run two-year Leaving Certificate or one-year repeat Leaving Certificate programmes for those who did not perform well enough first time round.

All students must complete at least three years of secondary education, and more than 90 per cent stay on for the full period (5 or 6 years) to sit the terminal Leaving Certificate examination, the equivalent of A-levels in the UK. Post-primary education consists of a three-year Junior Cycle (aged 12–15 typically) followed by a two-year Senior Cycle. In addition, most schools offer a Transition Year (TY)

– optional in most schools, but compulsory in others – intercalated between Junior and Senior Cycles, so that secondary schooling typically lasts six years (aged 12–18). Transition Year, it is claimed, provides an opportunity for students to experience a wide range of educational inputs, including work experience, during a year free from formal examinations, but opinion is divided about how effective and desirable this intercalated year is for subsequent senior cycle study. The content of Transition Year is determined by the school itself to suit its resources, the local availability of work experience and the wider intellectual interests of staff. Schools are not permitted to teach the formal Leaving Certificate curriculum, so as not to disadvantage those students *not* doing TY, but this rule is frequently (perhaps even generally) flouted. Students follow courses such as Law, Philosophy, Creative Writing and Public Speaking, and do projects that under normal circumstances they would not have time to do. TY is intended to help students mature academically, to give them a more informed basis for making their Leaving Certificate subject choices and to develop them into better and more self-directed learners, but critics – and there are many – believe that TY breaks the study habit established in the first three years of post-primary education and that students 'return' to Leaving Certificate study more distracted.

The Junior Certificate examination marks the end of the Junior Cycle. Students usually take ten or eleven subjects in addition to non-examination subjects like Physical Education (PE), and Social Personal and Health Education (SPHE). It is more generalist and broad than in NI or England. It aims to prepare students for the Senior Cycle and, as such, it is not a school-leaving examination like its UK counterpart, the GCSE.

During the Senior Cycle, whether via TY or directly from Junior Cycle, students follow one of three programmes, each leading to a terminal state examination: the traditional Leaving Certificate (LC); the Leaving Certificate Vocational Programme (LCVP); and the Leaving Certificate Applied Programme (LCAP). The traditional LC examination is typically taken when students are 17 or 18 years of age. Students must take at least five subjects, which must normally include Irish, but most study six or seven, and the best six grades are used for university entrance. The LCVP is similar to the traditional LC, but has a concentration on technical subjects and modules with a vocational focus. And finally, the LCAP is a self-contained two-year course designed to meet the needs of students who are not academically inclined to either of the other two programmes. It is person-centred and involves a cross-curricular rather than a subject based approach, but it is not recognised for entry to higher education.

The post-primary curriculum is generalist like its Scottish counterpart but unlike the NI and English systems. The emphasis is on breadth rather than depth. Students typically study seven subjects at either Higher (Honours) or Ordinary (Pass) level, as opposed to three (at a common level) in the A-level system of NI and England. Approximately 88 per cent of pupils stay on in school to study for the LC, which is a much higher participation rate than in other EU countries at the equivalent stage. Typically, a pupil entering the RoI system at age 4 will do

8 years at primary and 5 or 6 at second level school,[13] leaving at age 17 or 18, whereas in NI a typical pupil will do 7 years in primary phase and 5 in the secondary phase (or 7 for those who stay on to study A levels).

Education remains a high-value commodity in Ireland, and teaching is a highly esteemed profession. The RoI also ranks above average in academic attainment/ examination performance in both OECD and EU comparisons, with the second best reading literacy for teenagers in the EU, after Finland.

School holidays in RoI

Holidays in the RoI system vary from school to school, or in the case of vocational schools, from region to region, though there is widespread coordination locally to minimise transport costs and family disruption. Primary and post-primary schools have similar school years: beginning at the start of September; a mid-term week off at the end of October; a two-week vacation over Christmas; a mid-term week off in February; a two-week vacation at Easter; and a long summer vacation (June, July and August for post-primary students,[14] and July and August for primary pupils). There are historical reasons for this structure and for the widespread uniformity. It is not, as some have suggested, religious, but rather for agricultural reasons: historically, children were needed to help with farm work in a country that was, and still is, largely rural and non-industrial.

School leadership on the fault-line of conflict

Schools along the political border between NI and the RoI, and therefore on the educational fault-line of two different schooling systems, cater for communities and students for whom the border is (in an everyday sense) a meaningless political construct: they might live in NI, come from a farming family whose fields are divided comically by a line on the map, go to primary school in one jurisdiction and secondary school in the other. Families typically shop and attend church in different jurisdictions, and often have political allegiances at odds with the dominant view where they are resident: Protestant and unionist on the RoI side; Roman Catholic and republican on the NI side. However, for those who believe that all children are entitled to, and need, education in a supportive environment free from terror of whatever sort and from whatever source, institutional or political, this presents some challenging professional imperatives.

Defining the mission

Prime among these imperatives is the need for school leaders – heads, principals, curriculum leaders, boards of management, governors and the wider school community – to define explicitly the purpose of their school. Mission Statements have had bad press in recent years, with good reason. Too often they have been a substitute for good management. Children seldom come home from school enthusing (or complaining) about the latest version of the Mission Statement framed on the wall beside reception. Instead, they talk about particular teachers, subject difficulties, class relationships and the like. However, in conflict and post-conflict contexts, a Mission Statement is an opportunity to set the ethos of the school in a way that differentiates it from, rather than reflects, the context in which the school is situated. It can determine the pupil catchment of the school, its staffing (recruitment, retention and promotion) policies, its curriculum and examination policy, its funding streams and ultimately its chances of survival. Perhaps the term 'Statement of Intent' is a better moniker than 'Mission Statement'; for example, 'To cherish all children equally, irrespective of political or religious background' is a powerful statement of intent for a community that has suffered decades of sectarian violence, and to aspire to parity of esteem between opposing political aspirations is an educative, as much as a political, purpose.

Recruitment, retention and promotion of staff

It is axiomatic that the communities which suffer most from violence and disruption, whether political or otherwise, are those that are the most deprived. Those who can move out do so, and these are the people who can forge a living elsewhere: the middle classes; the families whose parents have already benefited from education; those with in-demand skills. Those who are left behind or those who choose not to leave find themselves living in an increasingly impoverished context; perhaps not in a cultural sense or in the sense of lacking community spirit, but in an economic and educative sense. For schools, this dynamic establishes a spiral of decline for staff recruitment and retention. How do heads entice the best staff to stay in the most deprived and challenging schools – young, motivated, dynamic, missionary types, intent on 'making a difference' – and having lured them to what often turns out to be the most satisfying context in which any teacher can work, how can schools keep them from moving to other schools for promotion; or while staying at the same school, moving to live in more prosperous 'satellite' towns away from the community in which the school is situated? Effective leadership in such a context is about having strong personal values, a set of skills that includes systems thinking and conflict management, and a desire to engage positively and sustainably with the local community. The goal in the Irish borderlands is to create a teaching staff *in* the community and *of* the community.

Recruitment and retention of pupils

The potential spiral of decline described above also applies to the recruitment and retention *of pupils*. Those who move out – high socioeconomic status (SES) children and those whose parents themselves have high levels of education – are disproportionately those children with high attainment. Sometimes they move at a certain age for educational reasons – say, to a bigger school with a broader curriculum – but more often, they move at the primary–secondary transfer point to a more selective school simply because they can. For the headteacher, the most sensitive manifestation of this issue is when the children of teachers also make that choice. Clearly and incontrovertibly, it raises the question in the minds of other parents with similar SES: 'If the school isn't good enough for the teachers who work there, why should it be good enough for my children?' And they have a point. In Ireland as elsewhere, teachers' children do very well from the education system, and other parents look to, and follow, their decisions in relation to school choice. Sociologists will construct all this as middle-class hegemony – the 'chattering classes' perpetuating their economic advantage – but there is a better way to conceptualise it: as simple risk management. Parents can choose a school – in Ireland, they do so with no restriction – but they cannot choose the other parents who make the same choice. They can pick the school with all its attendant baggage – uniform, ethos, curriculum, history, facilities, sporting prowess and geographical location – but they cannot pick their child's classmates, and thus they cannot control their child's learning environment for the coming three to five years. It is a non-trivial consideration. So, in choosing 'another' school, perhaps a fee-paying or more academically selective one rather than their stand-alone community school, they are reducing the risk of having the same choice made by parents who do not share their aspirations.

This theorisation has the same result as the alternative sociological theorisation, but the motivation is different. It is not a case of the middle classes consciously perpetuating their advantage, but rather of them reducing the risk of having their ethos diluted or eroded, as they would see it, through lack of effort on their part. It is more a *guilt* trip than a *power* trip: understand this and one is well on the way to tackling the issue, which for a head is about reassurance and celebrating engagement in such a way that achievement is extended beyond the narrow confines of examination success (to the sporting, artistic and cultural arena) so that all pupils get their fair share of time and resources, and all are valued for what they can achieve. Frequent school-stakeholder engagement is critical: parent–staff evenings; board of management meetings; one-to-one governor and parent meetings; attendance at community events; and having student representatives. Visibility is reassurance. Parents who care need to know that their caring is appreciated. Those who do not yet care need to be encouraged to do so. Absentee landlordism has a long and unhappy history on the island of Ireland; absentee headship is not the way forward!

Adapting the curriculum

Leaving aside the challenge for stand-alone community schools in small Irish border communities providing the full range of academic subjects, the teaching of History within the formal/provided curriculum is often a challenge in this context. The most successful schools have faced this challenge and have turned the challenge into a strength. History can achieve, in a way that mathematics for example cannot, an engagement with current and recent political upheaval, explaining its origins in a balanced way that is usually absent from the media (for example, were

Protestant fears justified about the creation of the Irish Free State?), challenging preconceptions (for example, are all Catholics anti-Union?), questioning the assumptions (for example, is a united Ireland or a United Kingdom still a meaningful notion in the context of EU and global economic imperatives?) and presenting the complexities (for example, why were 200,000 Irishmen fighting as part of the British Army in World War I, and how best should the sacrifice of the 50,000 who were killed be commemorated?). Done well, the teaching of what I call 'history-for-tolerance' can transform a school in a conflict setting; done badly, it can effectively make a nonsense of the entire school mission.

Allied to this challenge in post-conflict schools is the question of dispassionate service and impassioned teaching. The teaching of English and Irish Literature is a case in point. Inspectors and watchful heads have seen teaching of the very finest order, but there have been times when it has been imbued with inappropriate 'emotionalism'. There is a tyranny to this type of delivery that can too easily spill over. Post-conflict schools are, by definition, schools with a recent history of, and proximity to, civil unrest, as a result of which they are inherently unstable and have unknowable tipping points that can easily turn them from post-conflict schools into conflicted schools. So above all else, headship in this context needs to be watchful. Successful heads know that good teaching serves both the subject and the whole school.

Funding, buildings and infrastructure

Conflict takes its toll on human life, on social mobility and on economic well-being. Money flees from conflict and jobs with it, so it is always a challenge to maintain a good built environment for schools operating in such a milieu. In the Ireland borderlands context, the European Union was, and is, a backstop to economic deprivation, and in a wider context, a reason for antagonistic groups to work together as part of a 'cross community movement'. The fact that both Ireland and the UK are friendly and cooperating members of the EU helps in a significant way. The EU does not fund school-building programmes, but for those headteachers willing to invest the time in circumventing bureaucracy and exploiting opportunities, there is plenty of financial support for educational programmes. Educational leadership in this context – and the same would apply to regions like the former Yugoslavia, for example – is about putting in the time and effort to access all possible sources of financial support on behalf of the school community, whether that is from the US, the EU or other sovereign stakeholders.

On a day-to-day basis, schools that serve diverse communities and which seek to accommodate that diversity have greater costs than ordinary schools: there are more sporting and cultural activities to attend[15] with smaller groups so that transport costs are relatively large; there are more frequent disruptions to the delivery of the formal curriculum so there are more significant staff-cover costs; and there are huge capital estate costs. Essentially, the task for the head is to 'play the system' on behalf of stakeholders, so that alongside 'watchfulness', 'pragmatism' is the watchword, notwithstanding long-standing ingrained affiliations which must be dealt with on a daily basis.

Buffering staff

Another feature of headship in post-conflict and conflict schools is the need, unlike anything in normal schooling contexts, to buffer staff and students from external turmoil and from those who would seek to drag the school back into divisiveness. Anecdotal evidence suggests that this is exhausting and requires no small degree of diplomacy. The irony is that if it is done right, it goes unnoticed. There will be conflicts with local political and religious leaders, often over relatively trivial matters such as where to hold Christmas carol services (say), who to invite to assemblies and who to choose for the guest-list at prize-giving. All are laden with a perceived importance out of all proportion to the real problems facing the school. At other times the task is to buffer parents and children from internal *staff* conflict, but at least here the 'combatants' are professionals and employees, so if one cannot appeal to their professional ethic, one has recourse in law.

Involving students

Traditionally, schools have offered little to students in terms of their own leadership development, but nowhere is it more needed than in post-conflict communities.

School leavers must be prepared simultaneously to compete globally in economic terms and domestically to contribute to forming a just society, and experience suggests that students with no opportunity to shape their own educational experience will adopt a passive attitude towards these broader issues. Research suggests that students who are involved in leadership activities also improve their academic outcomes (Patterson, 2012) and become more confident and engaged members of society. These positive effects are not limited to students, but happily also accrue to their schools as institutions in helping them construct good relationships with their local communities. Schools are key to enhancing social responsibility among young people through the development of skills, like their ability to work with others, being aware of the beliefs and emotions that motivate action, understanding and being consistent with one's own values, commitment and collaboration, and the ability to deal with conflicting opinions and people. These values function at individual, group and societal level, but students first need to cultivate an understanding of their own leadership roles in the community, and themselves in relation to it, before they can be part of any solution.

Notes

1 Some of this description is taken from Kelly (2012).
2 The D'Hondt method (mathematically, but not operationally, equivalent to the Jefferson method) is a method for allocating seats in party-list proportional representation. It is also used in the London Assembly and in the European Parliament. There are two forms

depending on whether the parties use their own pre-election ordering of candidates or whether they use a post-election ordering. Proportional representation allocates seats to parties in proportion to the number of votes won, but exact proportionality is not possible because that would produce fractions of seats. The D'Hondt method is designed to overcome this: it preserves proportionality while allocating seats to parties in whole numbers that sum to the correct total, though in comparison with other methods like Hare-Clark, it is slightly biased in favour of larger parties.

3 The Programme for International Student Assessment (PISA) is a survey of the educational achievement of 15-year-olds organised by the Organisation for Economic Cooperation and Development (OECD). The 2009 results were published in 2010.

4 To replace the abolished 11+, the majority of grammar schools now set their own entrance exams, of which there are two versions. It has been reported that the majority of people in NI would prefer the 11+ to be reinstated because the new system involves children taking multiple entrance exams as opposed to a single test.

5 The Dickson Plan is a two-tier transfer system in which pupils can sit transfer tests at age 11 or age 14.

6 Monday, 7 July 2014.

7 Unlike NI, RoI has a written constitution, which allows education to be provided in the home, though the constitution does not explicitly require the State to define minimum standards for that provision.

8 The terminal 'Primary Certificate Examination' was abolished in 1967.

9 Secondary schools educate nearly 60 per cent of all pupils, but this has fallen dramatically since its heyday in the 1970s. The state pays 90 per cent of teacher salary costs and 95 per cent of other (non-pay) costs in these schools.

10 Vocational schools educate approximately 30 per cent of all second-level pupils, with 93 per cent of all costs met by the state.

11 The Education and Training Boards (2013) Act replaced the existing 33 local Vocational Education Committees (VEC) through a process of county-to-county mergers. Community Schools and Community Colleges are both managed by Boards of Management with various membership permutations, but essentially the former are types of secondary school and the latter come under the aegis of the local ETB.

12 Comprehensive schools were established in the 1960s in mimicry of what was happening in Britain and were founded by amalgamating secondary and vocational schools. Comprehensive schools are 100 per cent funded by the state and are run by boards of management at school level, rather than on a district level as with Vocational schools. Nearly 15 per cent of all second-level pupils attend comprehensive schools.

13 Six years if they do a transition year; five if they do not.

14 Post-primary students doing public examinations sit them for three weeks in June, at the start of the summer vacation.

15 According to Veronesi and Gunderman (2012), extracurricular activities in schools and colleges can foster the development of leadership abilities and can move students from passive to active roles. Evidence also suggests that extracurricular student organisations serve as catalysts for the development of student leadership skills by helping students work more closely and more effectively with one another.

References

Bradshaw, J., Ager, R., Burge, B. and Wheater, R. (2010). *PISA 2009: Achievement of 15-year-olds in Northern Ireland*. Slough: NFER.

DENI (2007). Pupil Religion Series. Available online at:
www.deni.gov.uk/pupil_religion_series. Accessed 3 March 2010.

DENI (2011a). Statistics and research. Available online at: www.deni.gov.uk/index/32-statisticsandresearch_pg/32-statistics_and_research_statistics_on_education_pg/32_statistics _and_research-numbersofschoolsandpupils_pg/32_statistics_and_research-northernireland summarydata_pg.htm. Accessed 12 February 2011.

DENI (2011b). Compendium of Northern Ireland education statistics, 1996/97 to 2008/09. Available online at: www.deni.gov.uk/index/32-statisticsandresearch_pg/32_statistical_publications-indexofstatisticalpublications_pg.htm. Accessed 14 February 2011.

Dugan, J. P. (2006). Involvement and leadership: A descriptive analysis of socially responsible leadership. *Journal of College Student Development*, 47(3), 335–343.

Gallagher, T. and Smith, A. (2003). Attitudes to academic selection in Northern Ireland: Research update. 16. Belfast: Ark NI, Social and Political Archive.

HMSO (1989). *Education reform (NI) order*. Belfast: HM Stationery Office.

Kelly, A. (2012). Educational effectiveness and school improvement in Northern Ireland: Opportunities, challenges and ironies. In C. Chapman, D. Muijs, D. Reynolds and P. Sammons (eds). *Challenging the orthodoxy of school effectiveness and school improvement* (pp. 81–96). London: Routledge.

OECD (2004). Policy brief (February). *Education and equity*. Available online at: www.oecd.org/dataoecd/17/10/29478774.pdf. Accessed 29 December 2010.

Patterson, B. (2012). Influences of student organizational leadership experiences in college students' leadership behaviors. *E Journal of Organizational Learning and Leadership*, 10(1), 1–12.

SELB (Southern Education and Library Board). (2011). Education Services: post-primary education (11–18 years). Available online at: www.selb.org/pupilparent/webpages/post primary.htm. Accessed 20 February 2011.

Veronesi, M. and Gunderman, R. (2012). The potential of student organizations for developing leadership: One school's experience. *Academic Medicine*, 87(2), 226–229.

Wright, M. and Scullion, P. (2007). Quality of school life and attitudes to Irish in the Irish medium and English-medium primary school. *Irish Educational Studies*, 26(1), 57–77.

7

SCHOOL LEADERSHIP IN INUIT AND MI'KMAW CONTEXTS IN CANADA

Fiona Walton, Joanne Tompkins, Jukeepa Hainnu and Denise Toney

Introduction

This chapter focuses on educational leadership in two indigenous schools in Canada. The first is Quluaq School in Clyde River, an Arctic community in the new Canadian territory of Nunavut, created on 1 April 1999. *Kangiqtugaapik*, meaning 'nice little inlet', is the Inuktitut name for Clyde River. Jukeepa Hainnu, an Inuit educational leader who was born in the community, was the co-principal and then the principal of the school over a period of 12 years from 2000 to 2012. She is currently on leave from her position for health reasons but is hoping to return to the school. In Nunavut most school leaders and teachers are non-Inuit (Nunavut Tungavik Incorporated, 2011). A co-principal model was introduced in the territory in the early 1990s to encourage capable Inuit teachers to take on the role of school principal in collaboration with experienced administrators who usually come from Southern Canada. Jukeepa is one of the long-term Inuit educational leaders who worked successfully for many years to influence Inuit education in her community as well as in Nunavut.

The second indigenous school is We'koqma'q First Nations' School in Cape Breton, Nova Scotia, in Eastern Canada. We'koqma'q is surrounded by low mountains and located along the shores of the Bras D'Or Lakes. A M'kmaw educational leader has been the school principal for the last decade. After considerable reflection, this principal has chosen to remain anonymous because she believes the leadership of the school is not a result of her own accomplishments. Instead, she feels that leadership emerged in the community and involved a collaborative effort among the staff, the parents and the Band Council. Naomi was previously chosen as a pseudonym for the principal when Denise Toney, another long-serving Mi'kmaw educational leader and scholar, used that pseudonym in her graduate research which involved a case study of the school in We'koqma'q. Denise Toney, who is currently the principal of the middle school in Eskasoni, another Mi'kmaw community, completed much of the material from which this chapter is drawn to describe school leadership in We'koqma'q. Naomi was born in a nearby community, but her mother, who is an advocate for the Mi'kmaw language, is from We'koqma'q where there are many family connections. The school is now recognised as one of the most successful Aboriginal schools in Canada (Education Canada, 2014).

While the two Aboriginal contexts described in this chapter differ geographically, politically, culturally and linguistically, Jukeepa Hainnu and Naomi share many of the challenges facing Aboriginal school leaders in First Nations, Inuit and Métis communities across Canada, including low socioeconomic levels, the impact of colonisation and intergenerational trauma which results in social issues, the complexity of offering culturally-based bilingual education to maintain precious legacies of indigenous knowledge and language, and the struggle to overcome academic struggles based on a difficult educational history. Persistently low academic achievement and graduation levels in many First Nations and Inuit educational systems in Canada have resulted in Aboriginal education being identified as having a very high priority (Council of Ministers of Education, Canada, 2010; National Committee on Inuit Education, 2011).

Aboriginal is the generic term used in Canada to describe First Nations, Inuit and Métis people whose ancestors were the original indigenous inhabitants of the geographical space now called Canada. Indigenous is a broader term encompassing groups of original inhabitants of countries across the world though it is increasingly used when referring to Aboriginal people across North America.

Inuit denotes the plural of Inuk, which is singular. Throughout this chapter, Mi'kmaq is used as a noun and can be either singular or plural. Mi'kmaw is used as an adjective. The rules for creating adjectival forms of words in Mi'kmaq are complex. In this chapter we follow the recommendations of Sherise Paul-Gould and Starr Sock from Eskasoni, a Mi'kmaw community in Cape Breton. Variations in Inuktitut or Mi'kmaq words may occur based on regional and dialectical differences.

Educational leadership in an Inuit context in Canada

Inuit have occupied Nunavut for over 5,000 years (McGhee, 1996) and were the only inhabitants of this part of the Canadian Arctic until 1,500–1,000 years ago (Crowe, 1991). For four centuries, from 1500 to 1900, whalers, explorers, fur traders and missionaries brought their tools, weapons, food, alcohol, religion and ways of life to Nunavut and other northern contexts in a process of colonisation that is ongoing, with evidence of a strong neocolonial and neoliberal influence having an impact on education at this time (Brody, 1991; Crowe, 1991; Nunavut Tunngavik Incorporated, 2011; Walton, 2014).

The formal educational system in Nunavut is relatively young, with day schools being established in the small Arctic communities in the early 1950s, first by the Government of Canada and then by the newly established Government of the Northwest Territories (McGregor, 2010). Prior to this time, missionaries, as they travelled around the Arctic regions, provided some basic education as well as religious instruction in the original Inuit camps on the land. In 1894, a teaching mission was established at Blacklead Island, near Pangnirtung, Nunavut (Macpherson, 1991).

Residential school experiences had a negative impact on the Inuit in Canada as children were removed from homes and families to receive an education, often for long periods of time and far from their own communities and regions. This left a deep sense of dislocation and a loss of identity among the students who were placed in institutional contexts and subjected to forms of indoctrination, punishment and abuse. Parents and grandparents were also left behind in camps and communities without the presence of their children, something that caused anguish and deep loss. Many indigenous people in Canada who attended residential schools and missed time with their families struggled with aspects of parenting and some also faced challenges with such social issues as addiction and suicide (Milloy, 1999; Chrisjohn and Young, 2006; Truth and Reconciliation Commission, 2012).

Intergenerational trauma marks Inuit communities because of the negative impact of both residential schools as well as schools built in the communities by the Federal Government or the Government of the Northwest Territories that initially provided an assimilationist curriculum and a colonial form of schooling (Nunavut Tunngavik Incorporated, 2011; Truth and Reconciliation Commission, 2012; McGregor, 2010). The generation attending schools at this time are affected in ways that may not have been identified until the Truth and Reconciliation process took place quite recently. Also, younger Inuit sometimes fail to understand the behaviour or attitudes of Elders because the difficult history may not have been shared or taught in the school system (Truth and Reconciliation Commission, 2012). Intergenerational recovery takes many years.

Modernisation and exponential change in Inuit communities in Nunavut and other Inuit regions of Canada have tended to brush aside history and the loss of Inuit 'ways of being' as each new generation grows to adulthood in a fast-paced technological age that is affecting all facets of society, including education. The Arctic also faces significant climate change because of melting glaciers breaking up sea ice far earlier than in the past, affecting permafrost, raising water levels across the globe, and negatively affecting the way of life of Inuit who live in northern Canada and have drawn their livelihood from the land and sea for thousands of years.

The establishment of Nunavut represents the largest land claim in Canadian history (Nunavut Tunngavik Incorporated, 2004). Home to the largest population of Inuit in Canada, it occupies 21 per cent of the Arctic landmass (2,093,190 square kilometres) and offers a public government to its citizens. Nunavut is the only territory or province in Canada with a majority Aboriginal population. The 2011 Canadian census reported a majority-Inuit population of 27,070 representing 85.4 per cent of the total population of 31,905 (Statistics Canada, 2011). There are 25 communities in Nunavut, all reached by air during the winter months, with many being accessible by ships and barges once the sea ice melts in the summer.

The cost of living in Nunavut is far higher than it is in southern Canada, with food costing almost twice as much as it does in the rest of the country (Peritz, 2014). Peritz also documents income inequities, as median income for non-aboriginal residents in Nunavut is $86,600 a year; for Inuit, it is $19,900. These factors contribute more challenges for a school system that is struggling to meet the needs of students (Auditor General of Canada, 2013).

The educational system in Nunavut is administered by the Department of Education, Government of Nunavut, with Regional Operations Offices (RSOs) located in each of three regions established by the Government of Canada in 1967. The Department of Education and the RSOs, in conjunction with locally elected District Education Authorities (DEAs) representing parents in each Nunavut community, administer education, including the hiring of staff and the curriculum offered in all subject areas, as well as the teaching of Inuit languages, culture and values in accordance with eight Inuit social values, or principles, defined in the Nunavut Education Act and developed in consultation with Inuit Elders (Government of Nunavut, 2008). These *Inuit Qaujimajatuqangit* (IQ) principles include relating respectfully to others; being inclusive, welcoming and in good spirits; serving your family and community; making decisions through collaboration and consensus; developing skills through perseverance and practice; working together for a common cause; being innovative and resourceful; and respecting and caring for animals, land and the environment.

Nunavut has a bilingual educational system (Inuktitut/English) and also delivers programmes in French as a second language in some schools. Educational services for students who qualify because of French first-language rights are provided for by La Commission Scolaire Francophone du Nunavut in Iqaluit, the capital of Nunavut. In order to distribute employment opportunities across Nunavut, the RSOs are not located in Iqaluit, which is in the Qikiqtani region. Instead, they are based in smaller communities within each region: in Pond Inlet in the Qikiqtani region, in Baker Lake in the Kivalliq region and in Kugluktuk in the Kitikmeot region.

In accordance with the Nunavut Education Act (2008), each community elects seven members of a DEA to serve for a three-year term and take responsibility 'for the administration of schools under its jurisdiction' (Government of Nunavut, 2008, p. 68). The Coalition of Nunavut District Education Authorities (CNDEA) acts as a society, or a corporation, that brings all DEAs together into one decision-making body with legislative power to work with the Minister of Education to ensure that shared concerns and needs brought forward by the communities are discussed and addressed (Government of Nunavut, 2008).

In response to persistently low educational outcomes across Inuit jurisdictions in Canada, a *National Strategy on Inuit Education 2011* (National Committee on Inuit Education, 2011) was recently led by the National Inuit organisation, Inuit Tapiriit Kanatami (ITK) and developed by all four Inuit regions of Canada. The strategy established six core themes: bilingual education; mobilising parents; Inuit-centred curriculum and teaching practices; post-secondary success; capacity building; and collecting and sharing information. Ten recommendations provide priority directions and an implementation plan is now progressing with leadership from the *Amaujaq* National Centre for Inuit Education (2014).

Clyde River, where Jukeepa Hainnu lives, is a small community of 975 people, with approximately 5 per cent being non-Inuit (Statistics Canada, 2011). Situated in a coastal and mountainous part of the Qiqitktani Region on Baffin Island, an abundance of wildlife, sea mammals and migratory birds are available on the land and in the ocean, making hunting accessible to community members. Inuktitut, as well as English, are spoken in the community and Inuit cultural activities continue to be practised. A new Inuit cultural learning centre, *Piqqusilirivvik*, administered by Nunavut Arctic College (NAC), was opened in Clyde River in 2011 offering a variety of programmes related to the maintenance of Inuit culture and knowledge and offering accommodation for individuals interested in learning more about Inuit practices and skills (Nunavut Arctic College, 2014).

Clyde River also established the *Ilisaqsivik* Society, an award-winning, not-for-profit organisation 'dedicated to promoting community wellness' (*Ilisaqsivik*, 2014). *Ilisaqsivik* provides a wide range of programmes and learning opportunities designed for pre-school children, adults and Elders in the community. Founded by Inuit in the community, including Jukeepa Hainnu, *Iliksaqsivik* actively raises funding and develops resources to expand and enrich the opportunities and programmes available to residents of the community.

Quluaq School in Clyde River offers educational programmes from the kindergarten to the grade 12 level. The school was recently renovated and rebuilt, and is an attractive and modern building with spacious classrooms to accommodate students' needs. A fine gymnasium, large library, resource rooms, a shop facility, offices for the school administration and the DEA, a kitchen and dining area that can accommodate community and school groups, and a large open area with a raised platform where groups can gather for announcements and attend events, help to make the school a vibrant and community-based facility. While Jukeepa Hainnu was principal, the school was open from the early morning when a breakfast programme was provided to students, to the late evening when sports and other events including music and hip-hop took place in the gymnasium. An Elders' lunch took place each week following school-sponsored hunting trips involving students. Students served the lunch to the Elders. *Going Places: Preparing Inuit High School Students for a Changing Wider World* is a documentary video which tells the story of two high school students in Nunavut, including Shawn Sivugat who attended Quluaq School (Walton *et al.*, 2011).

At this time, there are four qualified Inuit teachers, five Inuit language specialists, an Inuit school community counselor, four Inuit special needs assistants and an Inuit office manager working at the school. In addition, several non-Inuit teachers, a school principal, vice-principal and student support teacher also work in the school. In the 2011–2012 school year 262 Inuit students attended Quluaq School and no non-Inuit students were registered. The average student–educator ratio is 13:1 (McGregor, 2014, p. 34). The numbers of Inuit staff, many of them male, help to provide a strong Inuit presence and sense of safety and warmth with positive role models and the Inuktitut language being spoken in the hallways by both the staff and visitors to the school. The school has a high level of staff retention at 76 per cent (McGregor, 2014, p. 35).

In 2012, the attendance levels for the school were low at 60.6 per cent, which remains a significant challenge (Nunavut Department of Education, 2012). Recently completed ten-year historical and statistical profiles on high school education in Nunavut in four locations, including Quluaq School in Clyde River, track patterns related to attendance and graduation levels (McGregor, 2014). The graduation rates vary considerably from a high level for Nunavut and Aboriginal schools in Canada of 67.5 per cent in some years with much lower rates in several other years (McGregor, 2014, p. 39). McGregor's research was based on an analysis of statistical data available at the Department of Education, not on an investigation of factors contributing to the graduation levels; however, these higher rates of graduation need to be acknowledged as significant.

Jukeepa Hainnu was raised in a large family with strong Inuit roots. She was very close to her maternal grandmother and learned many stories that included Inuit myths and legends passed down orally over generations. Jukeepa is also very knowledgeable about Inuit history and ways-of-being. Fluently bilingual and biliterate in Inuktitut and English, Jukeepa started school in Clyde River when she was six years old. The first territorial school was established in 1960, a few years before she was born, and she attended when it included four small portable classrooms. At that time, Inuit classroom assistants were already teaching in the school so Jukeepa was able to complete several of the first years of her education in Inuktitut. By the time she was 12, Jukeepa was acting as an interpreter-translator at the Nursing Station and her fluency in both Inuktitut and English led to a job as a classroom assistant at the school in 1981 when she was just 17. Jukeepa completed the Certificate in Native and Northern Education as well as the Bachelor of Education (BEd) from McGill University through a university-certified programme offered at the Eastern Arctic Teacher Education Program (EATEP) in Iqaluit. The programme is now known as the Nunavut Teacher Education Program (NTEP). Returning to Clyde River to teach, as well as provide leadership for over 25 years at the school, Jukeepa is one of the longest serving Inuit educational leaders in Nunavut and has taught almost every grade from kindergarten to grade 12.

University certified professional qualifications for aspiring educational leaders working in the school system in Nunavut have been available since the early 1980s and Jukeepa completed the Educational Leadership Program (ELP), going on to act as the ELP principal or member of the team that developed and offered the programme at a summer school held each year. ELP is now called the Certificate in Educational Leadership in Nunavut (CELN), and is offered in the territory through a partnership between UPEI and the Department of Education, Government of Nunavut.

In 2000, Jukeepa accepted a role as co-principal at Quluaq School and shared this position with a non-Inuit educator for six years. In 2006, the DEA in Clyde River asked Jukeepa to take on the position as principal on her own, but she decided that before accepting this role she needed to complete a Master of Education degree. Therefore, in late June 2007, Jukeepa moved her family to Charlottetown, Prince Edward Island, where she completed her Master of Education (M.Ed.) at UPEI, returning to Clyde River as principal in August 2008. In interviews conducted for ongoing research related to Inuit educational leadership and high school education in Nunavut, Jukeepa commented on her reasons for leaving Clyde River to pursue a graduate degree:

> I wanted to be part of initiating change for the better, for the students. I returned home stronger and with a vision. . . . I knew more of what I wanted to see in our school and what else needed to happen, including what our students should be like. . . . To be competent . . . and if they go down south, to be capable also, yet proud of being an Inuk and [to] believe in themselves . . . to have a goal of working and raising their children properly.

Jukeepa's leadership and commitment to Inuit education have been captured in the documentary video already mentioned (Walton *et al.*, 2011).

Jukeepa identified several key issues and challenges that she faced as a school principal, including the difficulty parents in the community experienced supporting their children to complete school when their own levels of education were low and they did not understand the school system. Some of the parents who attended residential school are wary of schools, or doubt the ability of Inuit educators to offer educational programmes. Jukeepa addressed this challenge by encouraging the community to be involved in the activities at the school, including the school breakfast programme, assemblies, sports events, graduations and cultural celebrations. She mentioned how important it is to really listen to parental concerns and then respond in a way that would encourage parents to support their children to attend school and work hard. Jukeepa also mentioned that parents were critical about the levels of Inuktitut instruction offered at the school. She felt this was related to the complexity of offering a fully bilingual education programme with limited resources, particularly with the lack of books and materials in Inuktitut.

Jukeepa believes the students' levels of competency in Inuktitut and English are weak and mentioned that: 'We need more English, but we must preserve our culture. . . . We can't do everything. . . . Our society is losing the Inuktitut language and we see a lot of children speaking English.' She also said: 'It's hard, you have a clear mission, you have to spark each other.' It was clear that motivating teachers and maintaining a high level of commitment with limited resources and supports was sometimes difficult, but Jukeepa believes that having a strong relationship with the DEA members 'really helps'. She tried to show the DEA members that she could 'walk the talk' because, as she put it, she 'would never be comfortable talking about something that I was not doing myself'. In 2011, Jacob Jaypoody, the long-time Chair of the DEA in Clyde River commented as follows:

> Having an Inuk Principal who supervises in the Inuktitut language has improved morale amongst the staff, students, and the parents all around. It has even opened the lines of communication. If either one of the parents has a family issue with another parent, we can now sit them down and discuss what the problem is amongst them. That in itself has been revived, the Inuit traditional way of counseling.

Optimism and hope are evident in Jukeepa's responses about her leadership of Quluaq School and she spoke about the importance of having 'Inuit role models to encourage our students to be better.' Her grandmother had urged her to 'always try to respond in a positive way', and Jukeepa stressed her commitment to 'never being harsh, giving everyone a chance and being fair, kind, and compassionate'. Her vision is focused on the 'long term benefits of being educated'.

Conceptually, Jukeepa draws on her commitment to the IQ values, principles and beliefs gained in her upbringing as an Inuit child and young person with a strong-willed grandmother and a 'humble father who followed a very Inuit way of living'. Developed after extensive work with Inuit Elders, these Inuit beliefs and values are incorporated into the 2008 Nunavut Education Act as a foundation for Nunavut schools to follow. In Jukeepa's case she has always lived by these values and that is evident in the way she welcomed the community into the school, built consensus, collaboratively solved problems, and remained positive, resourceful and in good spirits at all times over many years in a challenging context. Tempered and honed by her years of experience and practice as a school leader, as well as by extensive professional education and studies at the graduate level at a southern university, her values and beliefs come together to form an Inuit conception of educational leadership that has withstood the test of time and many challenging situations in a school located in an Arctic community in Canada.

Educational leadership in a Mi'kmaw context in Canada

For over 10,000 years Mi'kmaq have lived in Mi'kmagi, the traditional land occupied by Mi'kmaw. The area included the northeastern corner of the United States, parts of Atlantic Canada, and the islands in the Gulf of St Lawrence. The Mi'kmaq experienced early contact with French settlers, who came in the 1500s to fish and later establish settlements. When French settlers were defeated by the British, treaties were signed between the British Crown and the Mi'kmaq in 1725 and 1752. A royal proclamation in 1763 asserted recognition of the Mi'kmaq as a sovereign nation and guaranteed hunting and fishing rights for them in return for their loyalty to the Crown. Over the years treaty rights were either ignored or broken by the Crown, but recent challenges from Mi'kmaw communities (Aboriginal Affairs and Northern Development Canada, 1999) are upholding the rights of Mi'kmaw people to make a moderate living from fishing and hunting. As more settlers arrived and appropriated land, Mi'kmaq moved into smaller land areas until today their land base 'is [metaphorically] the size of a postage stamp – less than the amount of land devoted to provincial parks in this province' (J. J. Paul, personal communication, 4 May 1999). In Nova Scotia, Mi'kmaq were gradually removed from their traditional territories and clustered into 13 Mi'kmaw communities. To speed up the process of assimilation a residential school was established at Shubenacadie in 1923 and operated until 1967 (Benjamin, 2014). As the only Indian Residential School in Eastern Canada, its damaging and enduring legacy impacted on Mi'kmaw children and their families and has been chronicled by the Truth and Reconciliation Commission (2012) and in accounts by Knockwood (1992) and Benjamin (2014).

In an attempt to streamline the management of Mi'kmaq, the Federal centralisation policies of the 1940s caused further dislocation of communities by trying to move all Mi'kmaq into one of two reserves in Nova Scotia. While generally recognised as a failed policy attempt, it caused considerable disruption within Mi'kmaw communities. Federal day schools were developed in Mi'kmaw communities during the 1950s with governance structures, personnel, teaching practices and curriculum placed in the hands of non-Aboriginal people. Aboriginal children across the country were generally unsuccessful in these schools where the mission remained assimilationist (McGregor, 2010; Paul, 2006; Schissel and Wotherspoon, 2003). This applied to We'koqma'q where the federal day school opened in 1956. This federal school did not provide programmes at the high school level and as a result Mi'kmaw students had to travel to a provincial school outside the community. Most of these students dropped out before completing high school.

In the late 1950s and 1960s a growing discontent arose among Aboriginal communities across Canada because of the Eurocentric education system imposed upon Aboriginal children and in 1972 the National Indian Brotherhood released a *White Paper* advocating Aboriginal control of Aboriginal education 'in which our children can develop the fundamental attitudes and values which have an honoured place in Indian tradition and culture' (The National Indian Brotherhood, 1972, p. 2). This led to the establishment of band-operated schools in Mi'kmaw communities. While the initiative enabled more opportunities for local control of education, staffing the schools with Mi'kmaw leadership at both the classroom and the administrative level proved to be a continual challenge.

Awareness that local control of education in Mi'kmaw schools required additional support at the governance level led to a historic agreement in 1997 signed between the federal government, the province of Nova Scotia and Mi'kmaw communities, creating an innovative governance structure, Mi'kmaw Kina'matnewey (MK), an educational jurisdiction that brings all 13 communities together. The aim of MK is to support Mi'kmaw communities to deliver education programmes and services to students from kindergarten to grade 12. MK is responsible for programming, special education services, post-secondary education, educational technology and capital funding. The management of tuition agreements with the Federal and Provincial Governments for the on-reserve students, as well as in provincial schools, is also MK's responsibility. Accountability and reporting structures on student attendance, student achievement and discipline are established between MK and regional school boards in Nova Scotia with frameworks to ensure that schools report to communities and families. Over a period of 17 years, this governance model has led to groundbreaking success for the Mi'kmaw students attending MK schools (Education Canada, 2014).

The Faculty of Education at St Francis Xavier University (StFX) has supported MK over this period of time by certifying 120 Mi'kmaw teachers with B.Ed. degrees, by providing access to graduate education through their M.Ed. programme and offering professional learning and in-service opportunities for Mi'kmaw teachers. This has included certificate programmess in Mi'kmaw language immersion pedagogy and mathematics education. Research partnerships between the Faculty of Education at StFX and MK respond to articulated needs within the schools and support improvements in Mi'kmaw education. This long-term collaborative partnership has made a significant difference for education in MK schools and the Aboriginal Knowledge Exchange Project (2008) highlighted the StFX programme as an exemplary programme nationwide (Tompkins and Orr, 2008). The impact of having Mi'kmaw educators teaching in Mi'kmaw communities, coupled with supports provided by MK, has led to results unequalled across Canada in Aboriginal communities. The school in We'koqma'q now has a graduation rate of 89.3 per cent (*Chronicle Herald*, 2012).

The school website (2011) describes the community as mid-sized, comprising 800 residents. The location of We'koqma'q 'has served the community well providing an abundant source of marine life, deer and other game that also provided food and clothing for Mi'kmaq families' (Toney, 2012, p. 26). The community is situated about 100 kilometres west of Cape Breton University where Unama'ki College has, for over 20 years, offered university programmes in Mi'kmaw studies. To the east, StFX is 100 kilometres away. Nova Scotia Community College (NSCC) programmes are also offered within 50 kilometres of the community. This close access by road to a range of post-secondary educational opportunities has contributed to higher levels of educational attainment in Mi'kmaw communities, particularly in the fields of M'kmaw studies and education.

Naomi, the school principal in We'koqma'q, finished high school outside her community. Following completion of her Bachelor of Arts degree from Cape Breton University with a focus on Mi'kmaw Studies, she went on to take a B.Ed. degree from StFX and, after teaching for several years and working as a resource teacher, she graduated with her M.Ed. in Literacy Education from Mount Saint Vincent University (MSVU) in Halifax.

Naomi's family members are strong advocates of Mi'kmaw language and culture, and her mother is a leader in Mi'kmaw language revitalisation. In spite of the fact that Naomi describes herself as having limited skills in speaking Mi'kmaq, she remains a strong advocate for the language and culture (Toney, 2012).

Several years ago, The Learning Partnership, a national not-for-profit organization that awards excellence in educational leadership across Canada, recognised

Naomi's leadership. The Learning Partnership highlighted the unique challenges facing principals who work in on-reserve schools and Naomi received an Honorary Aboriginal award for her exceptional leadership. Naomi is one of the longest serving and most respected principals within the MK system.

It was with great excitement that in 2008 the community opened a new state-of-the-art school. We'koqma'q Mi'kmaq School has an enrolment of approximately 300 students from the primary to the grade 12 level. The school building reflects Mi'kmaw culture, is environmentally sustainable, and offers the most up-to-date new learning technologies. Toney (2012, p. 26) has commented that 'the present school . . . reflects Mi'kmaw life. The architecture is pleasing and efficient with Mi'kmaw culture incorporated into the design'. Evidence of Mi'kmaw culture is immediately visible as one approaches the school. Flags of the Mi'kmaw Nation and Canada fly over a monument dedicated to the Mi'kmaw war veterans. Another monument is engraved with the names of the 39 children from the community who attended the Shubenacadie Residential School. The front of the building welcomes visitors into a large area with glass windows creating openness to the surrounding context. The traditional eight-point Mi'kmaw star decorates the floor and there are photographs and cultural artefacts displayed in glass cupboards. A teen wellness centre located in the school allows for comprehensive services to be offered to students. The classrooms are spacious and well lit. Multi-purpose rooms provide space for community events and community feasts. A large gymnasium is well used by the school and the community. Many examples of student artwork are displayed throughout the school and a visitor senses that arts-based education is an important part of the school curriculum. The vision and leadership brought to the school by Naomi, in collaboration with her staff, community members and the Band Council, have resulted in many enhancements and innovative programmes. As such, the school reflects the Mi'kmaw community in which it is located.

The school has a strong film programme with students researching and producing community documentaries. The documentary, *Our Legacy, Our Hope*, produced by grade 12 students, followed community Elders to the Truth and Reconciliation Commission hearings in 2012 and was later presented at the United Nations in New York. A recent graduate of We'koqma'q School, in a presentation to a graduate class at StFX, spoke of the school as being a 'second home' (T. Cremo, personal communication, 2 October 2014). The relationships between students and teachers are comfortable as there are many blood and marriage connections in this small community. The feeling and ethos in the building is informal, safe and warm.

From primary to grade 12, Mi'kmaq is taught as a core subject and not used as a language of instruction. Naomi explains: 'while Mi'kmaw language is very important, they don't have an immersion programme due to lack of resources (material and human)' (Toney, 2012, p. 30). Research on Mi'kmaw and Maliseet immersion programmes in Atlantic Canada cited inadequate and unstable funding as key barriers for schools aiming to implement and sustain Aboriginal immersion programmes (Newhouse and Orr, 2013).

Since 2008 the school has benefited from the First Nation School Success Program (FNSSP), designed to help First Nation educators on reserve (kindergarten to grade 12) improve school results in literacy and mathematics and encourage greater student retention (FNSSP, 2014). MK worried that mainstream school improvement models might be incongruent with notions of school success held by Aboriginal educators (Toney, 2012), therefore, *A Framework for School Improvement for Schools* (Orr and MacCormick, 2007) was developed, ensuring more cultural relevance in terms of knowledge and measures of success. In this framework, MK schools develop school success plans that focus on literacy, numeracy, Mi'kmaw language and student retention. The effect of including a Mi'kmaw language goal cannot be overstated as it validates the importance of the language and culture in MK schools. Student learning assessments support the school success plan and the performance measures established to facilitate, access and accelerate both student and school performance. FNSSP allocates funding for a variety of supports that allow access to mentors and consultants who travel to support Mi'kmaq teachers and principals. Prior to FNSSP, educators in MK had little access to these second level services that are common in public schools in Canada. As a principal Naomi now has the range of supports to assist her school with continuous improvement.

In 2014, the Mi'kmaq staff at We'koqma'q School included 47 teachers, teaching specialists and assistants with 35 being Mi'kmaw, representing 74 per cent of the school personnel. All of the teachers who teach from kindergarten to grade 6 are Mi'kmaw teachers who received their B.Ed. degrees at StFX. High numbers of staff create a low student–staff ratio of 6.4 staff to each student. Staff members who are not teachers are included in this ratio as they have a significant impact on the ability to provide academic and personal support to students. Orr *et al.* (2002) conducted research with three Mi'kmaw educators and found they exhibited relentless caring for their students while holding them to high expectations for success. It is this combination of high standards as well as support that has resulted in most impressive achievement levels at the school. MK, as an Aboriginal self-governance educational jurisdiction, is now drawing national attention as a possible model for First Nations' education in Canada. Recently, Scott Haldane, Chair of the National Panel on First Nation Elementary and Secondary Education for Students On Reserve Education for the Assembly of First Nations (AFN) was most impressed with the graduation rates that are 'double the national average and close to triple the average of what we saw in some of the worst performing schools' (Education Canada, 2014, p. 2).

In its relationship with the 13 communities in its jurisdiction, MK operates on a model of consensus decision-making and serving community. While it provides services for its members it does not direct activities at the school level, allowing MK schools to be more responsive to their local context. This is a key element in the success experienced at We'koqma'q, for Naomi and her staff can make decisions based on the needs in the community while at the same time benefiting from supports provided by MK.

A significant issue facing Naomi as an educational leader is the enduring effect of colonisation in the community. Schooling was a key vehicle in the colonisation process and former residential and federal or provincial school students were affected by trauma and loss. Trust between the education system and Mi'kmaw people was broken and Naomi continues to face this legacy as some community members have come to believe that the knowledge, language and ways of the colonisers are superior to those of the Mi'kmaq. This raises doubts about education that focuses on Mi'kmaw knowledge, history and culture and is occasionally the basis of questions about having Mi'kmaw staff at the school. However, this attitude is now changing as the positive news about the school success in We'koqma'q is shared in the community, the province and the country. The positive media coverage has helped Naomi to address the colonial attitudes as she no longer needs to defend the school programme or her Mi'kmaw staff. The results speak for themselves.

Naomi is also concerned about the declining levels of Mi'kmaw fluency among the staff and the students in her school where students are more fluent when reading and writing Mi'kmaw than they are when using it orally (Toney, 2012). A decline in Mi'kmaw oral fluency among young people in all MK communities was recently documented with worrisome results (Paul, 2013). The current model of core Mi'kmaw instruction will produce an appreciation of the language and allow students to speak and understand at a very basic level, but it will not produce the high levels of fluency many Mi'kmaw communities, including We'koqma'q, are now starting to ask for as the language declines. At this time, Naomi is assessing the degree of community support for the Mi'kmaw language programmes and is hesitant to make any major changes in the model of language instruction at the school because of the need for additional resources and expertise.

High unemployment in We'koqma'q results in incomes that are well below the provincial and federal levels (Wilson and MacDonald, 2010), which influences students' health and ability to learn. Poverty affects food security in families and is often associated with type 2 diabetes (Seligman *et al.*, 2007). Finding that funds at home are often insufficient, Naomi is trying to provide the extra material, physical, social and emotional resources some students need to make the school that 'second home' mentioned by a school graduate. Providing access to adequate nutrition, proper learning materials, wellness programmes and enough qualified personnel to meet the needs of a community impacted by poverty and food insecurity is a significant concern at the school.

Mainstream conceptions of educational leadership emphasise the importance of vision as the starting point of leadership (Barth, 2001; Lyman *et al.*, 2012; Murphy, 2013; Sergiovanni, 1992). In his research examining how seven school leaders lead with 'a vision of schooling that included social justice and equity for all the students in their care, particularly those who were most vulnerable', Theoharris (2009, p. 147) noted that all the leaders maintained a 'fierce commitment to their vision of social justice'. This is reflected in the way Naomi and her staff members extend relentless caring for the students that includes providing for their health and well-being (Orr *et al.*, 2002). They realise that unless the students are eating well and their psychological needs are met, it is very hard to expect them to learn and perform academically at a high level.

Naomi has also identified Eurocentric practices that do not serve Mi'kmaw students well and, working with the community, she developed a shared vision and conceptualisation for the school based on the seven sacred teachings of Mi'kmaw culture: respect, honesty, courage, love, truth, humility and wisdom. These values are central to the Mi'kmaw worldview and describe how Mi'kmaq are to conduct their lives in a good way. The values are also present and modelled by the many Mi'kmaw teachers and Elders from the community who work in the school and they build strong Mi'kmaw identity among the students, which leads to high levels of confidence and pride. The seven sacred teachings are integrated as a daily part of the formal curriculum throughout the school, particularly in the primary to grade 9 levels.

Recently, a Mi'kmaw pre-service teacher at StFX, who worked in We'koqma'q School for 14 years, commented on the behaviour of non-Mi'kmaw students while visiting a provincial school. She found the students in the mainstream school to be immature, disorderly and generally disrespectful. She felt these young people needed a teacher to tell them what to do. She contrasted this to the Mi'kmaw students at We'koqma'q, stating: 'The students in our school know how to be in charge of themselves' (S. Googoo, personal communication, 21 October 2014). This teacher believes the focus on the seven sacred teachings has taught the students in We'koqma'q to be a L'nu and act like a L'nu. L'nu is the Mi'kmaw word for person.

Toney suggests that 'one gets a sense of the "Mi'kmaq way of being" in the school' (2012, p. 46). Conceptualising and actualising the school as a 'second home', has required that Naomi change some of the taken-for-granted practices and structures that guide mainstream schools. For example, Naomi's authority as a leader comes from her ability to work collaboratively with staff and parents to develop a shared and well-articulated vision for Mi'kmaw education. Toney (2012) describes Naomi as a leader who can be found participating in many different roles that include leading a curriculum mapping meeting, talking with parents or helping students solve problems. Her leadership is congruent with the seven sacred teachings and emerging understandings of traditional Mi'kmaq leadership (Paul, 2006). It is producing impressive educational results that Mi'kmaq have dreamed about and waited for over many years.

Conclusion

This chapter has focused on two indigenous schools in Inuit and Mi'qmaw contexts in Canada. The schools are led by an Inuk and a Mi'kmaw school principal. Leadership in both schools has revealed that when education is based on foundations grounded in Inuit and Mi'kmaw ways of knowing, doing and being, education can succeed. This is made possible by legislation as well as educational practice in

Clyde River, Nunavut, and is supported by the overall policies developed by MK that enable the Mi'kmaw language and culture to become a grounding for the school in We'koqma'q. Students in both schools are being challenged to succeed in the Inuktitut and Mi'kmaq languages, but also in English up to grade 12 level, with expectations that they perform well in provincial, national and international tests at levels comparable to the mainstream. This establishes and maintains very high standards for indigenous students who face a significant array of challenges. While expectations are vitally important, in most Aboriginal contexts in Canada a wide range of supports as well as parental engagement and belief in the possibilities of education are required for students in Inuit and First Nations' communities to meet mainstream Canadian levels of achievement.

Based on the evidence provided by Jukeepa Hainnu and Naomi after their long-term experience as school principals, it is possible to address the impact of colonisation, poverty, food insecurity and social challenges, when system-wide and school-level administrators, consultants, teachers and staff all work collaboratively towards the same goals over an extended period of time. Depending on both the community leadership as well as the supports provided by the system, it is possible for graduation rates to reach or exceed mainstream levels of performance. In order to achieve this level of success, truly significant levels of support for students and a school ethos committed to caring in a way that fosters a feeling of being part of a family are necessary. In addition, parents need to be involved in efforts to get their children to school every day over the years from kindergarten to grade 12, which requires the regeneration of hope and belief in educational systems based on indigenous ways of knowing, doing and being.

There are some significant differences between the two communities considered in this chapter. Services and educational supports are more readily available in We'koqma'q. Consultants and support staff from MK can drive to We'koqma'q relatively easily and the additional personnel and resources provided by the FNSSP mean that students benefit from small group and individual attention focused directly on their academic skills. The staff to student ratio in We'koqma'q is double that of Clyde River and higher levels of support can be provided to students.

The importance of the proximity of StFX and Cape Breton University to We'koqma'q cannot be overstated for providing access to post-secondary qualifications and professional education for large numbers of Mi'kmaw staff. They have helped to raise professional skill levels in the community and promote a deep understanding of the issues and challenges facing Mi'kmaw learners. In addition, research partnerships between MK and StFX have addressed important questions and concerns raised by communities over a period of 17 years, building a substantial body of knowledge that can be applied relatively quickly within a school system that is nimble and responsive. Achievement levels are carefully monitored and tracked, successes are celebrated, and encouragement is offered at every step along the way. This has required a consistent and focused long-term effort. Low staff turnover and long-term leadership at the school level have helped to ensure that the educational mission at We'koqma'q is achieved.

In Nunavut, the Department of Education, as part of a public government, must address multiple issues, including political demands, legislative responsibilities and significant challenges related to developing and delivering a bilingual curriculum for all grade levels across a geographical area that is one-fifth the land-mass of Canada (Auditor General of Canada, 2013; Berger, 2006). Each layer of bureaucracy in any school system increases the challenges of communication and in a developing educational system, the roles of the Department of Education, the CNDEAs, the RSOs and the DEAs continue to be clarified. Given the urgent need for higher numbers of more qualified Inuit staff and the turnover of educators hired from southern Canada, it can be a challenge to fill and then retain staff in all positions in schools as well as at the programme and administrative levels making capacity building of Inuit educators a crucial factor for future success. Above all, unless significant additional supports are available at the school level in Nunavut, where they impact on students' learning; regardless of the talent, ability and wisdom of a school principal like Jukeepa Hainnu who has led hopeful change against many challenges, making sustained, long-term change is very challenging.

While the M.Ed. programme offered by UPEI has produced 37 Inuit graduates, it is difficult to increase the numbers of Inuit educational leaders in all Nunavut schools without providing more access to ongoing professional learning at both the professional and graduate levels. Critically informed leadership is vitally important when making change in a complex Indigenous school system. Support for Inuit leaders must be maintained in order to develop a wide range of leadership skills and a deeper understanding of the challenges facing the school system in Nunavut.

In Clyde River, the RSO provides administrative support to the school with the DEA addressing many of the issues at the local level. However, given the bilingual educational mandate and new legislation and policies, the CNDEA has continued to express the need for more training for DEAs at the community levels. In contrast, at We'koqma'q administrative support is provided by a structure much like a board of education that can focus directly on the needs of each school while allowing room for local control. There is a lighter administrative weight in the MK system and more ability to focus on curriculum, programme and student support.

Issues of equity and social justice are present in Inuit and First Nations' contexts in Canada, adding many extra challenges and increasing the need for exceptional leadership based on a deep understanding of community history and needs. When school leaders are from the community, they know every student and their families. They are part of large extended families in small communities where everyone is connected. School can feel like 'home' when school leaders consciously foster an ethos that mirrors a healthy and happy Indigenous family. Lena Metuq, a long-term Inuit principal in Nunavut has talked about 'surrounding' the students (personal communication, 27 May 2005). By this she means that families, school staff, principals, community members and the entire educational system need to provide high levels of caring, commitment and support for students. When the 'surrounding' works well it carries each student forward to graduation so they can pursue their lives with bilingual academic skills, a strong Indigenous identity, self-confidence and a sense of integrity that is based on the principles and teachings that have been passed down over millennia in their communities and schools.

School principals like Jukeepa Hainnu and Naomi are outstanding role models and educational leaders in their Indigenous communities. Their leadership is breaking cycles of failure and loss inherited from a difficult past, and they are forging a successful future for their communities, one that is filled with hope and strength.

References

Aboriginal Affairs and Northern Development Canada. (1999). *R vs Marshall*. Available at: www.aadncaandc.gc.ca/eng/1100100028614/1100100028615 (accessed 26 October 2014).

Assembly of First Nations. (2013). *Special chiefs assembly: Executive report 2013*. Ottawa, ON: Author.

Auditor General of Canada. (2013). *Report of the Auditor General of Canada to the Legislative Assembly of Nunavut—2013: Education in Nunavut*. Office of the Auditor General of Canada. Aailable at: www.oagbvg.gc.ca/internet/English/nun_201311_e_38772.html (accessed 28 October 2014).

Barth, R. (2001). *Moral leadership*. San Francisco, CA: Jossey-Bass.

Benjamin, C. (2014). *Indian road school*. Halifax, NS: Nimbus.

Berger, T. (2006). *'The Nunavut project' Conciliator's final report*. Vancouver, BC: Bull, Housser and Tupper.

Brody, H. (1991). *The people's land: Inuit, whites and the Eastern Arctic*. Maderia Park, BC: Douglas & McIntyre.

Chrisjohn, R. D. and Young, S. (2006). *The circle game: Shadows and substance in the Indian residential school experience in Canada*. Penticton, BC: Theytus Books.

Chronicle Herald. (2012). *An A+ for Mi'kmaw schools*. Available at: http://thechronicleherald.ca/novascotia/149588-an-a-plus-for-mi-kmaq-schools (accessed 17 October 2014).

Council of Ministers of Education, Canada (CMEC). (2010). Canada's ministers of education advance learn Canada 2020 priorities: A press release. Available at: www.cmec.ca/278/Press-Releases/Canada's-Ministers-of-Education-Advance-Learn-Canada-2020-Priorities.html?id_article=265 (accessed 28 October 2014).

Crowe, K. J. (1991). *A history of the original peoples of Northern Canada*. Montreal, QC: McGill-Queen's University Press.

Education Canada. (2014). *In Nova Scotia, A model for Mi'kmaw education*. Available at: www.cea-ace.ca/education-canada/article/nova-scotia-mi'kmaw-model-first-nation-education (accessed 15 October 2014).

First Nation School Success Program (FNSSP). (2014). Available at: http://kinu.ca/fnssp (accessed 20 October 2014).

Government of Nunavut. (2008). *Education act*. Available at: http://assembly.nu.ca/library/GNedocs/2009/000093-e.pdf (accessed 28 October 2014).

Ilisaqsivik Society. (2014). Ilisaqsivik. Available at: http://ilisaqsivik.ca. (accessed 28 October 2010).

Inuit Tapiriit Kanatami. (2014). *Amaujaq national centre for Inuit education milestone report*. Available at: www.itk.ca/publication/amaujaq-national-centre-inuit-education-milestone-report (accessed 28 October 2014).

Knockwood, I. (1992). *Out of the depths*. Halifax, NS: Roseway.

Lyman, L., Strachan, J. and Lazaridou, A. (2012). *Shaping social justice leadership: Insights of women educators worldwide*. New York: Rowman & Littlefield.

McGhee, R. (1996). *Ancient people of the Arctic*. Vancouver, BC: UBC Press.

McGregor, H. E. (2010). *Inuit education and schools in the Eastern Arctic*. Vancouver, BC: UBC Press.

McGregor, H. E. (2014). *Inuit Qaujimajatuqangit and the transformation of high school education in Nunavut: Historical and statistical profiles*. Charlottetown, PE: Faculty of Education, University of Prince Edward Island.

Macpherson, N. J. (1991). *Dreams and visions: Education in the Northwest Territories from early days to 1984*. Yellowknife, Northwest Territories: Department of Education, Government of the Northwest Territories.

Milloy, J. S. (1999). *A national crime: The Canadian Government and the residential school system 1879 to 1986*. Winnipeg: University of Manitoba Press.

Murphy, J. (2013). The unheroic side of leadership. In M. Grogan (ed.). *The Jossey-Bass Reader on Educational Leadership*, (pp. 28–40). San Francisco, CA: Jossey-Bass.

National Committee on Inuit Education. (2011). *First Canadians, Canadians first: national strategy on Inuit education 2011. Amaujaq* National Centre on Inuit Education, Inuit Tapiriit Kanatami. Available at: www.itk.ca/publication/national-strategy-inuit-education (accessed 28 October 2014).

National Indian Brotherhood. (1972). *Indian control of Indian education*. Ottawa, ON: Assembly of First Nations. Available at: http://64.26.129.156/calltoaction/Documents/ICOIE.pdf (accessed 28 October 2014).

Newhouse, D. and Orr, J. (eds). (2013). *Aboriginal knowledge for economic development*. Halifax, NS: Fernwood Press.

Nunavut Arctic College. (2014). *The latest piqqusilirivvik news*. Available at: www.arcticcollege.ca/piqqusilirivvik (accessed 28 October 2014).

Nunavut Department of Education. (2012). *Annual report 2010–2012*. Available at: www.gov.nu.ca/sites/default/files/files/FINAL%20Annual%20Report%202010–12_Eng%20low%20res.pdf (accessed 28 October 2014).

Nunavut Tunngavik Incorporated. (2011). *2010–2011 Annual report on the status of Inuit culture and society*. Available at: www.tunngavik.com/files/2012/11/2010–11-SICS-Annual-Report-Eng.pdf (accessed 20 October 2014).

Nunavut Tunngavik Incorporated. (2004). *Tukisittiarniqsaujumaviit: A plain language guide to the Nunavut land claims agreement*. Iqaluit, NU: Nunavut Tunngavik Incorporated. Available at: www.tunngavik.com/documents/publications/2004-00-00-A-Plain-Language-Guide-to-the-Nunavut-Land-Claims-Agreement-English.pdf (accessed 24 October 2014).

Orr, J. and MacCormick, F. (2007). *A framework for school improvement for Mi'kmaw Kina'Matnewey schools*. Membertou, NS: Mi'kmaw Kina'Matnewey.

Orr, J., Paul, J. J. and Paul, S. (2002). Decolonizing Mi'kmaw education through cultural practical knowledge. *McGill Journal of Education*, 37 (3), 331–354.

Paul, D. (2006). *We were not the savages*. Halifax, NS: Fernwood Publishing.

Paul, S. (2013). *Language use in MK communities*. Membertou, NS: Mi'kmaw Kina'matnewey.

Peritz, I. (2014). *Globe and mail*. 17 January 2014. Available at: www.theglobeandmail.com/news/national/the-north/why-is-food-so-expensive-in-nunavut-shop-for-yourself-and-find-out/article15915054/ (accessed 30 October 2014).

Schissel, B. and Wotherspoon, T. (2003). *The legacy of school for Aboriginal People: Education, oppression and emancipation*. Don Mill, ON: Oxford University Press Canada.

Seligman, H. K., Bindman, A. W., Vittinghoff, E., Kanaya, A. M and Kushel, M. B. (2007). Food insecurity is associated with diabetes mellitur: Results from the National Health

Examination and Nurtrition Examination Survey (NHANES) 199902992. *Journal of General Medicine*, 22 (7), n.p.

Sergiovanni, T. J. (1992). Why we should seek substitutes for leadership. *Educational Leadership*, 5, 41–45.

Statistics Canada. (2011). *National household survey, profile, Clyde River*. Available at: www12.statcan.gc.ca/nhs-enm/2011/dp-pd/prof/details/page.cfm?Lang=E&Geo1=CSD&Code1=1102037&Data=Count&SearchText=Clyde%20River&SearchType=Begins&SearchPR=01&A1=All&B1=All&TABID=1 (accessed 28 October 2014).

Theoharris, G. (2009). *The school leaders our children deserve: Seven keys to equity, social justice, and school reform*. New York: Teachers College Press.

Toney, D. (2012). *Exploring decolonizing practices in two Mi'kmaw schools*. Unpublished Master of Education Project. Antigonish, NS: St Francis Xavier University.

Tompkins. J. and Orr, J. (2008). St Francis Xavier University School of Education. In S. Niessen (ed.). *Aboriginal knowledge exchange project. Self-study compilation and report: Aboriginal ways of knowing in teacher education*. Regina, SK: Saskatchewan Instructional Development and Research Unity (SIDRU).

Truth and Reconciliation Commission of Canada. (2012). *Truth and reconciliation commission of Canada: Interim report*. Winnipeg, MN: Library and Archives Canada. Available at: www.myrobust.com/websites/trcinstitution/File/Interim%20report%20English%20electronic.pdf (accessed 27 October 2014).

Walton, F. (2014). Transforming indigenous education in Canada: A turning tide. In D.E. Mulcahy, D.G. Mulcahy and R. Saul (eds). *Education in North America*. London: Bloomsbury.

Walton, F., Sandiford, M. (producer), Pitsiulak, S. and Flaherty, E. (2011). *Going places: Preparing Inuit high school students for a changing wider world*. A documentary video. Charlottetown, PE: University of Prince Edward Island, Faculty of Education.

Wilson, D. and MacDonald, D. (2010). *The income gap between Aboriginal peoples and the rest of Canada*. Ottawa, ON: The Canadian Center for Policy Alternatives.

8

LEADING AN INDEPENDENT SCHOOL IN ENGLAND IN THE NEW MILLENNIUM

Ralph Townsend

Introduction

Almost everything I propound in this chapter is based on long experience, but even long experience is inevitably limited when it comes to schools. I have spent 40 years in the teaching profession, 30 of them in the United Kingdom. I have worked only in independent schools, though in recent years I have had increasing contact with the maintained sector in England. The great advantage of working in the independent sector is its relative independence from government interference. I write as Headmaster of Winchester College, most ancient of the so-called English 'public' (which means private) schools, an institution with a strong sense of its prestige and distinctive character and which enjoys, for better or worse, the public perception of being a nursery for intellectuals. Many of its alumni have distinguished themselves in academe, the law and the civil service, though they can be found too in every quarter of financial and business enterprise.

The reflections I have to offer bear the marks of Winchester's particular needs and challenges. While to some extent those needs and challenges are common to all schools in the independent sector in the UK, as they are indeed to those in the maintained sector too, they are in their detail peculiar to Winchester in the context of the times. There are many mansions among schools and long may it be so (Independent Schools Council, 2014). No doubt my opinions and actions betray my prejudices and preoccupations; in some aspects they are conservative, in some perhaps a little radical, in some perhaps even a little iconoclastic. Whatever they are, they are the views and actions of one who has tried to lead thoughtfully and boldly.

In trying to meet the purpose of this book I have organised my chapter around what I hope will be clear markers. I begin with some general points about leadership. This is followed by a summary of the skills independent school leadership requires. I then provide a brief account of the English context past and present, including the sensitive issue of elitism. An account of curriculum change at Winchester over the past decade is then presented. Finally, I offer some challenges to my successor.

Some general points on leadership

Institutions and organisations are like people. They pursue imaginative goals, high standards, hopes and aspirations; and they suffer from weaknesses, errors of judgement, disillusionment, bewilderment and failure. A new leader in any context:

- listens carefully and patiently to as many accounts as possible of the 'story of the past', including personal expressions of weakness, hurt and disappointment;
- organises systematic consultation throughout the organisation (via delegated area leadership) as to (1) the overall aims of the organisation; (2) what the organisation does well; (3) what has not been done well enough; (4) how the institution can do better; and (5) at the end of that process (which should be neither too long nor too brief) communicates a renewed vision for the organisation complete with coherent documentation and plan for action;
- based on listening and consultation, engages all stakeholders in writing together a new chapter of the organisation's story, learning lessons from past errors, building on established strengths, and leaving behind old rubble, with revitalised energy, courage and confidence.

Good leadership requires decisive action, but right action requires prior thought, reflection and critical independence of mind. Those of us leading schools these days can easily find ourselves trapped in a room with small windows. We are under immense pressures from various constituencies to show short-term quantifiable results in many different areas, from admission and graduation statistics to pupil learning outcomes, and from workloads to revenue streams and fundraising. Overwhelmed by these and other demands placed upon us, including the task of managing organisations that have had to become more bureaucratic in order to comply with increasing government regulation, many school leaders have turned to the business world for models of how to lead.

As efficient change managers we can talk about putting a computer on every desk, or improving student services, but we have trouble defining what a liberal education actually is, or explaining in anything but clichés why such a thing is worth defending. Most heads of schools don't have time to study. That is a great pity because those leading an organisation should embody the organisation's highest values. Finding a balance between the active and reflective life has always been difficult, and it is becoming ever more so in the fast-paced, future-oriented world of consumer capitalism, where the educational triad customer–competition–change has replaced wisdom–virtue–eloquence.

What does the Head do?

Not long ago I gave a talk to the pupils in my school entitled 'What do I do?' How does their Head spend his day? From the pupils' point of view, the Head's is the most mysterious of roles because they don't see as much of her/him as they do their classroom teachers. There are different ways of doing any job and how you do headship will depend on the character of the school, on its established organisational structure and on the personality, particular interests, strengths and weaknesses of the person doing it. I have been Head of three schools over a period of a quarter of a century, each of them different in character, though all of them concerned with the same basic constituencies of governors, parents, alumni, teachers and pupils; and beyond them, external groups like government departments, inspectorates, the press and the general public. Very few leadership roles require contact with, and accountability to, so wide a range of interested parties.

While I have the ultimate responsibility of managing the school day-to-day, I could not possibly do it all on my own. A lot of my responsibility has to be delegated to other people. Over the years I have taken to heart the golden rule: 'only do what only you can do'. So I delegate the direction of studies and the organisation of the curriculum, sport, music, fundraising, day-to-day pastoral care of pupils and the care of the grounds, to other people – many other people – about 500 of them.

'Only do what only you can do.' So what can *only* the Head do? I think this can be answered in relation to six main areas. First, the Head sets the tone of the school. This is a subtle matter. What language does he or she use when talking about the school to pupils, to academic staff, to prospective parents and other outsiders? What is the Head's personal style and manner? Is it extrovert or reserved? Does the Head come across as an efficient manager or more of a thinker or is the style more pastoral? Is the style intense or relaxed, earnest or humorous? Is the Head given to rousing speeches or a quieter mode of persuasion? The style needs to suit the school. The historic and prevailing tone of Winchester is basically scholarly: it is a place in which learning, high culture and good conversation (including humour) are what matter most. Most of its teachers fit that description and that is the model of the good life we commend to our pupils – the goal of lifelong learning.

Second, and closely allied to its tone, are the school's character and values, which need to be made consistent and clear. The school should have a strong sense of its history, its distinctiveness and its difference from other schools. Good teachers are more important than state-of-the-art buildings. In my opinion, schools should not buy too much into mission statements and the apparatus of the modern science of public relations. I think it is better to have a prospectus and website which are text-heavy and image-light, appealing to people who like to read prose and think seriously about education, who are sceptical about the extravagant claims some schools make and suspicious of glossy clichés that lack substance.

Third, the Head must ensure that the day-to-day order of the school is well understood and embraced so that people can live and work happily together. The prevailing experience must be one of harmony and not dissonance. Allied to this is the school's system of discipline, managed on a personal basis consistent with fairness. A good discipline system is one in which standards and values are clear, so that pupils respect their community and want to co-operate. The way the teachers relate to each other, and the way they treat the pupils requires an order and discipline which is so well understood that it happens naturally.

All academic, bursarial, grounds, catering, development and enterprise staff need the Head's support and encouragement – they all make an important contribution to a complex whole. The appointment of teachers is a key responsibility. I spend a lot of time talking to my staff, supporting them in their work, and helping them to find solutions to their difficulties, whether professional or personal. Most of them will work in the school for much longer than the pupils, or indeed me, and their professional fulfilment is important to them and their families. They are, as it were, the Head's apostles; the Head looks after them and they in turn look after the pupils, academically and pastorally.

Fourth, and for the most part invisible to pupils, but essential to their well-being, is the school's process of management. Pupils might get the impression that the Head can make any decision she/he likes and then impose it on everyone by fiat. I suppose it could be done that way, but it would not be very effective. It is important that decisions are taken with appropriate dispatch but after consultation. My Senior Management Committee meets under my chairmanship once a week. I meet the Housemasters (heads of pastoral divisions) every Monday morning. I meet with the Bursar (or Finance Director) every Monday morning too. Heads of department meet at least once a term. I meet with the School Prefects, who are an important part of my link with the pupil body, once a week.

Fifth, and also invisible to many, is my accountability for the day-to-day operations of the school to the Governors. In theory, they could tell me what to do, but in fact they avoid doing so, because they have delegated responsibility for ensuring the good order of the school to me. Their main responsibility is to ensure that the school's policies and finances are in proper order. I see the Governors a lot and keep them well informed.

Sixth, what happens in staff meetings and school assemblies is one of the Head's key responsibilities. These meetings are where the moral, pastoral and intellectual tone of the school is established; they are where the Head's personal stamp is put upon the school. They should always be carefully planned, and be where the Head's values and expectations are made clear, preferably spiced with a little humour. They should be long enough to project their seriousness, but not too long. Staff meetings should provide an opportunity for contribution from the floor while never losing the sense that the Head is in control.

All of this comes down, in the end, to good relationships among people who share common basic values and who enjoy working in a team. The metaphor that sums up best what the Head does in the school is that of the conductor of the orchestra, who has the whole symphony in his mind, ear and heart, who interprets the music to the players who can play all the instruments she/he cannot, so that every individual instrument can make its distinctive contribution to the complex and beautiful whole. The Head needs to be visible, not shut up in an office, be out and about in the school, greeting staff and pupils alike, sharing a joke, showing interest, showing enjoyment of the school community of which he or she is proud.

The English context

In 1901 every trainee teacher in England and Wales was presented with an edition of A.P. Stanley's *Life and Correspondence of Thomas Arnold, DD.* Arnold's biography is a model for any workaholic. His workload included running a school, preparing pupils for university entrance, dealing with parents, heading a boarding house with all the duties of a housemaster, conducting voluminous correspondence with former pupils and continuing to coach some former pupils by distance learning, latterly combining the headmastership of Rugby School with work as part-time Professor of Modern History at the University of Oxford. That could be matched by few, if any, twenty-first century Heads! It is hard to imagine any single book, let alone an exemplary biography, which could claim that kind of status among aspiring teachers in 2015. A guide to educational law, perhaps; or suggestions for self-defence in the classroom, or a plain man's guide to league tables, or strategies for the detection of plagiarism – these might be thought to have more general relevance.

Thomas Arnold's son, Matthew, who in the 1860s became Her Majesty's Inspector of Schools, espoused the concept of 'liberal education' as the basis of a modern curriculum. His view was that the aim of education is *to know ourselves and the world,* and that we have, as the means to this end, 'to be acquainted with the best which has been thought and said in the world' (Paul, 1902). Such liberal learning was to be based on the skills of reading, writing and arithmetic. Interpreted through a differentiated system of academically selective grammar schools and vocationally oriented secondary moderns, these over-arching skills and values remained in force in the English education system until the 1960s, when the Wilson Labour Government effected major reforms trumpeted as serving the common good and social integration. Almost all the grammar schools disappeared, to be replaced by comprehensives.

Progressively, and over the last twenty years in particular, however, it is not the three Rs, but the three Ts – tests, targets and tables – which have become the tightly imposed orthodoxies in English schools. From the baseline tests of 5-year-olds to General Certificate of Secondary Education (GCSE) targets, there is almost no aspect of school life which is not subject to a folder full of documents bearing the mark of the Department of Education. Heads of maintained schools have less and less say over what goes on in the schools for which they are responsible. The truth is that successive British governments have allied themselves to a market-based philosophy of education provision, though there is little sign that British society is any less economically and educationally polarised in 2015 than it was when this gruelling process began in the late 1990s. Education ministers have continued to ignore the evidence that crude performance tables punish working-class communities and encourage parents to make comparisons based on social rather than educational criteria. Here it is apposite to draw the reader's attention to the work of Professor Stefan Collini (2012) of Cambridge University, who has written trenchantly on the impact of market-driven government policy on higher education in general and on the study of the humanities in particular.

The debate about elites

The global community created by modern technology gives those of us working in education many challenges and opportunities. To meet those challenges we need the right elites, but for many years, 'elite' has been a dirty word in the politics of English education. It has not been so in other quarters. British governments have been keen to support elitist sport and elitist entertainment (celebrity), but the concept of elitism has not been welcome in talk about education. Sport and entertainment attract crowds and revenue and their spectacle has wide magnetic appeal across the social spectrum, but education (with its intellectual and social complexities) presents governments with a much more problematical issue; on this, it is instructive to recall the scrutiny under which independent schools came in the 1960s and 1970s (Rae, 1981).

The critical questions are these: Do we want any kind of elite at all in our society? And if so, what kind of elite do we want it to be? The debate about private education has raged for half a century. Should those who begin life with the financial and social privilege of their parents automatically succeed to influential and powerful positions in society? Should the institutions which they traditionally support, including schools and universities, enjoy favoured treatment in the political scheme of things and remain the preserve of the children of the ruling class? Does private education supply a hereditary elite of class and, if so, to what extent can it be tolerated? Regarding the latter, it is noteworthy that the French economic historian, Thomas Piketty (2014), has recently posited that Western capitalism has ironically returned to the nineteenth-century elitism of dynastic wealth.

As Britain has, for a long time, notwithstanding its class system, been a democracy, other questions have also been increasingly brought into the educational debate. Should the high culture of the traditional curriculum, with its emphasis on the study of classical literature and language, pure mathematics and theoretical science, be replaced by applied subjects that prepare people directly for the workforce? Should populism reign over elitism? Should meritocracy trump privileged inheritance?

The answers to these questions will be shaped by a number of factors giving rise to yet further questions. Which approach is thought to serve best the political, social and economic management of an advanced democratic society? Which will be the best tool to combine social stability with the means of production to sustain that stability? Which will promote the fundamental values and way of life that can hold society together? Which will provide the right kind of leadership for a free, diverse, globally financed society?

These far-reaching questions have pressed and continue to press themselves upon governments as they search for the answers, and the political response is never entirely complete or coherent. I would summarise the current prevailing state of British education in the following:

- Egalitarianism in the form of non-selective state education as a means to overthrow inherited class distinction and social division has been centre-stage for forty years. 'Equality of opportunity' has been the political goal.
- Populism has triumphed over academic rigour in educational discourse and political decisions about the curriculum taught in schools, partly as an attempt to eradicate class division, partly as an attempt to make education relevant to the perceived social and economic needs of modern society, and partly to keep children at school until the age of eighteen. For all these reasons the rigour of academic courses has unavoidably been sequentially reduced, while vocational courses (for which the majority of people are suited) have been insufficiently developed and looked down upon as inferior.

Governments have not succeeded in solving the problems they hoped they would. In recent years, a new materialist elite has emerged with scant regard for the communitarian values which hold a contented society together and which constitute the very origin of the social vision that motivated attempts to modernise our education system. The gap is growing between those who have great wealth and those who have none. Social unrest seems to be brewing.

I come back to my two questions. Do we want any kind of elite at all in our society? And, if so, what kind of elite do we want it to be? I am an elitist in a certain sense. A good elite sets high standards. It must be accountable. A well-led, creative society which cares for its citizens and aspires to give them reasonable opportunity, security and stability requires the leadership of an elite which is well-trained, adaptable and humane. That means a meritocratic elite of talent which is able to provide the trained competency, creativity and leadership essential to political effectiveness, economic growth and social solidarity.

These themes have in recent years come back with force on to the agenda of political and educational discussion in Britain as we try to recover from the financial crisis of 2008. There is an attempt to rediscover some of the strengths we have lost in our educational culture over the past generation and combine them with some of the advances which have been made in the name of increased equality. One key plank, promoted by governments of both stripes since 1997, known as the Academy movement, is partnership between state schools and independent schools (Adonis, 2012); in 2008 my school entered into a partnership with Midhurst Rother College, a failing state school 30 miles away, which, over the past seven years, has resulted in a dramatic improvement in the performance of that school while bringing to Winchester the benefits of a wider educational awareness and experience (Winchester College, 2014). There are now many similar partnerships in operation.

Independent schools (which educate only about 7 per cent of British youth), while increasingly called to account by governments, have managed to continue to flourish as a privately funded educational service. These schools have, in general, retained more of the strengths of the traditional curriculum and methods of teaching than the state schools, while adopting good modern practice and recognising opportunities to provide access to their educational programmes to children whose parents do not belong to the current economic elite. One valuable contribution that independent schools bring to state schools is the testimony that elitism does not have to be a dirty word – the best elite is one focused on leadership and service and not on preserving privilege as an end in itself.

Over the last decade or so independent schools in England have (rightly in my view) been required by government to justify the tax advantages they enjoy as registered charities in order to demonstrate their public benefit. They must explain and be accountable for the extent to which they provide wider access to their privileged status, a matter addressed by Winchester College under the heading of 'public benefit' (Winchester College, 2014). In fact, Winchester's greatest public benefit lies at the heart of its founder's vision, enshrined in its statutes of 1382 – that is, the provision of a good education for those who can profit and contribute by it, regardless of social background. Our social context is somewhat different from that of the fourteenth century, of course, but the provision of scholarships and bursaries to pupils who can excel and in turn contribute to the development of a free and civilised society, remains our principal objective.

Leading for old and new

The only real justification for a private education sector is its independence to conserve, experiment and lead to the benefit of society as a whole and to protect the democratic value of choice. Independent schools must participate in the democratic debate about education as one of the fundamental elements of a free and humane society. During the course of my career this responsibility has called independent schools to co-operate with governments in their well-founded intentions to break down long-established social barriers to opportunity among citizens, improve the quality of education for all, challenge where necessary the overly pragmatic and restrictive strategies of governments and demonstrate best practice when the necessary skills and resources are available.

The case for liberal education

The origins of Winchester College are a work of genius. They go right to the roots of the Western educational ideal. The founder, William of Wykeham, was twice Chancellor of England (prime minister) in the second half of the fourteenth century and Bishop of Winchester. His great project at the end of his life (he died in 1404) was to endow his double foundation, Winchester College and New College Oxford, to guarantee a competent educated clerical service for the government of the realm. In creating these two places of residential learning, meticulously planned in their architecture and their regulations, he established the model of the Oxbridge college.

The tradition of a liberal education has been intrinsic to the development of free Western society. It is a concept that goes back to the sixth century. The Latin Church, struggling in the ruins of the Roman Empire to hold on to as much civilised learning as possible, put together a basic curriculum, consisting of the seven liberal arts. As time went by the curriculum absorbed the great Greek texts that arrived from the Arabs and then from Constantinople. For a thousand years the monasteries, later also the cathedral schools, and later still the universities and grammar schools, kept the tradition of liberal education going.

I mentioned Matthew Arnold earlier in this essay. By the nineteenth century, the concept 'liberal education' had become definable as passing on to the young 'the best that has been said and thought'. Arnold was a school inspector afraid that the utilitarian training for work, which many Victorians saw as the only purpose of education, could well drive out of schools and universities both the disinterested love of learning for its own sake, and the handing on of 'the best that has been said and thought'.

Over the second half of the twentieth century Arnold's concept of liberal education came increasingly under scrutiny (Bloom, 1987). 'Political correctness' came to tell us that any idea is as good as any other because someone happens to hold it. Increasing information and technical skill have not been matched by a deepening wisdom or by growth in virtue in our time. Nevertheless, a school can still be sure that the best – the best books, the best ideas, the best ways of thinking and working in the pursuit of truth of all kinds – is *still* the best, and that the best can still be given to young people as their inheritance, with faith in its value for them as human beings growing up in a complex world (Proctor, 1998).

The curriculum

A rich curriculum is an invitation to young people to consider the historic roots of the humane tradition that we enjoy in a free society; the opportunity to hear and participate in fine music, the disciplines of sitting still, attending to reasoned argument, and reflection, all of which are relevant to the formation of cultural depth and social maturity. The disciplines that keep mature freedoms standing require steel at the centre. The world needs that steel more than ever and a good school will continue to do all it can to help supply it.

As Arnold's fears that secondary education might become a purely utilitarian exercise became a political reality by the end of the twentieth century, Heads with a strong commitment to intellectual quality became increasingly concerned about the reduced content, depth and challenge of A-level and GCSE courses, and also about the impact of coursework components and unreliability of marking. The prescriptive elements (both in specifications and in assessment objectives) now so characterised English A-levels that there was very little if any opportunity for individual thought or flair. Lack of differentiation at the top end, where the brightest could be identified, now created problems for universities in their admissions processes. An education culture for competency at the expense of flair and independence of thought and insight had come to prevail.

In response to this, some strong independent schools adopted several strategies to try to keep the challenge high, through the adoption of more demanding IGCSE courses (Cambridge International Examinations, 2014a) as distinct from the ordinary GCSEs, acceleration to AS-level and A-level where possible, and appropriate, and vigorous participation in such competitive programmes as Mathematics and Science Olympiads. Even so, these schools reached the point where the imposition of patch upon compensating patch had disfigured the structure of A-level beyond recognition, for A-level had become a mis-shapen garment shredded by relentless examination, coursework, retakes and depleted accounts of academic subjects. At least for those pupils with intellectual gifts, much of Sixth Form academic life had become busy, staccato and trivial.

Some schools found a remedy to some of these problems in the adoption of the International Baccalaureate (IB). Winchester considered that option but rejected it as too prescriptive in its structure. Our argument was that a pupil who has little aptitude for mathematics, for example, should not be compelled to study it for five years, while the same pupil, a gifted linguist, is confined to the study of only one foreign language in depth.

The requirements for the IB would also present obstacles to our maintaining Division (which simply means a class or form, abbreviation Div), a distinctive feature of our educational programme in which wide reading and daily discussion are required, and which we regard as essential in preparing our pupils for a good adult life of service and inner happiness (Winchester College, 2014). Div is a continuing programme of linguistic, historical, literary and cultural development, taught over five years, based on daily teaching and regular written tasks but subject to no examination. It was developed as the centrepiece of the Winchester curriculum in the late nineteenth century (anticipating Arnold's fears). Div has been adapted from time to time, but its continuing presence proclaims that at Winchester the study of the humanities constitutes one of the primary educational and cultural lifelines of Western civilisation and its future.

Most people today know the humanities only ahistorically, simply as a group of disciplines, such as the sciences, the social sciences and the arts, and with no particular connection to Western civilisation. Div at Winchester attempts to keep alive the rich insights that, through a dialogue with the tradition of the humanities, the historical, and ultimately aesthetic and moral knowledge, we can derive from a conversation with the past. The curriculum, therefore, in the spirit of Sacks (2011), presupposes that the humanities should be learnt and taught by everyone, including those gifted in the realms of mathematics and science.

In contrast to this, the curriculum of the standard modern school is fragmented and incoherent, as is the collective mind of the academic staff. Many men and women teaching today have not had the opportunity to acquire a good liberal education because their learning is narrow and specialised. Mainstream educational thought tends now to denigrate content and focuses instead on the teaching of skills. This approach of educational formalism, of skills divorced from content, combined with romantic notions of free and natural human growth and development, has reduced the demand and richness of what we teach. The Winchester principle is that we who teach can greatly improve the education we offer our pupils by improving the education we give ourselves. Studying and teaching the history of the humanities is an excellent way for all teachers, regardless of their academic specialisation, to continue to develop as teachers and thoughtful citizens.

The nature of contemporary parenting makes the content of our children's studies an important issue. Consumer capitalism ensures that it is increasingly difficult for us to be the parents we would like to be. Those of us who grew up in the 1950s and 1960s were unprepared, for the most part, to comprehend the effect on our children of the junk values fed them in the electronic community of rock music, television, videos and movies, where adulthood is presented as drinking, spending money and being sexually active. The mass media has the goal of making money from teenagers, while parents have the goal of producing happy, well-adjusted adults. Children can express individuality only in relation to the traditions of their society, which they have to learn; this cannot be achieved merely in response to a disorderly, uncertain and fragmented educational programme.

Happiness that lasts requires a number of elements: knowledge sufficient to acquire competency, self-confidence; values and disciplines that nourish lasting relationships; interiority which resists total dependency on external stimuli, gratification and affirmation. The books of great literature need to be our lifelong companions, as do the study of other world cultures and the modern age itself with all its experimentation and diversity in philosophy, science and the arts. The broader the learning, the better, but there must also be depth, which cannot be delivered by syncopated knowledge presented and examined in bite-size chunks. Indeed, such a reductive obsession of the modern world has been identified as having deep roots in a disfigured use and understanding of the brain itself (McGilchrist, 2009).

It was amid all this turmoil and dissatisfaction that, in 2002, a number of Heads of independent schools together approached Cambridge International Examinations (2014b) with the proposal that the syndicate might develop an alternative to A-level which would provide an option for increased space, measure, content and rigour in senior secondary school study. Our argument ran as follows. The academic content of science and the literary and cultural element in language courses, ancient and modern, in particular, had been progressively eroded. Those with the capacity to grapple with the full integrity of subject content needed full content to be restored to their courses; and universities, surely, would welcome such a restoration. While no one would contest the desirability of higher education for the majority of school leavers, it was surely in the interests of all that those who had the capacity for studying complex subjects at depth should be given the skills and opportunity to do so. They could only bring added value to their university cohort.

In response, CIE developed a new course known as the Cambridge Pre-U (Cambridge International Examinations, 2014c). Like the Cambridge International A-level, so widely used in such good Asian schools as Raffles Institution Singapore, the linear approach of Cambridge Pre-U (with exams taken at the end of the two-year course) provides for coherence and progression, and the chance to reclaim teaching and learning time at the end of the first year of the two-year course; and to decide the order, pace and depth of teaching and learning most appropriate for pupils. There is freedom to choose subject combinations without constraint. Winchester pupils take three subjects (or four if they are strong mathematicians, as the majority of them are). We use the Pre-U examinations as free-standing qualifications, for, as I have explained, academic extension is at the heart of Div, where we make the connections that allow us all (teachers and pupils) to assess the real value of cultural heritage and development.

Many Winchester Heads of Departments were involved in the development of Pre-U syllabuses, some of them chairing committees, and there was confidence among them that these two-year courses, without coursework and examined at the end of the second year of the Sixth Form, would suit the great majority of our pupils, and restore at least some of the quality of measured teaching and intellectual formation which had gradually disappeared during the curriculum revisions implemented by successive governments. CIE ensured that the Pre-U was accorded full recognition by all British universities.

My description above of Winchester Div was not merely a digression. Rather, it was by way of explanation of the values underpinning the school's decision to adopt a new structure to frame its cultural and intellectual goals. Our decision was not intended to deprecate other structures and models of academic and intellectual formation (though it is obvious we were critical of them), nor to set ourselves apart as an ivory tower; it was to take proper advantage of our independence to express our educational goals as best we could, within the constraints of modern political realities, and to offer leadership and encouragement to those who continue to believe that a spacious formation of young minds and hearts, with an examination structure which supports it, offers the best future for them and for the society in which they will take their place. Now, since 2008, while few schools have adopted this new credential in its entirety (as Winchester has), hundreds of schools, independent and maintained, have combined it with A-levels to enhance their programmes.

Sport and spirituality

The tradition of strong sport in English independent schools is well known (Mangan, 1981). In some it is indubitably the first priority. In a school which sets such store by the vibrancy of its intellectual life, it goes without saying that the excellence of its music, theatre and general cultural life follows naturally. Sport, however, in the current prevailing culture of sports celebrity, requires both careful explanation and special care in securing its connection with Winchester's cultural ethos. In broad terms, Winchester's educational aim is to equip its pupils to live a good life – that is to say, a life worth living, a life that is satisfying and a life that takes a critical interest in what is going on in the world.

Socrates and Plato understood ethics to be concerned with two areas – namely, right action and life's greatest good. Ethics may be defined as the study of right conduct and the good life. How does the concept of the good life relate to sport? It is arguable that we are more fascinated by sport now than at any time in our cultural history, and that the concept of the good life has something to do with that fascination. The values upon which physical team games are based make them more than pleasant diversion and recreation. If exercise can help us blow off angry steam, soothe jangled nerves, push along bulky food, teach us to respect and co-operate with others, and then smile at the limits of our bodies, we can call exercise a faithful friend and a contributor to our spiritual growth.

The human qualities underlying athletic activities are the same as those underlying spiritual life activities. Discipline, dedication, enthusiasm and perseverance are among them. They are the same qualities that will get us out of bed at dawn to meditate, or enable us to protect fifteen minutes a day for reflective study or the reading of a book of spiritual wisdom. The spiritual person is the one who is interested in and dedicated to the artful handling of the world, the artful shaping of the self, and the artful forming of a life into something good. This artful fashioning of life seldom results from coercion or regimentation. It is best achieved by virtue of spontaneous desire and the qualities of determination and commitment such as are embodied in the approach to playing games well.

Thus, soccer, basketball and cycling can be disciplines of the spiritual life inasmuch as they help develop qualities that also lend themselves to the spiritual life. Through skiing, rock climbing and white-water rafting, we learn how to deal with and overcome fear and anxiety. Through running, swimming or rowing long distances we develop endurance and willpower, and learn how to deal with boredom. Through golf one can practise intense concentration and subtle control. Team sports can teach us the value of co-operation.

Discipline, freely chosen, fully experienced, is essential if we are to do anything well, including playing a game. Meditation can be such a discipline, but so can running; both prevent the world from filling our lives to such an extent that there is no place left to listen. Further, if an activity is good for the body, it is also good for the mind and the spirit. Sports set in motion our mental faculties of attention, observation, analysis, order, judgement and evaluation. We need all of these qualities finely honed if we are to live the good life. As Socrates and Plato observed, no one with a sense of serious moral purpose can journey through life without these qualities. Deep thinkers enjoy sport as much as anyone, though they will be disinclined to be fanatical about it. I include these remarks to show the terms in which sport is consistent with scholarly and intellectual formation.

The global community of schools

With the rise of communication technology and ease of travel over the course of my career, schools have assumed membership of a global community of learning.

Exchange schemes and conferences abound. Approaches of so many schools seeking a connection with Winchester presented me with a management problem, since I could not oblige them all. As an example of a solution to this happy but daunting challenge, I set out here my scheme for the coherent management of international links with the global school community. As with all solutions to problems, it has required the clear identification of principles consistent with Winchester's values and ethos, or, to put it another way, the establishment of rewarding but limited objectives. Here is our manifesto:

- Ongoing links with schools operating in different educational systems provide challenge to Winchester's educational outlook and practice and valuable professional development for our staff.
- We should provide first-hand experience of other languages and cultures for our pupils.
- We should ensure a constructive place for Winchester on the world stage.
- We should maintain our links with prudent management of time and resources.
- Limited but long-term links with other schools provide depth of relationship and are preferable to the superficial buzz of large international conferences.

About half our pupils (350/700) travel outside Britain under the school's auspices every year. Our regular links with schools in other countries take four forms:

- Established exchanges with schools in countries whose languages we teach – i.e France, Germany, Russia, Spain and China.
- The Winchester European Symposium with reciprocal links with schools in Italy and Romania.
- Reception of groups of pupils from selected schools for a month or a term for academic and/or cultural enrichment: these include Montgomery Bell Academy, Nashville, Tennesee, USA; Colegio Claustro Moderno, Bogota, Colombia; Germantown Friends School, Philadelphia, USA; Nada High School, Kobe, Japan; and HAS Fudan Shanghai China. Two pupils from Johannes Kepler Grammar School Prague come for a term every year.
- The Winchester International Symposium is a defined group of schools covering every major region of the world. These are: African Leadership Academy Johannesburg South Africa; Colegio Claustro Moderno, Bogota, Colombia; Garodia International Centre for Learning Mumbai, India; Johannes Kepler Grammar School, Prague, Czech Republic; Karachi Grammar School, Pakistan; Liaoning Province Shiyan Co-operation High School, China; Montgomery Bell Academy, Nashville, Tennessee, USA; Nada High School Japan; Raffles Institution Singapore. Two senior pupils and a teacher from each school, together with the Heads, meet for a week each year, rotating annually around the schools, to discuss in depth a matter of common interest, for example leadership, poverty, world water shortage, global finance structures, art and architecture in society.

Through our Winchester Junior Fellowship scheme we maintain links with US universities that assist us with selection of young graduates to come and teach in the school for one or two years. Our main links are with Columbia University and the University of Pennsylvania. The scheme opens up familiarity with the sphere of university study in the USA for our pupils (of whom an increasing number choose to go to university in the USA) and provides us with a resource for their SAT preparation.

The leadership challenge continues

The last fifty years have shown that where public education is concerned, modern central government tends to abrogate to itself more and more power, leaving less and less scope for responsible delivery of education to Heads and teachers. In England, government has tightened its grip on the educational system as a whole, creating a bureaucratic apparatus which is increasingly felt to be pedantic. This is the regime of targets and directives where, despite everyone's best intentions, things all too easily go wrong.

Britons are sicker than ever, says Oliver James (2007), who contends that the inhabitants of English-speaking nations are more than twice as likely to suffer from mental illness as their counterparts in Western Europe. Some 23 per cent of us are troubled in this way, he suggests, though the proportion falls among those who give regular attention to community religious practice and discipline. James issues some bracing challenges for future reflection. Here they are:

- Aggressive, materialist-inspired consumerism is driving us mad. The more we want, the worse we feel. We need tighter restraints on the advertising industry, particularly on the use of attractive people to market goods.
- There is a correlation between television viewing and depression, including eating disorders, among the young. We need a less exam-driven school system, which has been suborned by economic imperatives. We need to spend more time with our young children.
- The gnawing wants and desires created by the advertising industry affect not just grown adults, but schools, children and even the nature of childhood itself.
- 'Affluenza' – the doomed search for material success offers some explanation for the madness inflicted on the UK's classrooms for the last two decades, where the goal has become to produce good little producers and consumers rather than enquiring minds. Hence, the failed regime of tests and targets, which has dominated school thinking in Britain since 1997 when it was introduced, an approach that came at the direct expense of the arts, drama and music. Schools with an insistence on community values seem, in contrast, unusually attractive to parents.
- The result of this hoop-jumping mentality that sees learning only as a means to a material end is rock-bottom levels of pupil satisfaction, among the lowest in Europe, and a tail of under-achievement.

- There is worrying evidence that the attempt to drive up exam results has been damaging for a group rarely considered at risk: able girls, particularly those from well-to-do families. The pressure on them to conform to parental expectations seems to be acute – much more so than for boys – and the consequences for their mental stability are sometimes serious. The most conformist do the best – and suffer the most.
- Why have examples such as this been deliberately ignored by those in favour of materialist models? Because a consumer economy works better when people are driven by selfish rather than collective impulses, and who dares challenge such a force?
- The consensus about our growing mental distress is hard to ignore and evidence of alienation and unhappiness in our schools mounts on a daily basis.

We cannot afford to ignore these observations; they are at the very least cause for serious reflection among all who care about young people and the education they receive. The key to successful schools is the motivation of young people to desire learning. The focus has to be, as ever, on the skills of literacy and numeracy, which are needed to develop anything creative, as well as embracing subject matter that is relevant to the economic, social, political and ecological problems of the times. A *sine qua non* is a strong and steady stream of talented people to take up the creative challenge of teaching:

> While technology can be put to good use by talented teachers, they, and not the futurists, must take the lead. The process of teaching and learning is an intimate act that neither computers nor markets can hope to replicate. Small wonder, then, that the business model hasn't worked in reforming the schools – there is simply no substitute for the personal element.
>
> (Kirp, 2014, n.p.)

This is achieved best where Heads have the capacity and the freedom to implement a clear vision of the content, standards, tone and style they want to cultivate and sustain in their schools and are given the resources to pursue their vision.

It is neither conceivable nor desirable that we should dispense with a guiding politically legitimate system in conducting the affairs of modern mass education, but let us not forget that the enterprise of education flourishes best where there is a measure of independence sufficient to protect and enhance the freedom of the human mind and spirit. When those of us who teach feel most dispirited, beset by the crush of modern institutional and political rhetoric and bureaucracy, we can do worse than seek solace in the words of Michael Oakeshott:

> Each of us is born in a corner of the earth and at a particular moment in historic time, lapped round with locality. But school and university are places apart where a declared learner is emancipated from the limitations of his local circumstances and from the wants he may happen to have acquired, and is

> moved by intimations of what he has never yet dreamed. He finds himself invited to pursue satisfactions he has never yet imagined or wished for. They are, then, sheltered places where excellences may be heard because the din of local partialities is no more than a distant rumble. They are places where a learner is initiated into what there is to be learned.
>
> (1989, p. 24)

It is the duty of those responsible for the delivery of an education that really nourishes young lives to continue to press that perspective upon our political masters.

References

Adonis, A. (2012). *Education, education, education: reforming England's schools*. London: Biteback Publishing.

Bloom, A. (1987). *The closing of the American mind*. New York: Simon & Schuster.

Cambridge International Examination (2014a). Available at: www.cie.org.uk/programmes-and-qualifications/. . .2/cambridge-igcse (accessed 28 October 2014).

Cambridge International Examination (2014b). Available at: www.cie.org.uk/ (accessed 28 October 2014).

Cambridge International Examination (2014c). Available at: www.cie.org.uk/qualifications/academic/uppersec/preu (accessed 28 October 2014).

Collini, S. (2012). *What are universities for?* Harmondsworth: Penguin.

Independent Schools Council (2014). Available at: www.isc.co.uk/ (accessed 28 October 2014).

James, O. (2007). *Affluenza*. Manville, IL: Vermillion.

Kirp, D. (2014). Teaching is not a business. Available at: www.nytimes.com/2014/08/17/opinion/sunday/teaching-is-not-a-business.html?emc=edit_th_20140817&nl=todaysheadlines&nlid=67311590 (accessed 28 October 2014).

McGilchrist, I. (2009). *The master and his emissary: the divided brain and the making of the western world*. Yale, CT: Yale University Press.

Mangan, J. A. (1981). *Athleticism in the Victorian and Edwardian public school: the emergence and consolidation of an educational ideology*. Cambridge: Cambridge University Press.

Oakeshott, M. (1989). *The voice of liberal learning*. Yale, CT: Yale University Press.

Paul, H. (1902). *Matthew Arnold*. London: Macmillan.

Piketty, T. (2014). *Capitalism in the twenty-first century*. Cambridge, MA: Harvard University Press.

Proctor, R. E. (1998). *Defining the humanities with a curriculum for today's students*. Indiana, IN: Indiana University Press.

Rae J. (1981). The public school revolution: Britain's independent schools 1964–79. London: Faber.

Sacks, J. (2011). *The Great partnership: God, science and the search for meaning*. London: Hodder & Stoughton.

Winchester College (2014). Available at: www.winchestercollege.org/ (accessed 28 October 2014).

9

LEADING AUTONOMOUS SCHOOLS

Academies, leadership and the self-improving school system in England

Christopher Chapman

Introduction

Education systems across the globe are constantly developing and experimenting with new policies designed to raise educational outcomes for young people. One important trend that has emerged over recent decades is the idea of 'autonomous' schools or 'independent state-funded schools' (ISFS). These schools are funded through public taxation, usually free at the point of delivery, and operate without the control of traditional school district or local government bureaucracies. The extent to which they offer a superior quality service to their traditional school district controlled counterparts remains contested. The political ideology that underpins them has also been part of a wider political debate in several systems.

ISFSs can operate as stand-alone schools or as part of a network or chain of schools under the control of a central organising body, such as a Charter Management Organisation in the United States (Wohlstetter *et al.*, 2011). In this chapter, I draw on the emergence of academies in England as an example of ISFSs and reflect on our programme of research that has explored new models of leadership emerging within the English system and the impact of federations and chains to consider the potential for a self-improving school system. The chapter is organised into four sections. The first provides the background context to the growth of academies in England. The second section provides an overview of academies in relation to change, improvement and leadership, while the third section reflects on the key messages from our programme of research in this area. The fourth and final section reflects on three key fault lines and offers a possible way forward to create an authentic self-improving system.

Context

In the United States the rise of the charter school movement has been a contested area, although these schools have only accounted for around 6 per cent of all schools nationally (http://nces.ed.gov/fastfacts/display.asp?id=30). Similar projects are underway in a diverse range of countries, including Chile, Australia, Colombia and New Zealand (Bettinger, 2009; Bellei, 2009). It has been argued that this trend is occurring in parallel with a broader range of policies underpinned by an overarching neoliberal agenda involving a transition of governance arrangements (OECD, 2005).

Turning attention to England, a relatively compact system operating approximately 22,000 schools, the ISFS trend is seen most acutely through the rise of the academy movement, the English equivalent of independent state-funded schools such as America's charter schools and free schools in Sweden. Academies can exist as stand-alone schools, as individual schools, or as part of a chain of schools under the control of a Strategic Management Executive (SME) (Chapman and Salokangas, 2012) in the same way that CMOs co-ordinate charter schools in the United States. It should also be noted that England has introduced free schools. These are much fewer in number and operate under the same legislation as academies (Higham, 2014).

We can trace the emergence of academies and academy chains to the neoliberal agenda and the transition of governance arrangements promoted by the Conservative government elected in 1979. Their policies eroded the power of local councils, including 150 Local Educational Authorities (LEAs) which managed and allocated resources to state schools under their control and also provided a broad array of services ranging from school meals to professional development courses and school inspection. Following the 1988 Education Reform Act the pace of change has been relentless and a zero tolerance approach to failure has dominated the discourse (Chapman and Gunter, 2009; Sammons, 2008). Significant changes have included the introduction of school-based management and the systematic dismantling of local authority control over schools, the introduction of a national inspection agency in 1992, and the launch of the academy programme by the New Labour government in 2000. These politically driven reforms have led to successive governments building on, rather than replacing their predecessor's policies. This has created a layered education system underpinned by a complex mix of competition and collaboration within a high-stakes' accountability framework. The pace and tenacity with which these reforms have been implemented have been fierce and their boldness has led some researchers to liken England to a real-life laboratory (Finkelstein and Grubb, 2000).

The academies programme: politics and policies

New Labour government academies (2002–2010)

The academies programme was first announced in England in 2000, by the then Education Secretary, David Blunkett, as a replacement to Fresh Start Schools, the

English version of the United States' 'Reconstitution'. The programme was specifically aimed at addressing long-standing educational underachievement in economically deprived areas. The creation of academies initially drew on the idea that poorly performing schools, defined in terms of low attainment, should be closed and then reopened as academies. They were mainly government-funded but are independent of local government control.

Under the New Labour government, academies had individual, faith or corporate sponsors which were initially required to provide £2 million to support the new school (although this requirement was removed in 2007). Subsequently, sponsors included high-performing schools, universities and the voluntary sector. More recently, local authorities (LAs) have been encouraged to become 'minor' sponsors. Section 65 of the Education Act 2002 provides for the establishment of academies and specifies their core characteristics. The final policy documents of the New Labour administration, the 21st Century Schools white paper (DCSF, 2009) announced the extension of the academies programme to include 300 new schools by the end of 2010.

Under New Labour, local authorities were involved in the process of setting up an academy from the outset and played a key role throughout, from initial, informal discussions between the LA, sponsors and the DCSF to the final decision-making process. However, some studies have highlighted concerns that, in spite of this level of involvement in the process, some LAs had no official policy on academies and suggested that, particularly with regard to the sponsors, the DCSF was in the driving seat (Hatcher, 2008). The whole process, including consultation took between 15 and 18 months (DCSF).

Initially, academies operated within a more permissive framework that offered:

- freedom to work outside local authority management and scrutiny;
- no requirement to participate in local authority strategic planning for children and young people;
- flexibility in relation to staff pay and conditions;
- freedom to have new and innovative approaches to governance;
- different financial and accounting arrangements;
- more flexibility with the curriculum;
- control of admissions as their own admissions authority;
- management of their own arrangements for exclusions;
- different appeal structures for exclusions and admissions;
- exemption from requirements to publishing exam results, or a breakdown of curriculum areas covered.

The Coalition government academies (2010–)

The Conservative/Liberal Democrat Coalition elected in May 2010 announced that all schools would be able to apply for academy status, including primary schools. Those schools graded as outstanding by the Ofsted inspection agency have, from

2010, been given the opportunity to become academies on a fast-track scheme (DoE, 2010). However, the rate at which schools have converted to academies and the nature of local authority responses to Academies have not been uniform (Abbot and Smith, 2014).

The Education Act (2010) removed any obligation to consult with the LA, community, parents or pupils during the application process. It allowed the Secretary of State for Education to issue a closure order for existing schools without consultation. Government advised consultation with trades unions prior to the completion of the process to avoid the invocation of employment law. The application process was to be simplified into four steps, taken over a period of about three months:

1 Registration of interest.
2 Application to convert.
3 Achievement of funding agreement and Pre-opening agreements (such as Criminal Record Bureau checks).
4 Setting up new financial systems etc. with support from the DoE.

The Education Act (2010) also introduced further freedoms for schools wishing to become academies. Fundamentally, this legislation altered the nature of the academies programme. Academies were initially conceived of as a means of addressing the quality of education in disadvantaged areas and as a way of replacing failing schools in order to ensure improved outcomes. Policy now focuses on opportunities for schools deemed to be 'outstanding' by Ofsted, the State's inspectors of schools, to become academies. This marks a significant change in the stated purpose of the programme and a clear departure from the rationale that underpinned its introduction.

The key changes to the academies programme introduced by the Education Act (2010) included the following:

- Academies no longer required a sponsor and could be created at the behest of school governors.
- The Local Authority was removed from involvement in the decision-making process on whether to create an Academy. This decision was placed in the hands of the Board of Governors and the Secretary of State for Education.
- There was no longer any obligation to consult parents, the community or pupils.
- The academies programme was expanded to include primary and special schools, as well as secondary schools.
- New academies could keep selective admissions policies if they were already in place in the predecessor school (i.e. grammar schools).
- Academies could keep 'any surplus balance they hold' (DoE 2010).
- Although new academies would automatically become charities they would be exempt from inspection by the Charities Commission.

By 25 June 2010, 795 schools described as 'outstanding' by Ofsted had registered an interest in becoming academies, alongside 605 schools that were not so designated (DoE, 2010). More recently, the political mantra has become one of developing an 'academised' system whereby all schools are constituted as academies and therefore free from local authority control. By April 2012, 50.3 per cent of English secondary schools were reported to be either already operating as academies, or to be converting to an academy (Shepherd, 2012). By November 2012, there were 2,456 academies, an increase of 2,253 from May 2010. By February 2015, there was a total of 4,460 academy schools open in England, again almost double the number that had been open in November 2012.

The number and size of academies working as 'chains' or Multi-Academy Trusts (MATs) has also grown dramatically. Hill *et al.* (2012) reported there were over 48 chains of academies containing three or more schools in the autumn of 2012. By January 2013, 91 chains had between two and nine sponsored academies in their chain. Nine chains had ten or more academies in their chain (Pearson/RSA, 2013). This number continues to rise as more schools convert to academy status.

An overview of the terrain: academies, change, leadership and the self-improving system

Change and academies

The aspirations of the academies programme are radical and there have been some impressive examples of turning around the fortunes of underperforming schools in particularly challenging contexts. There are also examples of where such transformations have not been possible, even within the same chain (Chapman, 2013). Various analyses have compared academy performance and progress against non-academy schools without providing consistent evidence (Muijs *et al.*, 2013). The National Audit Office (2012) reports that almost half of academies have been judged as inadequate or satisfactory (now reclassified as 'requiring improvement'). Other research has highlighted issues of access, inequity and segregation and negative impacts on other local schools and their communities (Gunter, 2011). The evidence relating to the success of the academies programme, therefore, is very mixed.

There is, however, one area of consensus. It is widely accepted that the programme is highly politicised, quickly polarises opinion and raises emotions. For those with views on the left of the political spectrum, academies are viewed as part of a wider neoliberal project underpinned by an anti-democratic agenda designed to promote privatisation of the education service with little evidence to support improved outcomes (cf. Gunter, 2011 and The Anti-Academy Alliance). For those on the right of the political spectrum, academies are seen as an attempt to increase choice and diversity within the education service by promoting innovation, injecting new freedoms, energy and ideas into the system (cf. Policy Exchange, 2009, for example, and the New Schools Network website).

Empirical research undertaken by Machin and Vernoit (2011) explores the impact of academy conversion on pupil intake and pupil performance. In their conclusions they argue that conversion to academy status has had a significant and positive impact on both pupil intake and pupil performance. The authors also report a significant impact on these areas in neighbouring schools. It is interesting that the authors highlight the fact that despite sharp (on average) decreases in the 'quality' of intake in neighbouring schools, these schools can also experience significant gains in pupil performance. This situation may offer some evidence of a ripple effect of improvement from academy schools into their non-academy local neighbours.

In their recent report The Academies Commission (Pearson/RSA, 2013) maps out the broad terrain, distinguishing between four types of Academy (Sponsored Academies; Converter Academies; Enforced Sponsor Academies and Free Schools) and offers an analysis highlighting the complexity of the programme. In conclusion, the Commission identifies three key imperatives for the future development of the programme if it is to fulfil its potential. These are:

> 1 To ensure there is a forensic focus on teaching and learning and its impact on pupils' learning so that the gap between the vision for academies and practice in classrooms is reduced and the words 'academisation' and 'improvement' become inextricably and demonstrably linked.
> 2 To ensure an increasingly academised system is fair and equally accessible to children and young people from all backgrounds.
> 3 To ensure academies demonstrate their moral purpose and professionalism by providing greater accountability to pupils, parents and other stakeholders. The role of governors is more important than ever in an academised system, and their scrutiny and challenge should ensure effective accountability.
>
> (Pearson/RSA, 2013, pp. 4–5)

The Commission recognises the ambition of the project but is cautious about linking the programme to the impact it has on academic outcomes. The Commission also highlights issues of access and inequities as a specific concern and takes on broader issues relating to democratic values, including the role governors play in ensuring that academies are accountable to stakeholders.

Leadership in academies

As previously noted, the 1988 Education Reform Act heralded the devolution of more resources to schools and the introduction of local management of schools in England. Over the following years several studies, including *Fifteen Thousand Hours* (Rutter *et al.*, 1979) and *School Matters* (Mortimore *et al.*, 1991) argued for the importance of leadership in schools. The leadership and management of schools became accepted as a key characteristic of an effective school (Sammons *et al.*, 1995) and a core area of evaluation within England's standardised inspection system.

The belief that the solution to educational failure can be found in securing better leaders and better teachers rather than by harnessing contextual and sociological explanations now dominates much of the discourse of educational change (Payne, 2008). In England, this belief emerged in the 1990s, and was embedded in the 2000s. The establishment of the National College for School Leadership (NCSL) at around the same time as the development of the academies programme created a powerful narrative linking headteacher/principal leadership to school reform. This played an important role in placing academy principals as a primary catalyst for change. Principals command high salaries, often larger than the prime minister's salary; they hold influence over politicians and policy makers, and are frequently recognised in honours lists, receiving knighthoods and other orders of merit as recognition for their services to education. This public validation perpetuates the myth that these leaders have all the answers.

The government has commissioned much of the research on academies and educational leadership and its agencies. The findings of this research vary from highlighting the complexity of emerging practices such as the importance of localised decision-making, tensions between leadership at different levels within the organisation and the importance of context specificity (Chapman *et al.*, 2008), to generic solutions and categorisations of leadership models, including 'Academy Leadership' (PriceWaterhouseCoopers, 2007). To date, however, there remains a paucity of high quality empirical research into the complexity of leadership, management or governance in academy schools. Glatter (2011) argues that this should be a priority at both the local and national level. Since Glatter's call, this has become an even more challenging area to research. During the past five years the ideologically driven educational reforms have further intensified the politics around the development of an academised system, which has made gaining access to academies and chains even more problematic for fear that the findings generated could lead to negative media coverage.

The self-improving school system and academies

In 2010, the White Paper, *The Importance of Teaching* (DfE, 2010) highlighted continued commitment to groups of schools working in federations and academy chains by setting out policies where the best schools and best leaders should develop federated approaches to lead systemic change. As the academies programme has expanded, the terminology has shifted from 'federation' to 'academy chain', but the essence of the structure remains the same. These are groups of schools working together under one set of formal governance arrangements to support the improvement of other schools within the group and more recently beyond the group.

The idea of the best schools within the system leading school improvement, or a *self-improving school system* (Hargreaves, 2010, 2011, 2012), is rooted in collaborative practices developed in federations and academy chains, but also in the *London* and *City Challenge* initiatives that invested in such leadership development and collaborative school improvement activities as mentoring, peer learning, support and intervention. The legacy of the *Challenges* includes *Challenge Partners* and *By Schools for Schools* networks (see www.byschoolsforschools.co.uk). The former is a registered charity and national network, now with its own chain of academies (http://challengepartners.org) and the latter is a partnership of schools across ten local authorities in Greater Manchester that aspires to secure the highest quality of teaching, learning and leadership through collaboration to drive a self-improving school system that places schools and professional practice at the centre of change. Beyond these and other similar examples of 'new wave' school improvement networks, the concept of the self-improving system is driven by high performing academy chains and schools graded as 'outstanding' by the inspection agency that apply to become 'Teaching Schools' and the headteacher/principal[1] as a 'National Leader of Education (NLE).

Teaching Schools receive additional resources for leading the development of practice across an alliance or network of schools and for making a significant contribution to initial teacher education. Specifically, in return for the additional resource, Teaching Schools are required to lead:

- school-based initial teacher education;
- continuing professional development activity;
- the identification and development of leadership capacity;
- the supporting of improvement efforts of other schools;
- the designating and coordinating of Specialist Leaders of Education (SLE);
- the engagement in research and development activity.

In January 2015, there were almost 600 Teaching Schools in England. In the first instance, designation usually lasts for four years but can be removed as a consequence of a poor inspection. In return for providing additional services Teaching Schools receive £190,000 of additional funding and opportunities to generate more income through associated consultancy activity.

This lateral approach to school and system improvement transcends the traditional producer–consumer relationships based upon hierarchy and bureaucracy within the system, lending itself to Emile Durkheim's notions of social organisation and social integration. These ideas were used by Douglas (1982) to develop Grid Group Cultural Theory and subsequently applied to public service provision (Hood, 1998). In Grid Group Theory egalitarian cultures assume low grid characteristics with few central rules, low levels of regulation and ascribed behaviours combined with high group characteristics including strong collaborative relationships between group members within well-defined boundaries. It would seem that successful federations, chains and teaching schools would be likely to require organisational and regulative flexibility combined with strong collaborative relationships associated with egalitarian culture.

Furthermore, Hood (1998) has argued that public service provision within egalitarian environments comes in the form of 'mutual' organisations. These organisations are characterised by mutual relationships, which transcend traditional conceptions of service provider and user. Put simply, the concept of a service provider becomes redundant as the users collectively deliver services themselves, just as is intended in school federations, chains and teaching schools.

Reflections on academies, change, leadership and the self-improving school system

In this section I draw on our own programme of research on the impact of federations and chains (Chapman *et al.*, 2010; Chapman and Muijs, 2013, 2014; Muijs *et al.*, 2013), new models of leadership in federations and chains of academies (Chapman *et al.*, 2008; Chapman and Salokangas, 2012), and, most recently, teaching schools and their alliances (Chapman, 2013; Ainscow *et al.*, 2013) to reflect on six key themes and messages. These are as follows:

1 Local context plays an important role in the adoption and development of new patterns of leadership and structural arrangements such as federations and academies

Where new leadership practices do emerge they have to be understood in relationship to their particular contexts. Our research suggests a local catalyst is needed before local leaders and stakeholders gather the impetus to move towards new ways of working. More specifically, the research found that local catalysts took one or more of three forms, namely:

- *Local dissatisfaction with current arrangements and/or a sense of opportunity for improvement.* For example, this occurred in one context where radical change was deemed necessary to tackle a prolonged history of failure. In this case the Director of Education approached the headteacher of a very successful school and asked whether the school would consider building on the links created via the Leadership Incentive Grant to form a hard federation with a school having a prolonged history of difficulties and failures. After a period of consultation and negotiation, the federation was launched in September 2006. In 2011, the schools converted to academy status. Progress in encouraging the ethos and branding of the successful school seems to have permeated into the struggling school. Staff resources are shared, subject leaders are responsible for subjects across the two sites and the appearance, atmosphere, teaching and leadership in the two schools have improved. In March 2013, the academies in the federation received a 'good' and 'requires improvement' grading from the inspectorate and it was noted that the headteacher is building a vision for improvement in the academy requiring improvement (OfSTED, 2013).
- *Personal vision.* Increased choice and diversity within the system has presented school leaders with an unprecedented range of opportunities. Many headteachers viewed themselves as system leaders and were developing a portfolio of activities working as consultants with government and private agencies or leading federations, academy chains and Teaching School Alliances. Increased

choice and diversity within the system has also created the context for a mixed economy of provision with private and public agencies working with each other and competing for school improvement and other services. The emergence of academy chains has intensified the market as they compete with each other to secure newly converted academies and schools which have been identified as requiring a 'structural solution' (enforced academisation) because of low performance. In turn, this increases the size of the chain and adds to its power and sphere of influence within the system.

- *An act of philanthropy.* This third catalyst for change is exemplified by the case of a Housing Trust becoming involved in the creation of a new academy within the locality. The Housing Trust is seeking to extend the positive impact it has had within the community into two of its schools – amalgamating two of the most difficult and lowest performing schools in the authority to create a new academy and linking this school to primary academies to create a cross-phase chain.

These catalysts for change can act independently or in combination in different proportions in different localities; they are context specific. Therefore, there is no 'one size fits all' solution or response that is guaranteed to be successful.

2 Innovative and traditional approaches appear in combination

On one hand, federations and academy chains are adopting or are developing innovative or new organisational structures, some of which might be described as being at the leading edge of policy development. On the other hand, the findings suggest that innovative approaches to leadership do not necessarily emerge in these settings. That is not to say that the form of leadership seen in these settings is less effective because it remains traditional in nature as opposed to being innovative. Rather, it would appear to be shaped by the leader's personality traits and particularly in challenging school contexts. Those leaders adopting more traditional approaches tend to be recognised as 'strong', 'committed' and 'direct' by their colleagues, and often have a reputation in the local community or media for having led a school(s) through particularly turbulent times. Many of the leaders in the study demonstrated an especially high capacity for managing change. While often working with levels of commitment beyond the norm (Mortimore and Whitty, 1997), they hold high expectations (Maden, 2001) and are perceived to 'get things done'. These leaders also are very active networkers and entrepreneurial, encouraging staff to be outward looking and creative.

3 New leadership arrangements that are seen as liberating by some staff can be seen to increase constraints and pressures felt by others

The restructuring of schools is altering external accountability patterns, with some relocation of decision-making 'upwards' to newly created bodies (e.g. federation managers and academy governors). For example, one federation has established a strategic governance committee to discuss common issues and make policy decisions. The committee included the headteacher, a governor and another representative from each partner school. Each school within the federation retained its own governance and leadership but the strategic committee provided an additional layer of decision-making. This arrangement can provide interesting career opportunities, particularly for those headteachers who have an appetite for leading collaborative chains of schools and other agencies, and engaging with a wider range of agencies at local and national levels than they have previously experienced. However, there have also been cases where headteachers have felt disempowered and even demoralised by the development of new organisational structures. Some have reported that federating or joining an academy chain has reduced the power, autonomy and status previously enjoyed by a headteacher, without reducing the pressures – indeed, the pressure to succeed may seem even greater.

At the same time, restructuring often provides internal opportunities for senior and some middle-level leaders. In some cases heads felt that their own priorities and relationships were much clearer as a result of restructuring, which, in turn, made decision-making easier. In other cases this was experienced as a positive 'redistribution' of leadership, providing meaningful development opportunities for senior and middle-level leaders, at earlier stages of their careers than would have been possible in the past. This was perceived by some middle-level leaders and more junior teachers to be a significant shift in culture and attitude within the education system, suggesting that it is no longer necessary to serve your time to achieve leadership positions and that merit, in itself, is sufficient for being presented with worthwhile leadership opportunities.

The increased external demands on headteachers has created a shift in the leadership and management roles of deputy heads, who often tended to be focused more on lower level, day-to-day concerns in the past. Deputy heads were taking on more strategic roles and felt comfortable with being the most senior person on site for days and, on occasions, weeks at a time. This, in turn, has a knock-on effect on the role of assistant heads, many of whom are now engaged in significant managerial tasks, including timetabling, curriculum arrangements, or the management of substantial subject staff groups, activities which were previously the preserve of deputy heads. Of course, it has frequently been observed that deputy headship, as it was, was not a very satisfactory preparation for headship. At the same time, it is clear that some patterns of leadership distribution appear more effective than others (Leithwood *et al.*, 2006).

Some patterns of distributed leadership were providing teachers and middle-level leaders with opportunities for personal and professional growth that were simply not possible in the past. A common example was that of middle-level leaders being given whole school responsibility for a substantive piece of developmental work and to be seconded on to the senior management teams. In other examples, which occasionally came to our attention in this study, the least effective arrangements constituted little more than systems for holding people responsible for activities over which they seemed to exercise very little control, or decision-making power without freedom to take risks. The skills needed for senior leadership roles are unlikely to be developed according to such structures.

4 Changes in local arrangements are helping schools to cope with an increasingly complex educational agenda

School leaders have recognised that they face increased challenge and complexity within the fragmenting system. Many argued that new arrangements were enabling them to think more strategically about school organisation in relation to these demands. For example, one federation principal in the New Models of Leadership Project commented on how, as a leader, he had invested in internal capacity building as a strategy for succession planning. A teacher in this federation described the head's whole-school vision as 'directional and bringing it all together', moving middle managers on to the senior leadership team (SLT) and 'allowing them to grow together'. The principal argued that he had moved from a 'delegated form of leadership to a distributed *model*'. One member of SLT described this shift as an increase in autonomy and trust combined with lower levels of monitoring. On this, one teacher went on to observe, he now wants you to 'just go and sort it out' rather than having a long conversation about 'what, why and how, and I prefer this'.

Conversely, other principals have noted that their Strategic Management Executive (SME), which co-ordinates the chain's activity, provides variable support for school improvement, poor value for money from centralised resources and generally replicates the variation in support previously provided by the local authority. In this regard, one principal from the British Educational Leadership Management and Administration Society (BELMAS) study on academy chains reflected:

> We don't think it's a good idea to employ people to school improvement jobs, because then you get somebody like we had to start with . . . There is a permanent contention of 5 per cent. That's still an issue. I've said to X, we are outstanding why do we still need to pay that 5 per cent. We don't get 5 per cent worth of services . . . What we don't want in the group is the increased number of administrators and bureaucrats at the heart. There's a massive resistance from principals on that. All the 5 per cent pays for, it doesn't pay CPD, is running the head office.

It is noticeable that many were increasingly liaising and working beyond the school, collaborating with other schools and agencies to an unprecedented degree. Leaders are grappling with new approaches, and attempting to redefine their roles and responsibilities in an uncertain and rapidly evolving context. For example, in the New Models Project the senior team in one federation has expanded to incorporate collaborative work with the primary feeder schools. Eleven assistant headteachers each hold a specific leadership role for an issue or theme across all schools in the federation. In another example, an academy sought sponsorship from a university and FE college. The principal and other senior leaders have negotiated the university involvement to support the vision of establishing life-long learning in an area of severe socioeconomic deprivation. All these activities suggest that school leaders are increasingly finding themselves operating outside traditional school hierarchies and, therefore, need to draw on a wide range of sophisticated social skills, including those of negotiation, brokerage, facilitation and disturbance-handling, often within highly politicised environments where agendas and the balance of power and influence are unclear and unstable.

5 The picture is fluid and the pace of change rapid

The volume of change since the previous Coalition government in Britain came to power has been unprecedented. Our research evidence suggests that school leaders are increasingly experimenting with the range of statutory frameworks and, where appropriate, combining elements from different frameworks to fit their needs at a given time. With such an approach, many school leaders appeared responsive to the dynamics of their specific contexts and were not 'wedded' to a particular definition of the role. Some had taken an evolutionary approach, gradually shifting from one set of arrangements to another. For example, a number of federations within the sample were now exploring the possibility of moving towards trust status as a next step, and many have converted to academy status.

In some cases, extreme circumstances had led to revolutionary changes. These might be manifested in the closure of a 'failing' school, leading to a wholesale reorganisation and rebranding exercise, to launch a new school with new expectations, new staff and, most often, new leadership. Schools in less extreme situations tended to prefer combining models, drawing on elements of various new leadership and governance arrangements that were considered appropriate to meet their needs.

In such a rapidly changing landscape, it is not surprising that sometimes developments in practice appeared uneven and unpredictable. If we are to develop our understanding of emerging patterns of leadership, considering models of leadership to be closely aligned to structural arrangements is unhelpful, since no single pattern was apparent in the arrangements we scrutinised. However, our research found school context to be an overriding factor, determining to a great extent the arrangements that were put in place. Inevitably, although extremely interesting to catalogue, the impact and sustainability of many of these developments, particularly in academy chains and Teaching School Alliances remain unclear. As such, a longitudinal study tracking the progress and impact of selected examples would prove instructive.

6 Impact of these new arrangements on student outcomes

There are a number of clear messages emerging from our work on federations for student outcomes. However, there is less robust evidence relating to the impact of chains and it is too early to report findings about the relationship between

Teaching School Alliances and student outcomes with any confidence. In federations designed to improve student attainment by matching a high-performing school with a low-performing school(s) in 'Performance Federations', student attainment at GCSE in performance and academy federations is significantly higher than student attainment in their non-federated counterparts. However, there is lag-time of two to four years before this effect becomes evident. Also, there is a positive impact on student attainment in both the higher and lower performing schools. This suggests there is an additional benefit for the higher performing schools to engage in these partnerships. Our qualitative work highlights the importance of continuing professional development opportunities for staff and learning from pockets of excellent practice in the lower performing schools as sources of improved practice for those in the higher performing school. It is also worthy of mention that Secondary School Federations outperform collaboratives (a soft federation in which schools retain their own governing body but delegate some decision-making power upwards to a joint committee) and executive leadership structures with a chief executive outperform traditional leadership arrangements where a group of headteachers share leadership of the federation (Chapman and Muijs, 2014).

An initial quantitative analysis of academy chains undertaken by Muijs and colleagues (Muijs *et al.*, 2013) shows that they differ significantly in their level of centralisation, with no chain being fully centralised or decentralised. In terms of GCSE performance, chains do better than non-chain schools. Our qualitative work suggests that this is likely to be due to the benefits of shared resources and professional learning (Salokangas and Chapman, 2014). Early indications imply that the more centralised chains appear to be, the more effective they tend to be, an observation that provides initial support for a franchise model. There are, however, a number of caveats associated with this preliminary analysis including issues related to causality and missing data.

The impact of Teaching Schools and their alliances on student outcomes remains unresearched. It would seem likely that high-capacity schools provided with additional resources to support the work of other schools would be a sensible strategy for supporting improvement across a system. Indeed, evidence from the City Challenge initiatives in London, Manchester and the Black Country (West Midlands), where similar collaborative strategies were experimented with, indicate positive gains compared with 'non-challenge' areas. There is, however, some anecdotal evidence that suggests when leadership capacity is dispersed to support other schools, the stronger schools in the collaboration can experience dips in test scores. On this, Ainscow and colleagues' analysis of the implementation of Teaching Schools Alliance highlights a number of key issues and tensions in the way the system has attempted to control the development of the initiative which is stifling creativity and innovation (Ainscow *et al.*, 2013). Furthermore, the cultural conditions that pervade the system support the development of market-based organisations rather than an egalitarian culture, which is more likely to support the development of mutual organisations.

Autonomous schools and authentic self-improvement: the case of academies in England

The synthesis presented in the previous sections of this chapter clearly highlights some promising emerging leadership practices and interesting possibilities for further policy development within the English education system. However, our observations also lead us to reflect on three key fault lines in policy and practice, namely:

- Leadership practices and expectations – A leadership catastrophe?
- Collaboration and competition – A case of chain wars?
- Middle-tier arrangements – A crisis of coherence and confidence?

It seems that these fault lines are playing out across the system as issues, tensions and dilemmas affect actors in different roles and contexts in very different ways. Here, I argue that these issues limit the system to self-repair rather than promote self-improvement. Each fault line is now examined in turn.

While leadership practices and expectations within the system seem to be appropriate for the new arrangements in some contexts, in others there appears to be a leadership vacuum. For example, in one academy chain there have been a number of academies that have experienced unprecedented levels of principal turnover. Despite extensive support and interventions from successful leaders and school improvement initiatives from within the chain and other external sources, and a succession of new appointments, several of the schools in this chain continue to make little or no progress.

There may be a number of explanations for this situation. Payne (2008) might put it down to the ahistorical, non-sociological and decontextualised attempts at school improvement that are likely to be a contributory factor. However, it seems the supply of leaders with the appropriate qualities to lead multiple and complex educational organisations is insufficient. This is compounded by the obsession with the rhetoric of 'system leaders', 'system leadership' and 'National Leaders of Education'. Put simply, we have developed an over-reliance on charismatic system leaders and it is becoming evident that we just do not have enough of them. The situation is reinforced by research making generous claims about the importance and impact of school leaders (cf. Day *et al.*, 2010; Higham *et al.*, 2009; PriceWaterhouseCoopers, 2007), policy-makers' belief in the leadership cult, high-profile case studies of a small number of these successful system leaders and a cadre of leaders, of whom many are willing to perpetuate the myth for their own personal and professional gain. There is a major possibility we are heading towards a 'leadership catastrophe'. Continuous attempts at plugging the leadership gap make it very difficult to move beyond repairing the lack of progress which hinders the development of a self-improving school system.

Second, English policy makers have persisted with combining policies creating a volatile cocktail of competition and collaboration within the system (Ainscow and West, 2006). This is based on the assumption that a blend of competition and collaboration will facilitate knowledge exchange and generation across boundaries while challenging mediocrity and complacency within the system. To date, it would seem the optimal balance (if, indeed, there is one) has not been found. Furthermore, the high stakes accountability mechanisms that pervade the system continually push the system towards competition. It would seem that this has shifted the system from a bureaucratic to an individualised culture (Douglas, 1982) supporting the movement of public sector provision from hierarchical to market-based organisations (Hood, 1998). This is problematic because, as noted earlier in this chapter, Grid Group Theory (Douglas, 1982) would suggest self-improving school systems would be best suited to egalitarian cultures and mutualistic organisations (Hood, 1998).

Increasingly, schools and chains compete with each other at the expense of collaborating with their neighbours and this is magnified through chains of schools ferociously engaging in 'chain wars' to become the 'biggest' and 'best' within the system. Ironically, the ultimate conclusion of this exercise may well be the creation of a monopoly where a few chains run schools within the system as a franchise model where consistency of provision rather than choice and diversity, one of the policy aims of academisation, become the order of the day. This normalisation within the system will lead to isomorphism and ultimately reinforce the status quo. In turn, this will lead to the system focusing on repairing itself rather than improving itself.

Third, and related to the second fault line, is the erosion of the local authority (school district) power and control over schools. Since the 1988 (Education) Act, successive governments have pursued policies to shift the role of local authorities from providers of services to commissioners of services to schools. The current administration has reduced local authority involvement in education to a minimum and a fully academised system will operate, for the most part outside their control. This dismantling of the middle tier has created much uncertainty within the system and a lack of local co-ordination. The exception is in areas where previous initiatives (for example, City Challenge) mobilised cross-local authority collaboration and new relationships in which there was some sense of local co-ordination. These, however, are limited to a few outlier examples. There is also increasing evidence to suggest some chain SMEs are recreating inefficient structures and providing ineffective services that were often associated with less effective local authority predecessors. Put simply, there is a 'crisis of coherence and confidence'.

Perhaps, it is here that we see the most potent example of self-repair. It would seem that the attempt to develop new structures, particularly within the middle tier, to create new ways of working and thinking are replicating the practices and variations that existed in the past. For example, variations in academy chain performance are similar to those that were found in local authorities and many of the practices such as top-slicing school budgets and imposing services on schools replicate the practices of the old order.

As noted already, the academies programme and the Coalition government's reforms have resulted in the polarisation of opinions. There is growing resistance within the academy and among educational professionals. For example, one hundred English Professors of Education recently wrote an open letter to the Secretary of State expressing their concerns about the programme. The fault lines I have highlighted will no doubt add weight to the arguments of some of the critics who assert this is a neoliberal agenda designed to open up public education to the private sector, is inherently disempowering for the profession and anti-democratic for those working in education and living in the communities they serve. I have no interest in this ideological debate; this is not my intention and not my primary concern.

I am concerned, however, as to whether policies have positive effects on educational outcomes. The origin of these policies can be traced to innovative attempts to tackle low-attaining schools located in the most socioeconomically disadvantaged communities. My fear is that despite decades of reform and considerable investment of resources the policies have not created innovative classrooms or significantly raised the achievement of students from our most disadvantaged backgrounds. Furthermore, it may be that these policies are compounding achievement gaps and even reinforcing educational inequity. Put simply, what we have achieved is a *self-repairing* rather than *self-improving* system.

So what might be done?

It would seem necessary to tackle the three fault lines head on. The first requirement is a reimagining of educational leadership that challenges current notions of charismatic super-hero leadership and focuses on building collective capacity and deep understanding of managing change in complex arenas. This will require a fundamental rethinking of how we develop our leaders and conceptualise roles and responsibilities within the system. The second task is to redress the balance between competition and collaboration within the system. This will open up more spaces for purposeful rather than transactional collaboration. The third action is to develop local co-ordination rooted in and across schools and the communities they serve.

In order for all of this to become a reality, a significant cultural shift towards an egalitarian culture is needed. This will involve constructing professional identities and perceptions of roles and responsibilities within the education system. Those involved in education will have to rethink not only with whom they work, but also how and where they work. Inevitably, this will involve the blurring of institutional roles and boundaries. Frankly, it is no longer acceptable to hide in a classroom, school, town hall or university office replicating practices of the past.

It would seem that the key priorities for supporting this cultural shift can be distilled into three areas:

- *A focus on professional development*: This is the key to constructing a new genre of education professional, linking initial pre- and in-service education in a way that challenges assumptions about traditional roles and responsibilities to have a profound effect on how new and established education professionals view themselves and understand their work, and perhaps most importantly challenge established cultural norms within the system. This will require rethinking leadership practices and how they relate to different settings and developing forward-thinking leadership development that focuses on developing individuals' leadership capacity and potential to lead within schools, between schools and beyond schools with other public sector services, key stakeholders, including the private and third sector, and the whole community.

- *A commitment to ownership over what 'works and why'*: This galvanises and reinforces the appetite for change-Investing in a range of evidence-based, localised experiments, monitoring their impact and using findings to inform refinements to promote models of practice that are locally owned, tailored to specific contexts and more likely to meet the needs of all students. This will require leaders to access, analyse and assimilate the best knowledge about what works and why into their day-to-day practice.
- *A dedication to joined up public service provision*: This is a prerequisite for tackling educational inequity, mobilising elements of public services to provide a coordinated framework for within-, between- and beyond-school improvement to have the effect of challenging inequity that the educational system cannot deal with in isolation.

The challenge of tackling these fault lines is difficult and complex terrain requiring a fundamental rethinking of roles and relationships. Continuing as we have done in the past will only lead to a failure of implementation, and continue to reinforce a self-repairing rather than a self-improving education system in England.

Note

1 Headteacher is the traditional English title for a Principal. However, it is becoming common for Principals to be appointed in academies. For the purposes of this article the terms are used interchangeably.

References

Ainscow, M. and West, M. (2006). *Improving urban schools: leadership and collaboration.* Maidenhead: Open University Press.

Ainscow, M., Chapman, C., Dyson, A., Goldrick, S. and West, M. (2013). *Promoting equity in education: a study of the work of 'teaching schools' in England,* paper presented at the annual meeting of the American Educational Research Association, San Francisco, CA.

Bellei, C. (2009). The public–private controversy in Chile. In R. Chakrabarti and P. Peterson. (eds). *School choice international: exploring public–private partnerships.* (pp. 165–192). Cambridge, MA: The MIT Press.

Bettinger, E. (2009). Voucher schools in Colombia. In R. Chakrabarti and P. Peterson. (eds). *School choice international: exploring public–private partnerships* (pp. 143–164). Cambridge, MA: The MIT Press.

Chapman, C. (2013). *A study of Hub Teaching Schools in England and Scotland.* Interim report to BELMAS.

Chapman, C. and Gunter, H. (2009). *Radical reforms: reflections on an era of change*. London: Routledge.

Chapman, C. and Muijs, D. (2013). Collaborative school turnaround: a study of the impact of school federations on student outcomes. *Leadership and Policy in Schools*, 12 (3), 200–226.

Chapman, C. and Muijs, D. (2014). Does school-to-school collaboration promote school improvement? A study of the impact of school federations on student outcomes. *School Effectiveness and School Improvement*.

Chapman, C. and Salokangas, M. (2012). Independent state-funded schools: some reflections on recent developments. *School Leadership and Management*, 32 (5), 473–486.

Chapman, C., Muijs, D. and MacAllister, J. (2011). *A study of the impact of Federation on student outcomes*. Nottingham: National College for School Leadership, 25 (3), 351–393.

Chapman, C., Lindsay, G., Muijs, D. and Harris, A. (2010). The Federations Policy: from partnership to integration for school improvement? *School Effectiveness and School Improvement*, 21(1), 53–74.

Chapman, C., Ainscow, M., Bragg, J., Gunter, H., Hull, J., Mongon, D., Muijs, D. and West, M. (2008). *Emerging patterns of school leadership: current trends and future directions*. Nottingham: National College for School Leadership.

Day, C., Sammons, P., Hopkins, D., Harris, A., Leithwood, K., Gu, Q. and Brown, E. (2010). *10 strong claims about successful school leadership*. Nottingham: National College for School Leadership.

Department for Children, Schools and Families (DCSF) (2009). *Departmental Report 2009 – Presented to Parliament by the Secretary of State for Children, Schools and Families*. Available at: www.dcsf.gov.uk (accessed 11 July 2012).

DfE. (2010). *The importance of teaching: the schools white paper* 2010. Cm7980, Norwich: The Stationery Office.

DfES. (2005). *Excellence in cities: the national evaluation of a policy to raise standards in urban schools*. Research Report No 675A, London: The Stationery Office.

Douglas, M. (1982). *In the active voice*. London: Routledge & Kegan Paul.

Finkelstein, N. D. and Grubb, W.N. (2000). Making sense of education and training markets: lessons from England. *American Education Research Journal*, 37 (3), 601–631.

Glatter, R. (2011). Joining up the dots: academies and system coherence. In H. Gunter (ed.). *The state and education policy: the academies programme* (pp. 159–170). London: Continuum.

Gunter, H. (ed.). (2011). *The state and education policy: the academies programme*. London: Continuum.

Hatcher, R. (2009). Setting up Academies, campaigning against them: an analysis of a contested policy. *Management in Education*, 23, 108–112.

Hargreaves, D. H. (2010). *Creating a self-improving school system*. Nottingham: National College for School Leadership.

Hargreaves, D. H. (2011). *Leading a self-improving school system*. Nottingham: National College for School Leadership.

Hargreaves, D. H. (2012). *A self-improving school system in an international context*. Nottingham: National College for School Leadership.

Higham, R. (2014). 'Who owns our schools?' An analysis of the governance of free schools in England. *Educational Management Administration & Leadership*, 42 (3), 404–422.

Higham, R., Hopkins, D. and Matthews, P. (2009). *System leadership in practice*. Maidenhead: Open University Press.

Hill, R. and Matthews, P. (2010). *Schools leading schools II: the growing impact of national leaders of education*. Nottingham: National College for School Leadership.

Hill, R., Dunford, J., Parish, N., Rea, S. and Sandlas, L. (2012). *Growth of academy chains: implications for leaders and leadership*. Nottingham: National College for School Leadership.

Available at: www.thegovernor.org.uk/freedownloads/acadamies/the-growth-of-academy-chains.pdf (accessed 3 July 2012).

Hood, C. (1998). *The art of the state, culture, rhetoric and public management*. Oxford: Clarendon Press.

Leithwood, K., Day, C., Sammons, P., Harris, A. and Hopkins, D. (2006). *Seven strong claims about successful leadership*. London: DfES.

Lindsay, G., Muijs, D., Harris, A., Chapman, C., Arweck, E. and Goodall, J. (2007). *Final report of the evaluation of the federations policy*. London: DCSF.

Machin, S. and Vernoit, J. (2011). *Changing school autonomy: academy schools and their introduction to England's education*. London: Centre for the Economic of Education, April CEEDP123.

Maden, M. (2001). *Success against the odds: five years on*. London: Routledge.

Mortimore, P. and Whitty, G. (1997). *Can school improvement overcome the effects of social disadvantage?* London: Institute of Education.

Mortimore, P., Sammons, P., Stoll L., Lewis, D. and Ecob, R. J. (1995). *School Matters*. London: Paul Chapman Educational Publishing.

Muijs, D., Chapman, C. and Reynolds, D. (2013). The impact of centralisation: a study of chains of academies in England. *American Educational Research Association Annual Meeting, San Francisco, USA*, 27 April–1 May 2013.

National Audit Office. (2012). *Managing the expansion of the academies programme: Department for Education and Education Funding Agency*. Report by the Comptroller and Auditor General (HC 682. Session 2012–13). London: The Stationery Office.

OECD. (2005). *Teachers matter: attracting, developing and retaining effective teachers*. Paris: OECD. Available at: www.oecd.org/education/preschoolandschool/attractingdevelopingandretainingeᐩeffectiveteachers-homepage.htm

OfSTED. (2013). School X inspection report.

Payne, C. (2008). *So much reform, so little change: The persistence of failure in urban schools*. Cambridge, MA: Harvard Education Press.

Pearson/RSA. (2013). *Unleashing greatness: getting the best from an academized system*. Report of the Academies Commission, January. London: Pearson.

Policy Exchange. (2009). *A guide to school choice reforms*. London: Policy Exchange.

PriceWaterhouseCoopers. (2007). *An independent study into school leadership*. London: DfES.

Rutter, M., Maughan, B., Mortimore, P. and Ouston, J. (1979). *Fifteen thousand hours: secondary schools and their effects on children*. London: Open Books.

Salokangas, M. and Chapman, C. (2014). Exploring governance in two chains of academy schools: a comparative case study. *Educational Management Administration & Leadership*, 42 (3), 372–386.

Sammons, P. (2008). Zero tolerance of failure and New Labour approaches to school improvement in England. *Oxford Review of Education*, 34 (6), 651–664.

Sammons, P., Mortimore, P., Hillman, J. and Mortimore, P. (1995). *Key characteristics of effective schools: a review of school effectiveness research*. London: OfSTED.

Shepherd, J. (2012). Academies to become a majority among state secondary schools. *Guardian*. Available at: www.guardian.co.uk/education/2012/apr/05/academies-majority-state-secondary-schools (accessed 11 July 2012).

Smith, P. and Abbott, I. (2014). Local responses to national policy: the contrasting experiences of two Midlands cities to the Academies Act 2010. *Educational Management Administration & Leadership*, 42 (3), 341–354.

Wohlstetter, P., Smith, J., Farrell, C., Hentschke, G. C. and Hirman, J. (2011). How funding shapes the growth of charter management organizations: is the tail wagging the dog? *Journal of Education Finance*, 37 (2), 150–174.

10

LEADING AS STATE AGENTS

Narratives of Shanghai principals

Qian Haiyan and Allan Walker

Introduction

This chapter explores how neoliberal educational reforms have shaped the work lives of school principals in China and how Chinese principals have located themselves in relation to the two domains of the lifeworld and systemsworld in their schools. Using narratives collected from three high school principals in Shanghai, the chapter illustrates that Chinese schools, like their Western counterparts, face the challenges of an invading systemic power flowing from the state and the market. All three principals feel under pressure to meet the systemic expectations imposed on their schools. However, what makes the situation that Chinese principals face quite distinct is the strong presence of the state and relatively muted role of the market. The primary role of a school principal in China is as an agent of the state.

Harvey (2005) suggests that future historians may well look upon the 1978–1980 period as a revolutionary turning point in the world's social and economic history, with the world experiencing a 'neoliberal period' in the years since then (Lupton, 2011, p. 309). The education arena is no exception. Neoliberal reforms emphasising decentralisation, marketisation and accountability have reshaped the global education environment (Peters *et al.*, 2000). Sergiovanni (2000) contends that the increasingly strong policy emphasis on efficiency, outcomes, productivity and performance means that schools today are faced with the major problem of what Habermas (1987) refers to as the 'colonisation of the lifeworld by system imperatives' (p. 325). In other words, the systemic powers steered by the state and the market are exerting a dominant influence on schools. The colonisation of the lifeworld by the world of systems, or 'systemsworld', is thus shaping the work environments of most school principals, who increasingly dwell in both worlds (Blackmore, 2004; Sergiovanni, 2000).

Given that the educational policy reforms spawned in the US, the UK, Canada, Australia and New Zealand have spread across the globe like wildfire (Hallinger, 2005), it would be naive to believe that mainland China is immune to this universalising reform tendency. China launched its 'Reform and Opening-up' policy at almost the same time that the UK and US turned to neoliberal solutions (Harvey, 2005). The emergence of China as a global economic power since 1980 has been, in part, an unintended consequence of the turn towards neoliberalism by the advanced capitalist world (Harvey, 2005). This chapter explores how neoliberal educational reforms have shaped the work lives of school principals in China and how Chinese principals have located themselves in relation to the two domains of the lifeworld and systemsworld in their schools.

Using narratives collected from three high school principals in Shanghai, the chapter illustrates the ways in which neoliberal reform trends similar to those in the West have swept across the Chinese mainland. While the three participating principals led schools of differing status, their work environments were all characterised by the overwhelming control of systemic power. In other words, Chinese schools have witnessed the colonisation of the lifeworld by the systemsworld. Although schools in China face similar pressure to adhere to the system imperatives as their counterparts elsewhere, the patterns describing how systemic power exerts its influence over them appears to differ. In China, the systemic power imposed on schools comes primarily from the state, with the market playing a more indirect role. In other words, the primary influence on the expectations surrounding school principals is that exerted by a state agent. This difference is worthy of further study to elucidate the patterns underlying systemic influence.

The chapter is divided into four sections. The first section introduces the international reform context and the problems arising from the colonisation of the school lifeworld by the systemsworld. The second section briefly outlines the major reform initiatives in China. The third section introduces the background to the study and then presents the illustrative narratives of the three high school principals in Shanghai. The final section discusses how Chinese principals locate themselves in the school lifeworld and systemsworld and explains why the country's principals lead primarily as agents of the state. It also suggests possible directions for future research.

Neoliberal reform, lifeworld and systemsworld

In the 1980s, the newly elected Thatcher and Reagan governments in the UK and the US turned to a particular doctrine labelled 'neoliberalism' that positioned economic thought and management as its central guiding principles. Most educational reform initiatives introduced in that era reflected a neoliberalist interest that explicitly sought to 'link economic productivity and education (Walker, 2003, p. 974) and to maximise productiveness and effectiveness (Mok and Welch, 2002). Central to these initiatives were moves to dismantle centralised educational bureaucracies and to create in their place devolved systems of education that granted significant degrees of institutional autonomy (Pedroni, 2007; Power *et al.*, 1997). School-based management (SBM) was widely adopted, becoming perhaps the most common reform initiative worldwide. SBM's stated aim was to increase school autonomy in an attempt to unleash initiative, creativity and productivity at the local level, thereby driving higher quality education (Moos and Møller, 2003; Yimaki, 2012).

An equally visible cornerstone of neoliberal education policy was the introduction of market competition into the school sector (Ball, 2012; Lauder, 1997). The assumption was that the competition between educational institutions arising from enabling parents to exercise choice in a free market would lead to a rise in standards (Murphy and Datnow, 2003; Lupton, 2011). The role of the state, then, shifted from that of direct provider of educational services to that of umpire and market regulator (Chan, 2002; Sbragia, 2000). Schools were increasingly subject to greater output controls, more explicit standards and performance measures, and clearer goal definitions and targets and indicators of success, preferably in quantitative form (Blackmore, 2004; Dempster, 2000).

As a consequence of initiatives centred around decentralisation, marketisation and accountability, schools became faced with the major problem of what Habermas (1987, p. 325) refers to as the 'colonisation of the lifeworld by system imperatives'. According to Habermas (1987), all societal enterprises are made up of two mutually exclusive yet ideally interdependent domains: the lifeworld and the systemsworld. The lifeworld is a world of purpose, norms, growth and development, while the systemsworld is a world of efficiency, outcomes and productivity. The school lifeworld represents an individual school's particular culture, traditions, rituals and norms, while the school systemsworld provides management designs, strategic and tactical actions, and policies and procedures. When the systemsworld is the generative force, it can be said that the lifeworld has been colonised. In many schools, the lifeworld has been colonised by goals, purposes, values and ideals based on adherence to system requirements, and these are imposed on parents, teachers and students rather than created by them (Sergiovanni, 2000).

This shift has been accompanied by a fundamental rethinking of the role of the school principal, as he or she struggles against the flow of policy directives and increased expectations for implementing and making change work. Principals are held increasingly accountable for school success and failure in a dynamic education marketplace in which success is judged by how well they exercise their roles (Power *et al.*, 1997; Sugrue, 2005). Accordingly, school principalship has become the point at which the contradictions, tensions and ambiguities typifying reform movements have converged (Blackmore, 2004; Townsend, 2012). In a globalised society, policy makers can easily borrow educational policies and practices from other contexts (Hallinger, 2005). It is now widely accepted that educational reforms in the Asia-Pacific region, including China, share 'similar roots and mirror global, often neo-liberalist trends' (Walker, 2003, p. 974).

Educational reforms in China

China launched its 'Reform and Opening-up' policy in 1978, coinciding with the turn towards neoliberal solutions in the UK and US (Harvey, 2005). Before the adoption of this policy, almost everything of significance was under state control. The new leadership under Deng Xiaoping advocated that China should shift from a socialist planned commodity economy to a socialist market economy (Yergin and Stanislaw, 1998). While retaining its centralised political system, the country has adopted a particular kind of market economy, one that 'increasingly incorporates neo-liberal elements interdigitated with authoritarian centralised control' (Harvey, 2005, p. 120).

Education has also undergone fundamental changes within this macro reform context, with the central leadership reaching consensus that education is an important means of promoting economic development. For example, in May 1985, in an address to the country's first national conference on education, Deng Xiaoping stated: 'Our national strength and sustained economic development depend more and more on the educational qualifications of the working people and on the number and quality of intellectuals.' This statement signified the beginning of a process of educational reform and the gradual alignment of the education system with the newly emerging marketisation of the economy (Hawkins, 2000).

Table 10.1 maps out the reform context by listing the major reform initiatives in chronological order.

It is not difficult to discern that the themes and concepts underpinning these reforms mirror those prevalent in Western countries, including the UK and the US. The Western vocabulary of reform, including decentralisation, SBM, competition, performance and accountability, are now commonly used in Chinese policy documents, albeit operationalised in a different context.

The general trends emerging from these reform documents include diminishing party influence, reduced participation by the state, the devolution of authority to the local level and to school principals, and the increasing role of the market. First, the central government in China has consciously retreated from being the sole provider of social services, with some of the rights held by the state in previous decades now delegated to local governments and principals. For example, the curriculum reform launched in 2001 advocates the establishment of a hierarchical curriculum management system comprising state, province and school (Ministry of Education, 2001). Schools today are supposed to design school-based curricula adapted to local needs (Qian and Walker, 2011; Walker *et al.*, 2011).

Second, the reform policy encourages the adoption of a 'market-oriented' approach to education. The major marketisation initiatives include the encouragement of a diversity of educational providers, calls for multiple channels of educational funding, increased numbers of self-supporting students, reorientation of curricula to meet market needs, and the introduction of competition in the education sector to enhance the efficiency and effectiveness of educational service delivery (Mok, 2000; Walker and Qian, 2012). Principals today are encouraged

TABLE 10.1 Chronological description of major reform initiatives in China

Year	*Document release*	*Major initiatives*
1985	*Reform of China's Educational Structure: Decision of the Communist Party of ChinaCentral Committee*	Authority should be 'devolved' to lower levels Multiple methods of financing should be sought Schools should gradually adopt the 'principal responsibility system'[1] Party functionaries should be separated from the day-to-day running of schools
1993	*Outline for China's Educational Reform and Development*	Reaffirmed the direction of the educational reforms set by the 1985 initiative Provided sufficient space for those at the local level to take increased responsibility for basic education in terms of both management and finances Emphasised that the state remains the arbiter of rules and regulations Reaffirmed that all schools should adopt the 'principal responsibility system'
1995	*Education Law*	Confirmed the major principles of PRC educational funding under market-economy conditions, that is, the bulk of educational expenditure would come from central government grants, while schools were encouraged to also seek alternative funding channels
1996	*Ninth Five-Year Plan for National Economic and Social Development and the Long-term Outline Objectives for the Year 2010*	Called for switching the mode of training professionals from examination-oriented education to all-round quality education
1998	*Action Scheme for Invigorating Education towards the 21st Century*	Reiterated the move towards decentralisation and marketisation and towards achieving quality education
1999	*Cross-Century Quality Education Project Decisions on Deepening Education Reform and Promoting Quality Education in an All-round Way*	Requested that the focus of quality education be shifted from pilot projects to full-scale implementation
2001	*The Decision on Reform and Development of Basic Education by the State Council*	Further recognised quality education as a major goal of the nation's 10th Five-Year Plan

continued . . .

TABLE 10.1 Continued

Year	*Document release*	*Major initiatives*
		Proposed a new school review system under which schools could apply for an 'exemplary school' title, as long as it had seen some breakthrough or achievements in promoting quality education
2001	*Framework for the Curriculum Reform of Basic Education – The Trial Version*	Outlined a move away from pure knowledge transmission towards fostering learning attitudes and values Established a new system whereby the curriculum is managed at the central, local and school levels
2010	*National Guidelines for Medium- and Long-Term Educational Reform and Development 2010–2020*	Entrenched the twin goals of equity and quality as the future of educational improvements in China
2013	*The Professional Criteria of Principals at the Compulsory Education Stage*	Stipulated the professional responsibilities of principals

1 This system, established in 1985, attempted to reverse the structures established during Mao's chairmanship, which saw a party secretary with considerable power over all aspects of school governance and ideology posted in each school. The 'principal-responsibility system' repositioned the school principal rather than the party secretary as the key leader in the school.

to harness a variety of resources drawn from parents and the community to support school development (Walker and Qian, 2011).

Third, principals are increasingly expected to lead changes at the school level and to cater to the central government's demands for performance and accountability (Walker *et al.*, 2012; Walker and Qian, 2011). The adoption of the principal responsibility system has positioned the school principal rather than the party secretary as the person who actually runs the school. The system also promises principals greater autonomy in terms of school-based curricula, teacher development, recruitment and promotion (Qian and Walker, 2013; Yin *et al.*, 2014). However, an integral aspect of decentralisation is increased public accountability for academic performance and resource utilisation. Various performance indicators have been adopted to review the performance of schools, principals and teachers. Principals need to demonstrate that their school produces satisfactory academic results and is adhering to the requirements of curriculum reform. Principals themselves also need to meet the professional criteria stipulated in national policy documents.

As a result of these reforms, Chinese schools exist on ever-shifting ground – somewhere between the state and the market. The systemic power of the state and market is exerting a dominant influence over schools. In other words, the lifeworld of Chinese schools is increasingly threatened by the expansion of the systemsworld. Similar to their international counterparts, Chinese principals tend to place priority on managerial and market-oriented accountability (Moos, 2005).

Illustrative narratives

These narratives are drawn from a major study that explored the lived experiences of eleven high school principals in the context of the ongoing educational reforms in China. The study yielded rich data on how each individual principal interpreted his or her work environment and elucidated his or her relationships with significant stakeholders in implementing those reforms. We selected three of the eleven principals from differing school backgrounds, and here present their stories of how they interpreted the possibilities and constraints of the reform context and how they acted on the basis of those interpretations. Each principal represents a particular type of school – that is, a municipal-level exemplary school, a district-level exemplary school and an ordinary school.[1] Despite the three schools' varying degrees of prestige and status, their principals developed similar priorities when they had to respond to calls from within and outside the schools.

Narrative 1: Principal G

Principal G worked in a prestigious school in Shanghai. The school has more than 100 years of history, and boasts a wealthy and active alumni body. Before being appointed principal of this school, G worked in the district education bureau for six and a half years. G said he believed his government working experience had helped him to think about educational issues from a macro perspective. In his opinion, school development cannot be separated from the social context:

> The experience [of] working in the education bureau [was] very meaningful and valuable for my principalship. While working in the education bureau, you were governing different types of schools. Thus, you had to think about problems from a macro perspective, and a lot of policies had to take different types of schools into consideration.

The experience of working in government had helped him to become an acute 'policy reader', G believed. He provided an example to illustrate his acute ability to interpret government policy. A former reform initiative allowed municipal exemplary schools in Shanghai to admit students from other provinces for a fee of 50,000 yuan. As this was an additional income source, most schools were enthusiastic about the initiative. However, G recognised that the reform would not last very long, and the national Ministry of Education indeed ended the policy several years after it had been initiated. G attributed his acute judgement about this issue to his government working experience:

> I [was] clear that the policy would not last long, because I [had] been working at *jiguan*.[2] I [knew] it [would] not be a long-term policy. We [planned for] it as a short-term practice. Thus, the money we . . . made from [it] over the past few years [was not] used up.

Although the school made some money out of admitting students from outside Shanghai, G used only part of that income as bonuses for teachers, saving most of it for 'later and long-term use'. G was very proud of his acute judgement concerning this policy. If he had used all of the money for teacher bonuses, he risked elevating their expectations to an unsustainable level. In his words:

> If you increase their income to a high level and there is a sudden decrease, teachers will blame you. . . . They will be dissatisfied with you because you [have given] them a decrease instead of an increase [in] income. They will forget they [had] already got a lot [before the policy ended].

G expressed the belief that a principal has to read, sift and differentiate the information contained in a superior's words:

> When you judge a decision made by your superiors, you have to be clear whether it is a task, a regulation, a rule or a policy. If it is a regulation, then you have to follow [it]. . . . If it is a task, then you have to think clearly [about] whether it is a good or bad, big or small issue and, more importantly, whether it will become a one-off or routinised practice. You have to make your own judgement.

G developed a principle for dealing with his superiors that he called the 'combination of a fixed standpoint and flexible strategies'. He said he believed that, in principle, a principal needs to follow orders from the top as long as they meet legal and ethical requirements. However, a principal may have to be flexible in implementing specific orders:

> In dealing with specific issues, [there are] two things you need to avoid: disobeying your superiors and one hundred per cent faithfully following them. According to my understanding, if you do not listen to your superiors, then you violate discipline. . . . However, if you faithfully follow them, you will be accused of only emphasising upward accountability. . . . When you master this principle of [the] 'combination of a fixed standpoint and flexible strategies', you can take active initiatives.

As a keen policy reader, G was acutely aware of how a school was evaluated and where he needed to place his priorities as a principal. He admitted that developing a new curriculum was both necessary and important because it represented new frontiers the school needed to explore. If done well, the new curriculum could become a marketable school brand and so boost the school's reputation. However, he considered the major pressure on the school stemmed from parental and societal expectations for a consistently high university admission rate. He also recognised that the admission rate was a major criterion for the government in evaluating his work as a principal. Thus, pursuing a high admission rate was important because it was considered the very foundation of the school. In G's words, a school 'needs to explore the frontiers, but also has to keep the bottom-line'. G further justified his pursuit of a high admission rate by saying that 'a school needs to provide education that satisfies the people'. His rationale was that because parents and society as a whole are most concerned about the university admission rate, that rate has to be the focus of a principal's work.

Within the school, G preferred an approachable and flexible approach to motivate different types of teachers. For example, he encouraged teachers to experiment with their teaching approaches. He also expected teachers to involve students in research-based learning. However, G felt certain that a number of more senior and better known teachers at his school would prefer to stick with familiar methods. As he did not want these teachers to oppose change, given their high professional standing among the school's teachers, he tended to rely on younger teachers to develop the new curriculum while giving the better known teachers the title of mentor. G considered that he was giving these teachers 'high-sounding titles' and more discursive power in exchange for their loyalty. He explained:

> They [well-known and senior teachers] [are] in charge of the training of younger teachers. They . . . represent our [school when engaging] in . . . external exchange activities with other schools, and we may also consult them for . . . important school issues. Their words [attach] some authority [to] the school development[s]. Of course, you need to make sure that your words and their words conform to each other. If you cannot [achieve] good coordination, and these teachers often disagree with you, you will be in trouble. Thus, you and these teachers need to have a shared discourse and then try to turn it into the public discourse of the school.

Thus, G was clear about the importance of co-ordinating various kinds of relationships both within and outside the school, and he had also acquired the ability to deal with the range of relationships important to a principal. He explained:

> Now you have to run your school [as an] open system. A school is related to various stakeholders such as superintendents, different government agencies, and neighbouring enterprises and residents. If [a principal] does not have the awareness and ability to deal with these relationships, in a sense it will result in a major problem [for] Chinese education.

As an example of a prestigious school principal, G embodied the following characteristics. First, he seemed to know intuitively how to relate to higher government officials, teachers and other stakeholders. Second, he was a sophisticated policy reader. His acute reading of government policies and orders seemed critical to setting the right direction for the school. Third, he knew that demonstrating his stance about following the curriculum reform was important but that what really mattered for a school and principal were good academic results in high-stakes exams.

Finally, while being a highly approachable and visible principal at his school, G also adopted many exchange-based strategies to win teachers' support.

Narrative 2: Principal T

The school at which Principal T worked is a district-level exemplary school. Although its designation suggests that the school is not as prestigious as a municipal exemplary school, it is highly popular among students whose scores are insufficient to meet the entry requirements of a first-tier school.

Although not a young man, T was a new principal. He worked in a municipal key school as a politics teacher until 1996 when he was summoned to work at the district education bureau. In the education bureau, he worked as an executive officer before being appointed principal of his current school. T said he appreciated the opportunity to be back in a school:

> [When] working at *jiguan*, you are mainly involved in administrative affairs. You may not know what you have done over the. . . . You do not have a sense of accomplishment. Furthermore, as a mid-level administrator, you had better keep quiet and not express your views. There are bureau heads and party secretaries above you; how can you freely say something? Under the cadre system of China, a subordinate needs to obediently perform [his or her] job. . . . I like challenges. This is my last chance. Since I [came] from a school, I [am happy to be] back [in a] school [before retirement].

Like many new principals, T did not risk initiating much change when he first came to the school. Instead, he retained most of his predecessor's practices, as he explained:

> After I came to the school, I recognised the job of my predecessor. I chose not to deny the efforts of previous principals. Even if I ha[d] some new ideas, I need[ed] to combine them with what the school already had. . . . The first step [was] to ensure stability.

When asked what he did after he had ensured school stability, he recited a collection of popular and somewhat hackneyed sayings about education:

> First, I need[ed] to make the school stable. And then I [promoted] these ideas around the school: Reform and development are complementary. Teaching quality is the lifeline of the school. Teaching should be the central concern of the school.

T implemented a set of measures intended to improve teaching. However, most of these measures were based on input-process-output models. In his school, teachers were subjected to myriad judgements, measures, comparisons and targets, and material rewards were regarded as the most effective way to motivate them. T explained:

> We have some required tasks for each teacher. For example, they are required to teach a certain number of classes. They also need to ensure the quality of teaching. Each teacher is also required to submit a research paper. These are required. . . . There are also tasks not required for every teacher. For example, if a teacher also takes the job of a class head teacher, then we will give him/her a sum of additional money as a reward. If [his/her] research paper wins a prize, [he/she] can also get [a monetary] reward.

A teacher had to meet the criteria set by the school. T further explained:

> When new students are admitted to my school, we enter their scores into a data base and rank them according to their scores. Then we will track [the] scores they achieve in monthly exams [and] mid-term and final exams. We may also track the gaps between different classes. In this way, we can see whether and how the teacher has helped students to progress. . . . All these results will be publicised. If you do not teach well, it will not be me who comes to blame you. Instead, parents, students and your peers will blame you. If a teacher cannot meet the criteria, he/she will be constrained in a lot of aspects. He/she will have less income and be less likely to be promoted.

T said he believed that teachers take their own financial welfare into careful account when they evaluate a principal. He explained:

> Teachers definitely [take the income they can get at the school into consideration] when they evaluate a principal. For example, if I gave each teacher a 500 yuan bonus as a celebration for, let's say, International Labour Day last year, then they would expect me to give them more this year. When I first came to the school, some teachers said that here [comes] a new principal. Then how about giving each teacher 1000 *yuan* as a gift for the first meet[ing]? We have nearly 170 staff members. If I distribute each of them 1000 yuan, what will be the total sum? You see, you cannot avoid talking about money.

In addition to 'spare' government funds, T said he actively gained access to various channels for money. For example, although T's school operates under district administration, it is located in a town (a smaller unit under the governance of a district). On the third day of his principalship, he went to visit township government officials, and they gave the school 50,000 yuan. T said this visit was part of forming a reciprocal relationship. T's visit showed his respect for the township office and made the officials feel they had been afforded 'face' (*mianzi*). The money formally recognised the new relationship. T said he worked hard during his tenure to further strengthen that relationship:

> When local enterprises have celebrations, we lend our auditorium for their use. Our dancing teams and chorus also perform [at] their celebration parties. They are very happy about it. This is actually serving the society with school resources. In return, the school can [make] a good impression and [win a] favourable social evaluation. It is reciprocal. Schools today cannot be isolated from the society. . . . You have to make use of all kinds of resources. Some of them cannot be exchanged for money . . . because Chinese society emphasises relationships.

T admitted that, as a principal, he had to focus on improving the school's admission rate, and he used various measures to monitor and evaluate teacher performance. He saw the process as 'a summative index' by which society evaluates school quality. As a new principal, he felt pressure to prove his performance.

As a district-level exemplary school principal, T exhibited the following characteristics. First, he was anxious to demonstrate his performance, particularly by showing that he could help to improve students' academic results. Second, he adopted a range of performance measures to monitor and motivate teachers, as he expected them to produce better results in a relatively short time. Finally, he was also conscious of the importance of establishing good relationships with a variety of stakeholders that were not limited to his direct supervisors, but also included the community leadership.

Narrative 3: Principal X

Principal X worked at an ordinary school, the designation assigned to the lowest ranking public schools. These schools usually admit students who do not receive high scores in the senior secondary school entrance exams. X is not a Shanghai native. In 2000, the P district of Shanghai launched the open recruitment of school leaders (principals and vice principals) via media advertisements. X applied, and was appointed principal of his current school. Before moving to Shanghai, he had worked as a principal in a neighbouring province for ten years. After arriving in Shanghai, the changes he initiated in the school garnered him such prestigious titles as 'the first person who eats crabs'[3] and 'an adventurous principal' in media reports. He was invited to speak at numerous forums, conferences and leader development courses, and his school received visits from educators across the nation. Compared with T's school, his school had greater publicity and visibility. As he somewhat immodestly claimed, he had managed to 'make an ordinary school extraordinary'.

X demonstrated a strong sense of entrepreneurship. He noted that a principal is like a brand manager, winning resources to help to promote the school. He saw brand as a very important concept. However, he admitted that when he first became a principal in his early thirties, he was more prone to being an educator and made teaching and curriculum issues his top priority. He soon encountered difficulties in doing so:

> I soon encountered [this problem]: I did not have enough funding. Relying on funding [from] the education bureau [alone] could only meet the basic needs of the school. . . . I had to motivate my teachers. Spiritual rewards were important but they could not replace material rewards. I had to make our teachers both spiritually and materially rich. Then I had to get money and win resources. For example, parents could be an important resource. I could also get resources from the school district and neighbouring enterprises. I invited alumni to our school anniversary celebrations and asked them to donate. I opened a factory within the school. Then my role actually turned into [that of] an entrepreneur. School is part of society. A school principal has to be a resource-winner and a mediator of public relations. Then, [the question is] how to develop [those] resources. You have to seek sources of resources from both within and [outside] the school. Thus, I have developed the awareness [needed] to win multiple resources. . . . If I still only focus[ed] on the teaching, pedagogy and observation of classes, I [might] not get recognition [from] teachers. I have to seek more economic support. Then, sometimes I have to change my role [to contact neighbourhood leaders and parents]. As a public school principal, I also need to frequently go to the local education bureau to establish [a] good relationship with them.

Keeping brand awareness foremost in mind, X said that when he first came to his current school his main concern was to identify its distinct characteristics and then implement measures to advertise and magnify those characteristics and turn them into a recognisable brand. He further explained:

> The school is not a key school, and it does not have a long history that we can boast of. How can the school be distinguished from others? I [had to conduct] an on-site investigation before I could properly design the school development route. . . . I had to be clear about the advantage[s] and the tradition of the school. Then, I found [that] the school [had] taught Japanese as a foreign language since 1972. This was a selling point, and I had to maximise it and [transform] it into [the school's] brand.

X implemented a number of strategies to 'sell' his idea. For example, he applied to change the school's name from XX Middle School to XX Foreign Languages Middle School. As the alteration of a school's name must be approved by several layers of government, the process took two years. X also established a Japanese Language Research Institute, the first of its kind to be established in a secondary school. This move, in turn, helped to advertise the school brand, X said.

X seemed to be instrumentally oriented and performance-focused. He embraced market values, using words such as 'selling points' and 'the market' regularly. However, this does not mean that he did not depend on the government. He was 'multilingual' in the sense that he could move relatively easily between the old language of being a state agent and the new language of school management. He was pragmatic about how to get what he wanted. X explained:

> You have to rely on both government policies and market effectiveness. You cannot give up either of them. I believe in multiple values, and I pursue whatever [is] effective and valuable. You need to be clear [about] what the bottleneck is that constrains . . . school development. If it is [a] funding problem, then try to get more funding. If it concerns [certain] people, then try to solve their problem[s]. If it is due to policy constraints, then try to get political approval. If it is due to disagreements within the school, then organise a school-wide conference to [reach] agreement.

The foregoing declarations make it clear that X made a distinction between the state and the market. Relying on the government could help him to 'solve the basic feeding problems of the school'. If the school wanted more nutrition, then he had to proactively seek out resources from other, mainly market-based, channels. He believed that this approach was the only way to invigorate the school. X further believed that the government would provide additional support once the school had demonstrated performance improvements:

> [As a] principal, [you] should be clear [about] when and what to report to your superiors. You should not [make a] report whenever your school [has] difficulties. Instead, you [may] have to report more [information] when your school [is] running smoothly. . . . In this way, the government [will] regard you as a competent principal, and then your superiors [will] have the desire to invest in your school. After all, competence determines status. The government will invest only when they can see some returns. You see, the government has invested a lot in my school over the past few years. Our new teaching building and new stadium [were made possibly primarily by] government funding.

As with many other principals, X did not hesitate to admit that the state maintains tight control that constrains his power. However, he also recognised that the situation was simply China's 'national condition'. Thus, as a subordinate, he chose not to disagree with or confront his superiors but instead to adopt a more flexible approach in dealing with the government. He explained:

> There are too many tasks assigned by the education bureau. We have to deal with a lot of inspections, and these tasks and inspections lead us by the nose. I would rather that the government [did] not interfere [in] any school affairs and [gave] us more space. However, you have to accept it because it is the national condition of China. [Even if you have disagreements], you have to keep them to yourself instead of conflicting with [officials].

> You have to adapt yourself to changing conditions. For example, you may not perform [certain] assigned tasks very well, but you need to report to your superiors [that] you [performed them] beautifully. You have to differentiate and make judgements because for some tasks you can muddle through while for others you cannot. You need to have acute insight.

X also demonstrated flexibility in his relationships with teachers. He implemented a number of personnel reforms in the school. He expressed the belief that 'shock therapy' does not work when it comes to personnel issues. Accordingly, as the redistribution of interests was involved, he adopted an incremental approach to implementing reforms to win support:

> You cannot abruptly start a reform. Sometimes you have to make your reform intentions known long before you actually propose a change. When the thunder [is] heard long enough, people [anticipate] rain. By then your change initiatives will not be so unacceptable.

X is representative of the type of principal who can overcome the constraints of working in a lower status school by seizing every opportunity to render his or her school (and him or herself) more visible. He exhibited the following characteristics. First, he could speak different 'languages' when dealing with different stakeholders – namely, the languages of the state and market. He was an adept manipulator of relationships with those parties he deemed significant. Second, he was able to develop a clear sense of priorities. As indicated by his food metaphor, while the market could provide the school with supplementary 'nutrition', it was the government that essentially fed the school. Thus, losing the support of the government would threaten the school's very survival. Finally, he also believed that material rewards were needed to motivate teachers.

Discussion and conclusion

The three narratives show that principals working at schools of different status have different opportunities and constraints in the reform context. For example, the two principals whose schools were the most prestigious of the three tended to have access to better resources, and thus found it easy to capitalise on their distinct features and long traditions. The narratives also indicate that the personal context – namely, the three principals' individual experiences and leadership approaches, mediated the way in which they interpreted the reforms. For example, Principal X seemed to be more market-oriented than the other two participants.

However, many commonalities can also be identified in the principals' narratives, some of them in alignment with those depicted in the international literature (e.g. Gewirtz and Ball, 2000; Townsend, 2012). These include the strong influence of managerial ideology and awareness of the need to win resources from various sources and the need to sufficiently motivate teachers to meet the systemic requirements imposed on schools. For instance, all three principals had exchanged material rewards for better output from teachers. The narratives also reveal the overwhelming control of systemic power in Chinese schools. What appears different from the case in the West is that the systemic power being imposed on schools comes mainly from the state, with the market playing a more indirect role. The government remained the significant other in all three principals' interpretation of the reform initiatives. When the principals talked about themselves in relation to the domains of the lifeworld and systemsworld, it was clear that they identified themselves primarily as state agents.

Since the 1980s the world has turned to a particular doctrine labelled 'neoliberalism'. Consequently, there has been a fundamental change in the relationships among the state, the education sector and the market. The ideology of neoliberalism and the concomitant strategies of marketisation, devolution, choice and privatisation have reshaped education policies over the past three decades (Henry *et al.*, 2001; Lupton, 2011; Terosky, 2014). As a result, most schools now face the pressure of the dominant systemic influence, and principals have to place priority on responding to the systemsworld of their schools.

Although spawned in Anglo-American countries, these neoliberal reforms have spread to many non-Western settings, including China. However, while similar textually, these travelling reforms may take on 'different readings and effects because of the different histories, forms of governance, industrial relations systems, level of centralisation/decentralisation, cultural attitudes, and welfare systems when articulated in local contexts' (Blackmore, 2004, p. 270). This exploration of how the reform context has shaped Chinese principals' work lives, and how Chinese principals relate to both the systems and lifeworlds, is thus of significant research interest.

The narratives of three high school principals in Shanghai presented herein show that Chinese schools, like their Western counterparts, face the challenges of an invading systemic power flowing from the state and market. They demonstrate the general trend towards increased emphasis on efficiency, outcomes, productivity and performance. All three principals felt under pressure to meet the systemic expectations imposed on their schools. However, what makes the situation facing Chinese principals distinct is the strong presence of the state and relatively muted role of the market. The primary role of a school principal in China is that of state agent.

There are three possible reasons for this situation. First, Chinese school principals are first and foremost accountable to the state rather than to the market. All three principals interviewed worked in the public sector. Although the state had retreated as the sole resource provider, it remained the schools' major source of income. The three principals were also appointed by the government, and their career progression (and indeed survival) thus depended on the government.

Second, the principals regarded themselves as state employees who occupied the lower echelon of the government hierarchy. Thus, loyalty to their superiors appears to have been taken for granted. For example, while all three principals mentioned that they were unable to follow every single instruction issued by the government, they all stated that they had to adopt, and strategically use, various approaches to avoid appearing disobedient.

Third, the market does not have a well-developed role in the school sector in China. As the three schools under study were state-owned, a loss of market attraction was not an existential threat. Because there is a hierarchy of schools in terms of status, schools do not compete with one another on a level playing field. It is implicitly agreed that municipal exemplary schools always admit the best students, while ordinary schools attract only those at the bottom academically. Thus, the principals interviewed for this study acknowledged the considerable pressure to ensure that their students performed well in high-stakes exams. However, their major concern was not that poor exam results might worsen their market status, but rather that their superiors would place sanctions on the school if their performance was not up to scratch.

Analysis of the three narratives suggests a number of areas in which further research can be conducted to enrich scholarly understanding of how Chinese principals locate themselves in relation to the systemsworld and lifeworld. The following are a few suggested directions for future research.

- This study suggests that principals adopt managerial strategies to motivate teachers. There is thus a need to explore how such strategies affect teachers and to elucidate the relationships between principals and teachers in China.
- Although the influence of the market on Chinese schools tends to be indirect and more obscure than that of the state, there is a need to understand the ways in which the market exerts its limited influence.
- While the primary concern of the participating principals is to meet the systemic requirements of the state, there also seem to be occasions on which they can bargain for greater autonomy. The intricate relationships between the state and principals thus require further study.
- The three participants in this study were all employed in public schools. Private school principals may face a different situation in relation to the systemic influence stemming from the state and market. Hence, there is a need to explore how private school principals and teachers narrate the way in which neoliberal reforms have shaped their work lives.

Notes

1 China adopted the practice of classifying schools into key and ordinary schools a long time ago. To overcome the problems caused by the concentration of quality resources in a few schools, the central leadership decided that an exemplary school system should be established to replace the previous key school system (The State Council, 2001). As a result, a hierarchical school system remains. At the top are the fifty or so municipal-level exemplary schools. Further down are district experimental exemplary schools, and at the bottom are ordinary schools.

2 *Jiguan* is a term used to describe a government administrative unit. In this chapter, it refers primarily to the district educational bureau.

3 This traditional phrase is used to refer to someone who is brave and adventurous.

References

Ball, S. (2012). The reluctant state and the beginning of the end of state education. *Journal of Educational Administration and History*, 44(2), 89–103.

Blackmore, J. (2004). Restructuring educational leadership in changing contexts: A local/global account of restructuring in Australia. *Journal of Educational Change*, 5, 267–288.

Chan, Y. C. (2002). Policy implications of adopting a managerial approach in education. In K. H. Mok and K. K. Chan (eds), *Globalisation and education in Hong Kong* (pp. 243–258). Hong Kong: Hong Kong University Press.

Dempster, N. (2000). Guilty or not: The impact and effects of site-based management on schools. *Journal of Educational Administration*, 38(1), 47–63.

Gewirtz, S. and Ball, S. (2000). From 'welfarism' to 'new managerialism': Shifting discourses of school headship in the education marketplace. *Discourse: Studies in the Cultural Politics of Education*, 21(3), 253–268.

Habermas, J. (1987). *The theory of communicative action. Vol. 2: Lifeworld and system: A critique of functional reason* (T. McCarthy, trans.). Boston, MA: Beacon Press.

Hallinger, P. (2005). Foreword. In C. Dimmock and A. Walker (eds), *Educational leadership: culture and diversity* (pp. vii–xii). London: SAGE.

Harvey, D. (2005). *A brief history of neoliberalism*. New York: Oxford University Press.

Hawkins, J. N. (2000). Centralisation, decentralization, recentralization: Educational reform in China. *Journal of Educational Administration*, 38(5), 442–454.

Henry, M., Lingard, B., Rizvi, F. and Taylor, S. (2001). *The OECD, globalisation and education policy*. London: Pergamon Press.

Lauder, H. (1997). Education, democracy and the economy. In A. H. Halsey, H. Lauder, P. Brown and A. S. Wells (eds), *Education: culture, economy, and society* (pp. 382–391). Oxford: Oxford University Press.

Lupton, R. (2011). 'No change there then!'(?): The onward march of school markets and competition. *Journal of Educational Administration and History*, 43(4), 309–323.

Ministry of Education (2001). *Framework for the curriculum reform of basic education* (trial version). Retrieved from: www.edu.cn/20010926/3002911.shtml (in Chinese).

Ministry of Education (2013). *The professional criteria of principals at the compulsory education stage*. Retrieved from: www.moe.edu.cn/publicfiles/business/htmlfiles/moe/s7085/201302/147899.html (in Chinese).

Mok, K. H. (2000). *Social and political development in post-reform China*. Basingstoke: Macmillan.

Mok, K. H. and Welch, A. R. (2002). Economic rationalism, managerialism and structural reform in education. In K. H. Mok and K. K. Chan (eds), *Globalisation and education in Hong Kong* (pp. 23–40). Hong Kong: Hong Kong University Press.

Moos, L. (2005). How do schools bridge the gap between external demands for accountability and the need for internal trust? *Journal of Educational Change*, 6, 307–328.

Moos, L. and Møller, J. (2003). Schools and leadership in transition: The case of Scandinavia. *Cambridge Journal of Education*, 33(3), 353–370.

Murphy, J. and Datnow, A. (2003). The development of comprehensive school reform. In J. Murphy and A. Datnow (eds), *Leadership lessons from comprehensive school reforms* (pp. 3–18). Thousand Oaks, CA: Corwin Press.

Pedroni, T. (2007). *Market movements: African American involvement in school voucher reform*. New York: Routledge.

Peters, M., Marshall, J. and Fitzsimons, P. (2000). Managerialism and educational policy in a global context: Foucault, neoliberalism, and the doctrine of self-management. In N. C. Burbules and C. A. Torres (eds), *Globalisation and education: critical perspectives* (pp. 100–132). New York: Routledge.

Power, S., Halpin, D. and Whitty, G. (1997). Managing the state and the market: 'New' education management in five countries. *British Journal of Educational Studies*, 45(4), 342–362.

Qian, H. Y. and Walker, A. (2011). The 'gap' between policy intent and policy effect: An exploration of the interpretations of school principals in China. In T. Huang and A. W. Wiseman (eds), *The Impact and Transformation of Education Policy in China, International Perspectives on Education and Policy* (Vol. 15, pp. 187–208). Bingley, UK: Emerald.

Qian, H. Y. and Walker, A. (2013). How principals promote and understand teacher development under curriculum reform in China. *Asia-Pacific Journal of Teacher Education*. 41(3), 304–315.

Sbragia, A. (2000). Governance, the state, and the market: what is going on? *Governance*, 13, 243–250.

Sergiovanni, T. J. (2000). *The lifeworld of leadership: creating culture, community and personal meaning in our schools*. San Francisco, CA: Jossey-Bass Publishers.

Sugrue, C. (2005). Putting 'real life' into school leadership: Connecting leadership, identities and life history. In C. Sugrue (ed.). *Passionate principalship: learning from the life histories of school leaders* (pp. 3–26). London: RoutledgeFalmer.

The State Council (2001). *The decision on reform and development of basic education*. Retrieved from: www.edu.cn/20010907/3000665.shtml (in Chinese).

Terosky, A. L. (2014). From a managerial imperative to a learning imperative: Experiences of urban, public school principals. *Educational Administration Quarterly*, 50(1), 3–33.

Townsend, T. (2012). The askers and the tellers. In M. A. Acker-Hocevar, J. Ballenger, A. W. Place and G. Ivory (eds). *Snapshots of school leadership in the 21st century: The UCEA voices from the field project* (pp. 209–236). Charlotte, NC: Information Age Publishing.

Walker, A. (2003). School leadership and management. In J. Keeves and R. Watanabe (eds), *The international handbook of educational research in the Asia-Pacific region* (pp. 973–986). Dordrecht, the Netherlands: Kluwer Press.

Walker, A., Hu, R. K. and Qian, H. Y. (2012). Principal leadership in China: An initial review. *School Effectiveness and School Improvement*, 23(4), 369–399.

Walker, A., and Qian, H. Y. (2011). Successful school leadership in China. In C. Day (ed.), *The Routledge International handbook of teacher and school development* (pp. 446–457). London and New York: Routledge.

Walker, A. and Qian, H. Y. (2012). Reform disconnection in China. *Peabody Journal of Education*, 87(2), 162–177.

Walker, A., Qian, H. Y. and Zhang, S. (2011). Secondary school principals in curriculum reform: Victims or accomplices? *Frontiers of education in China*. 6(3), 388–403.

Yergin, D. and Stanislaw, J. (1998). *The commanding heights: The battle for the world economy*. New York: Simon & Schuster.

Yimaki, R. M. (2012). Curriculum leadership in a conservative era. *Educational Administration Quarterly*, 48(2), 304–346.

Yin, H. B., Lee, C. K. and Wang, W. L. (2014). Dilemmas of leading national curriculum reform in a global era: A Chinese perspective. *Educational Management Administration & Leadership*, 42(2), 293–311.

11

LEADERSHIP AND EMOTIONS

Promoting social justice

James Ryan and Stephanie Tuters

Introduction

This chapter explores how a social justice-minded educational leader strategically manages her own and others' emotions. Employing a case study approach, we observed and interviewed a principal of a diverse elementary school and her teacher colleagues. The principal, whom we called Pearl, recognised that if she wanted to achieve her social justice goals, then she had to work at understanding her own and others' emotions. At the same time, she also recognised that she had to mask her own emotions, regardless of the potential fallout.

It has almost become a cliché to say that our schools and communities are becoming more diverse. Cliché or not, racial, class, cultural, religious, geographical and sexual orientation differences are more apparent now than they ever were in classrooms around the world (Milner, 2010; Sleeter and Cornbleth, 2011). Such differences, however, are more than merely curiosities; they have consequences for schools, the students who attend them, and their parents and educators who work in them. Most obviously, many of these differences generate advantages and disadvantages. For example, in most contemporary schools in the Western world, non-white, gay, lesbian, poor and differently abled students tend to achieve at lower levels, drop out in greater numbers and are less likely to attend post-secondary school institutions than their white, straight, middle-class and physically able counterparts (see, for example, Bennett, 2001; Darling-Hammond, 1995; Orfield, 1995; Sweet *et al.*, 2010; Trembley *et al.*, 2001). These inequities have not gone unnoticed; those who are concerned about them are taking action to change the practices that generate them. Many of those who do so identify with a social justice perspective (Ryan, 2012).

Nevertheless, promoting social justice is not an easy thing to do. This is because proponents routinely encounter resistance (Ryan, 2012; Theoharis, 2007). This is true in education just as it is for most other institutions. Educational leaders, for example, have to find ways to counter the ever-present resistance to their efforts. In order to do this, they need to be strategic about the ways in which they go about their advocacy work (Ryan, 2010). This requires that they understand the political environment in which they work, are able to size up the situations they encounter, and appropriately calculate actions that will produce the outcomes that they favour.

But promoting social justice involves more than rational calculations. It is also an emotional enterprise (Flam and King, 2005). Emotions intrude in at least two ways. The first way is in the emotions that leaders experience as they advocate for their social justice ideals. Theoharis (2007), for example, documents the emotional fallout from such efforts. He notes, among other things, that leaders experience considerable anxiety when they promote social justice. The other sense in which social justice-minded leaders encounter emotions is in the way they attempt to entice or suppress emotions in others that can either obstruct or support social justice efforts (Flam and King, 2005). They may, for example, nurture hope, while helping people deal with their fear (King, 2005). In doing so, they strategically manage emotions to promote social justice ideals.

Given the importance of strategy and emotion, how then might social justice-minded educational leaders strategically approach the emotional side of their activist work? While recent education literature has explored the emotions of leaders and teachers (Beatty, 2000; Hargreaves, 2001) and social movement research has looked at the political mobilisation of emotions (Flam and King, 2005), no research has explored the ways in which educational leaders strategically approach their own and others' emotional deployment in the service of social justice ends. The remainder of this chapter attempts to fill this gap. It explores how a social justice-minded educational leader strategically manages her own and others' emotions. The chapter is organised in the following way. First, we review the work that has been done in the area of emotions and strategic action. Next, we describe the methods we employed for the study and the setting. The following section probes the ways in which a school principal understands others' emotions, the actions she takes and the manner in which she manages her own emotions. This is followed by an example of how she puts these tactics into practice.

Emotions and strategic action

The work of educators is fraught with emotions; teaching, leading and learning are emotional activities (Beatty, 2000; Blackmore, 1996; Hargreaves, 2001). Not everyone, however, can agree on just what emotions are. One way to characterise emotion is as a 'self-feeling' process (Denzin, 2009). These self-feelings are associated first and most significantly with physiological or bodily changes like, for example, an increased heart rate, a reddening of the face or other more difficult-to-identify sensations within the body. But there is more to feeling than just bodily sensations; they are also accompanied by expressive gestures, like a change in vocal timbre, unique facial expressions, or a particular choice of words.

While emotion has a private element, the emotional process is also public – that is, it is also social (Denzin, 2009; Hochschild, 1979, 2012). Emotions are felt and expressed in social contexts. This occurs as individuals appraise situations in which they find themselves, bringing their socially acquired understandings of the world with them to make these judgements. This has an impact on what they feel. More than this, though, their physiological reactions, expressive features and appraisals reflect social and culturally conditioned meanings. Sociologists like Durkheim, Weber and Marx, for example, have acknowledged the social nature of emotions, situating them in rational rules, economic practice, power relations and rituals (Denzin, 2009).

Emotions are not just social phenomena, however, they are also political (Flam and King, 2005). Emotions are employed to establish, sustain or resist certain social arrangements. Marx, for example, contends that when certain (capitalist) economic conditions prevail individuals can be cut off from their practical economic activities and from one another, engendering in them resentment and alienation. When this happens they can be susceptible to subordination and exploitation. Contemporary scholars have also probed emotions and politics. Feminists and social movement advocates have been the most vocal in this respect. The former contend that women's socialisation into 'emotion rules' discourages them from getting angry and subordinates them to social conventions that do not work in their favour (Boler, 2007). Feminists contend that changing unfair social arrangements requires that advocates mobilise emotions like anger (Flam and King, 2005).

Although a comparatively recent phenomenon, researchers have begun to explore emotions in education. In particular, they have looked at how emotions are implicated in the work of teachers and administrators. They have also probed the social and political nature of emotions in educational institutions. Hargreaves (2001), for example, examines how teachers' emotions are shaped by the changing conditions of their work. He does so through the concept of emotional geographies – spatial and experience patterns of closeness and/or distance in human interactions that help, create, configure and colour feeling and emotions. Illustrating the social nature of the process, he contends that teachers both construct and are constructed by these emotional geographies of teaching. He demonstrates empirically how several forms of emotional distance and closeness – sociocultural, moral, professional, political and physical – can threaten emotional understanding.

One of the forms of emotional geography that Hargreaves explores is political. He acknowledges that not only is emotional understanding social, it is also part of a political process, bound up with people's experiences of power and powerlessness. Other scholars in education have also pointed out the political nature of emotions. Zorn and Boler (2007), for example, explicitly highlight the role that emotions play in gender, class, race and sexual orientation relationships and suggest ways in which emotions can be approached to change these inequitable relationships. In this vein, Zembylas (2007) contends that anger can be used to promote social justice. He maintains that it can stimulate people to act against injustice and inspire social change. Among other things, learning to listen to anger at injustices can lead to constructive classroom dialogue about the fairness of power relationships in society.

Education scholars have also explored leadership and emotions in education. This research is in its early stages (Beatty, 2000; Leithwood and Beatty, 2008; Zorn and Boler, 2007). Although not labelled as such, other research also features emotions (Blase and Blase, 1997). The focus of much of research into emotions is on the kinds of emotions that administrators experience, the situations that give rise to these emotions and the impact of others' emotions on administrators (Beatty, 2000). This research reveals that much of the emotional work of administrators involves the management of emotions – their own and others'. In the course of doing their work, administrators spend much time managing how they feel and expressing (or not expressing) these feelings in order to engender particular emotions in others. Leithwood and Beatty (2008) and Lambersky (2014) explore the latter, identifying leadership practices and working conditions that influence teacher emotions. While this leadership research highlights its social nature, it does not explicitly target the political nature of emotions, statements to the contrary notwithstanding (Beatty, 2000).

Other leadership studies in education touch on emotions, but do not feature them. Some of these studies are explicitly political in nature. They are part of a tradition that associates itself with the idea of social justice. These scholars draw attention to inequities in education – often revolving around issues of race, class, gender, sexual orientation and ability – and advocate for, or study ways to turn these injustices around (Anderson, 2009; Blackmore, 1996; Dantley, 2003; Furman, 2012; Shields, 2003). Some of these studies touch on emotions. For example, Blackmore (1996) explored the emotional labour of leaders in times of educational reform. She highlighted the ways in which women administrators attempt to cope with legislated changes with which they did not agree. Theoharis (2007) also alludes to emotions, but as part of a larger study about social justice leadership. He describes the anxiety that administrators experience when promoting their social justice agendas. This literature, however, does not explicitly attempt to connect emotions and efforts to strategically promote social justice.

The most intensive work on strategy and emotion has been carried out in disciplines outside education. Two well-known, but quite different approaches, look at the manner in which organisational members and leaders strategically employ emotions. Hochschild (1979) identifies the 'emotion rules' that people follow in particular situations. She illustrates how institutional norms dictate that organisational members cannot always show what they feel; instead, they must mask their feelings in order to generate a desired state of mind in others. For example, airline attendants cannot express anger at unruly passengers; instead, as part of their job they are expected to smile even though it may not be what they actually feel like doing. Hochschild refers to this process as 'emotional labour', drawing attention to the ways in which people strategically attempt to manipulate their own emotions to achieve organisational purposes. Her view is a negative one; organisations exploit members by requiring them to mask their feelings in order to generate profits or advance organisational interests.

Goleman (2006, 2014) advances another, more positive, view on strategy and emotion. He contends that organisational members, particularly leaders, need to be able to manipulate their own and others' emotions if they are to successfully achieve their goals. This requires that they possess or acquire a degree of social and emotional intelligence. He maintains that if leaders can understand their own emotions, read others' emotions, and diagnose the circumstances in which emotions occur, then they will be better able to act in ways that will advance their own and their organisations' interests. Like Hochschild, Goleman understands that leaders will have to mask their emotions. Goleman, however, differs from Hochschild in that he believes that this ability to mask emotions and to display situation-appropriate ones is a valued skill that leaders should seek to acquire and practice. Goleman's approach to strategy and emotion is not without its critics, however. Boler (2007), for example, criticises Goleman's approach as a marketable package that ends up moulding emotions for organisational profit.

Scholars in education have also begun to explore the connection between leadership strategy and emotions. Leithwood and Beatty (2008) and Lambersky (2014) look at the actions that administrators take to engender desired emotions in teachers. However, they do not examine the ways in which leaders strategically approach emotions to promote political, that is, social justice goals. The remainder of this chapter attempts to fill this gap by exploring the ways in which an administrator attempts to strategically manage her own and others' emotions in her attempt to promote social justice practices in her school.

Methods

We employed a case study research approach (Merriam, 1998). In particular, we focused our efforts on understanding the emotion-related practices of one particular principal, whom we called Pearl. As part of a larger study that explored the (micro) political actions of social justice-minded leaders, it focused on the ways in which Pearl dealt with her own and others' emotions in her efforts to promote her social justice agenda. Initially we looked at her political practices, but narrowed our efforts down to emotions as we collected the data and came to know Pearl's situation better. We initially chose Pearl from the sample of leaders we interviewed for the larger study. She seemed to be a promising selection for a more intense exploration because of the attention she gave to her (micro) political activities. In the spirit of case study research (Merriam, 1998), we gathered data to inform us of her activities. This included talking to people within her school who could tell us about what she did, talking to Pearl and observing what she did.

Data collection occurred over the course of five days of observations and interviews. The first day of observation started with a school tour and introductions to most of the staff members. It also involved observing Pearl as she went about her daily duties and her attendance at a New Teacher Induction Program (NTIP) meeting. At the meeting Pearl reviewed the goals and expectations for new teachers with the five new staff members. During days two and three, one of us shadowed her as she went about her day and talked to her about her practice. On the fourth day of observation we interviewed five teachers we felt could shed light on Pearl's activities and also observed her. The fifth day included observation of a parent council meeting, and a meal with Pearl and the parent council prior to the parent council meeting.

Data from observations and interviews were collected and recorded using a voice recorder. Hand-written notes were entered into a journal even when conversations and interviews were being recorded in order to keep track of key themes and new lines of inquiry as they arose. Post-observation notes were written in the journal at the end of each observation experience. The journal notes were analysed following each observation to reflect on each observation experience, consider what was covered/uncovered and plan what should be further explored or probed during the next observation date. Recorded conversations and interviews were transcribed at a later date, as were hand-written notes. All data were coded and organised using NVivo 9 qualitative data analysis software.

Antionnette Carlson School

The study was conducted in Antionnette Carlson elementary school (this is a pseudonym). It is a mid-sized school in a very diverse suburb of a large and diverse Canadian city. The school houses just over 500 students from junior kindergarten to grade three. The principal describes the student population as being very diverse with over 45 languages or dialects spoken in the home, including Farsi, Russian, Chinese, Urdu, Tamil, Cantonese, Mandarin, Persian, Russian, Italian, Ukranian and Greek. Students most commonly speak Cantonese, Chinese or Farsi (Persian) as their first language. Many of the students are first-generation Canadian citizens (over 80 per cent), hailing from over 65 countries. Although most of the students were born in Canada, half of them grew up speaking a language other than English as their primary language in their home and the first language that they learned. The students also come from a variety of backgrounds, socio-demographically and otherwise. However, the parents of many of the students identify with a higher socio-economic status. Approximately half of the parents have university degrees. The majority of the parents work in the field of management or business and the unemployment rate is lower than the provincial average, hovering around 4 per cent. The problem with this relative affluence is that sometimes the less privileged students get overlooked. Teachers often assume, wrongly, that all students at the school enjoy the benefits that accompany their relatively privileged home situations.

The teaching population is also very diverse; teachers on the staff come from many different continents and countries. The principal has made a considerable effort to encourage the teachers to incorporate their background as well as their students into their teaching. For example, students often speak multiple languages during school events to help make other students feel their backgrounds are appreciated, and to help create a sense of welcome and inclusion with the students' families and the broader community. The principal also often enlists the help of translators to help parents communicate with the school.

The shortage of school administrators in the school district has had an impact on Antionnette Carlson elementary school. Many schools in the area have lost their vice-principals entirely, or at least partly, over the last few years due to budget restrictions. Principals and vice-principals are also sometimes required to teach courses. While it has a full-time principal (Pearl), the school only has a part-time vice-principal because it is a mid-sized school. The vice-principal splits her time between this and another local elementary school; the two schools are about a ten-minute drive from one another. Ideally, the vice-principal spends 2.5 days per week at each school. However, due to the nature of the job, this is not always the case; sometimes she is at one school more than the other, or at both in the same day. The vice-principal is therefore very busy and often absent. When the vice-principal is at the other school, the principal (Pearl) acts as both principal and vice-principal.

Leadership and emotions

Administrative work for Pearl can be very emotional. Most of what she does in her position of principal – both routine and novel tasks – is tinged with emotion. When asked to talk about the emotional side of her work, she speaks about the more deeply felt emotions, like anger and fear – both others' and her own. The most mentioned emotion is anger. Pearl points to a seemingly endless series of situations in which members of the school community have expressed their anger. These include fights between parents and teachers in the parking lot, yelling parents, parents attacking teachers, parents 'going off', parents berating teachers, parents storming out of the office, parents going to the superintendent, teachers yelling, teachers going to the union and to the superintendent, abrasive teachers, rude teachers, harassing parents, name-calling teachers and angry students. But teachers, parents and students are not the only ones who get angry; Pearl also feels anger. She gets angry at things that teachers, parents and students do and say. Some of these instances are described below.

Other emotions coexist within the school community. One of these is fear. Pearl refers to others' fear as well as her own. She notes that many teachers fear change. 'I guess with any change there is fear, right? There is uncertainty . . . for some teachers, there is a lot of fear,' she said. Pearl also experiences fear. In one situation where a teacher complained to the union and the superintendent about her, Pearl confesses that she was fearful because she did not know what she was going to do. Pearl also mentions other emotions. It is interesting to note that Pearl speaks exclusively of negative rather than positive emotions. Rather than identifying joy, satisfaction or amusement – which also occur in abundance at the school – she recalls dealing with nervous, upset and stressed teachers, parents and students. When these emotions coincide with anger and fear they can provide a toxic mix, which can challenge Pearl and threaten to derail social justice plans.

Pearl experiences many of the same emotions that teachers, parents and students experience: fear, anger and anxiety, among others. But the way in which she expresses them often differs, given her strategic intentions. She attempts to manage her emotions in ways that the others do not – that is, she attempts to control the way in which anger manifests itself in her behaviour so that she can also manage the outcome of these situations.

Pearl's goal in the short term is to survive prickly situations. Doing so requires that she not express emotions that might escalate already intense situations. Instead, she does her best to rein in her emotions so that she can calm the angry, provide the fearful with hope and reassure the anxious. She says:

> If I'm not rational and careful about what I'm doing, outcomes and scenarios could be a lot worse potentially. Do I try to have people leave here happy during a difficult conversation? I do. . . . So I think that those emotions you use are so critical to the outcome.

In the longer term, though, she manages her emotions in ways that can best promote social justice.

Pearl is an advocate for social justice. In her leadership appointments to date she has done her best to provide conditions that will help marginalised students. She describes her 'core purpose' as a leader and an educator, to help all students achieve 'true dignity' and have 'a fair chance at being educated so they can contribute positively as civil people in society'. She recognises that the way in which schools are set up does not serve all students equally; some do better than others. She also knows that this is not an accident. She believes that 'there are certain groups of people that are more marginalised than others', and that these patterns of marginalisation often revolve around race, class, gender and sexual orientation relationships. Pearl is currently on a district-wide committee that is looking for ways to promote inclusion for marginalised students. She also finds ways to advocate for their inclusion in her current school. This includes employing strategies that acknowledge the place of emotions.

Strategic action and emotions

Pearl is strategic about how she approaches emotions. Managing the emotions of others in ways that promote her social justice goals, however, requires that she engages in a number of pursuits. Her first step is to understand the emotions of others.

Understanding

Pearl maintains that she needs to understand the emotions of others – that is, comprehend what they are feeling. She feels that her foray into emotional intelligence and cognitive coaching has helped her understand the importance of emotions and to 'read' or recognise the signs in people that reflect their emotional states. She also recognises that it is important to understand the circumstances that may have led to the expression of particular emotions.

Pearl believes that understanding these circumstances may help her better understand why people are expressing those emotions. She says:

> You need a high level of emotional intelligence. You really need to know your social context. You need social intelligence because every situation is different. Every situation needs a different kind of leadership [practice].

Part of this social/emotional intelligence for Pearl includes understanding the context that gives rise to emotional issues. She maintains that she needs to 'understand what other people are going through or facing, and helping them understand'.

Pearl recalled one occasion where her actions were tempered by the circumstances surrounding an infraction of school rules. A grade three student had been sent to her because he had been the instigator in an altercation with four other boys during a ball game on the playground. His classroom teacher had also noted his aggression over the past few days. In the meantime, though, Pearl had met with his mother and discovered that things at home were not good; the mother had taken out a restraining order on the boy's father. Pearl felt that it was important to take this into consideration when dealing with this emotionally charged situation. She said:

> It was knowing what's happening at home and trying to see from his perspective. But who knows what he witnessed from home? The parent has a restraining order so when you talk to parents and you say 'we have to be really cognizant and in-tune'. So when teachers really do see him outside doing this they can also see it from this perspective. So all that emotional piece is understanding it as much as possible from everybody's lens.

Once she understands or is able to read the others' emotions and the circumstances that have given rise to these emotions, she is in a position to take action.

Taking action

Pearl knows that if she is to influence emotions in desired ways, she has to acknowledge these emotions, be patient, put time into listening to what others have to say, provide support and perhaps, most important of all, manage her own emotions. When Pearl is able to do these things, then she is better able to resolve contentious issues, and in the end, promote her social justice agenda.

Pearl recognises the importance of acknowledging people's emotions. She has realised over the years that people respond in desired ways in difficult situations if she lets them know that she understands how they are feeling. She says:

> People appreciate that you try to deal with their emotions. The moment you say 'I can sense you're frustrated, please share with us or me what we can do to help you further,' you can see . . . parents take more time, right from the get-go. Some will calm down and I think it goes a long way.

Pearl knows the value of acknowledging others' feelings, particularly in volatile situations. She has learned over the years that people appreciate attempts to deal with their emotions. They notice these efforts, and when they do so, they tend to step back and calm down, diffusing these anger-charged moments and paving the way for more meaningful dialogue and a resolution to the issue at hand.

Pearl also does her best to exercise patience in emotionally charged situations. Recalling a meeting with a parent, she says:

> The meeting lasted an hour and 15 minutes. She just had to get it all out. But I think if I had interrupted her, they don't want to hear that. They don't want to hear 'no', they don't want to hear 'but'. They are triggers. Once that parent was kind of diffused, then I started to ask some questions. If it escalated again, I mean there are people, not particularly here, but I've had parents storm out of the office, right? Then you talk to them a few days later. But in this situation, I keep myself busy. I might take notes. And honestly, I do a lot of nodding, watch the breathing and I do eye contact and I think that slows them down.

Despite her busy schedule Pearl takes time to listen to people when they are angry or upset. She gives people time to have their say, and in those circumstances where they are particularly emotional, to vent. She takes care not to interrupt, contest views or signal an early end to these meetings. Only after they have had a chance to say what they need to say and she senses that they have calmed down, does she begin to ask questions or interject. Of course, this does not work in all cases, and Pearl notes that some parents have left her office in anger before the issues were worked out.

Just sitting and listening, particularly if it is for extended periods of time, is not an easy thing to do. So Pearl has developed strategies that help her through this time. One of the things she does is to take notes or at least pretend that she is taking notes. She also employs other techniques to move the conversation along. These include nodding and looking people in the eye at the appropriate times.

Support is also important for Pearl as she deals with emotional issues. She sees one of her most important roles as providing support to teachers, parents and students. She believes that those who are emotionally stressed are in need of help, and she does what she can to assist them. Pearl provides support to stressed individuals in the heat of the moment, as she attempts to help them understand the issue at hand and how they can resolve it. So, for example, she attempts to get parents to understand why a teacher might have told them that they could not park in a particular place or to help a teacher comprehend why a student might be acting out in class. But the support she provides also moves beyond trying to get teachers or parents to calm down in these emotionally charged situations. Pearl also helps parents, students and teachers to deal with the issue over longer periods of time. So she will attempt to work with a teacher who is having difficulties in the classroom or help a parent deal with an issue that her son is experiencing at school.

Managing her own emotions

Pearl makes an effort to control her own emotions on the job. She has learned over the years that if she wants to be able to generate outcomes that she favours she cannot express particular kinds of feelings. This is particularly the case in situations where emotions run high. In these cases, Pearl does her best not to show that she is angry, upset or fearful; she masks these and other feelings that she believes will not help her get what she wants. In place of any outward sign of the turmoil she may feel within, she attempts to present an even demeanour. She says:

> Well you don't show it, but your heart is palpitating I'll tell you, especially when the parent is yelling at you on the phone. You know, I think before I used to show my emotions. A lot of it [not showing emotions] is through maturation and growth. Finding myself as a leader. Figuring out what do I want the outcome to be. Do I want it all dramatic? Spiraled? Not benefit anybody? . . . Or do I want to try and make a positive outcome, despite being yelled at.

Pearl knows that she cannot express particular kinds of emotions, even in situations where she is under fire, especially in cases where others are raising their voices. Instead, she has learned with her maturation that if she wants to achieve her preferred outcome, then she has not to react in kind when, for example, parents are yelling at her. She has a number of strategies that help her mask her feelings. She pays attention to her:

> body language and the posture. I'm lucky I'm not one of those folks who turn all red. I might in a small heated room. But there are people physically, you'll start to see the redness. I have to work on . . . what is my breathing like, how do I speak.

Pearl is also conscious of the ways in which she reacts in emotionally charged situations. She recognises that she has certain proclivities that may reveal what she is feeling at the time. As a result, she has realised that she needs to work on her body language, posture, breathing and speech. She knows that if she can adjust these and other physical performances, she can successfully mask emotions that will get in the way of her agenda.

Masking emotions is not always an easy thing to do. It is easier to do in some circumstances than others, particularly if people are well intentioned. Pearl nevertheless contends that she has an obligation to do so. She says:

> For those who are well intentioned, I never hold a grudge. For those who have been malicious or backstabbed it is difficult not to but it's my duty as a leader. I can't allow myself to get angry, I might be inside and I won't lie to you. Some of those teachers or parents who wrote a letter to the board about me, you don't forget those people or names. But for every one of them there is a lot of good things that have happened. So for me it's not easy for those people who irk me to detach, but I have to take the high road. You're a leader. It's our duty. We have to be poised and make sure that it's not visual and how am I going to model what we need to do if I can't do it with one or two staff?

Masking her feelings, however, has consequences. It is not easy simply to change behaviour or forget things that people have said or done. And so there are times when leaders have to let their emotions out.

Pearl concedes that she is only human, so there have been times when she has had to take the time to express her emotions. She says:

> I'm not going to lie to you. There are times you go home and cry. You can't really cry here. Have I shut my door when it was a really bad situation and vented here? I'm not going to lie, in the four years I've been here I think that happened maybe two or three times. I don't think it's healthy to keep it suppressed. I have some amazing colleagues I could call, everything is held in confidence. I have a great VP, half time unfortunately and a great person . . . but I think that we are only human so I'll have the facade when I'm out there.

Pearl cannot simply change the way in which she feels, even though she may be able to erect a façade that disguises these feelings. As a consequence, she needs an outlet where she can express these emotions. Most often, she does so in private, away from the eyes and ears of those with whom she works.

Strategic action, emotions and social justice

Pearl puts some or all of the above practices into play when she promotes her social justice ideals. She recalls a particular instance when she had to exercise her skills to get the outcome that she wanted in a difficult and emotionally charged situation. She recalls:

> I had a situation with one teacher . . . and it's very vivid because it went all the way to the superintendent. And it had to go that far because it tested my emotions and another piece of that is I was fearful too because I didn't know what I was going to do. But it tested my emotions.

It occurred as she first took up her position as principal in March of the year. At the time, just before stepping aside, the previous principal had announced the teaching assignments for the following year. A number of teachers were not happy with his decisions and they showed up in force on that first day to voice their displeasure to Pearl. Apparently, in an effort to cut down on the number of parent complaints, her predecessor had planned to move a number of teachers to compensate for the shortcomings of a single teacher. The first thing that Pearl did was to try to understand the larger picture by listening carefully to what the complaining teachers had to say. She concluded that the former principal did not listen to them because their argument made a lot of sense to her. In this diverse school, students and teachers would suffer if the assignments proceeded as planned. Those students who needed the most help would not be getting it. The number of parent complaints might be reduced, but Pearl concluded that the cost to the most needy students would not be worth it.

Pearl decided that in the interests of students and teachers she had to change next year's teaching assignments. This meant that she could expect objections from the weak teacher and quite possibly parents of the students of this same teacher. Despite these looming prospects, she did what she felt was right. She believed that she had an obligation to help the weak teacher to develop pedagogy best suited for the diverse group of students in the class and appropriately place the other teachers. Her strategy was to support the teacher and try to survive the inevitable protests from the teacher and parents. These moves were consistent with Pearl's commitment to social justice. She firmly believed that she had to take this path in order to provide support and appropriate pedagogy for the students who needed it most.

It did not take long for the storm to break. The teacher was the first to complain as Pearl revealed her plans. In no uncertain terms, she let Pearl know that she was not happy. Among other things, she accused Pearl of being a racist. Her actions did not stop there, however. She complained to the superintendent and she called in the union. Parents were also upset. On the first day of school in September, Pearl found three unhappy parents waiting in her office for her. These and other complainants had to be dealt with by her over the next few months.

Through all of this Pearl did her best to maintain an even and calm disposition, even though she was both fearful and upset. She kept reminding herself, though, that if she was to successfully resolve the issue, she needed to follow through with her plan, without losing her cool. Even though the entire episode upset her, she felt that a socially just resolution required that she not reveal these feelings to the teacher or others when she met with them. She hoped that this strategy would enable her to do what was right in a way that was consistent with her commitment to social justice. She says:

> So it took a lot of months and stress but if you don't detach yourself or get too emotionally involved and angry about it. Then I think those situations can go a completely different direction. You always have to remember at the end of the day you can't make enemies whether it's parents, teachers. So was I upset? Yeah. I was by the fact that she called the union. Did she

> know I was? No. What am I going to do? Cry in front of her? You go home, have your glass of wine and get upset, but when she came I had to smile and be nice.

Over the subsequent months, Pearl persisted with her efforts to help the teacher.

According to Pearl, 'Things got progressively better.' She worked closely with the teacher and helped her try out different strategies. In the end, her actions paid off. The turning point occurred at a meeting she had with the union and the teacher. Pearl recalls:

> By January or February we had to sit down with the union and I was able to articulate how I supported her with this parent complaint, how I met with this other parent. So they looked at her and said they didn't need to go any further and she needed to listen to [me].

Eventually, the teacher's skills improved. In time, she became an exemplary teacher, to the point that teachers from other schools came to see her teach. In the end, Pearl's persistence, patience and her ability to mask her emotions enabled her to achieve her goals. Her support helped this teacher to improve, and in the process, she was able to provide what was necessary for the diverse student population and the community in general.

Deploying emotions and promoting social justice

Promoting social justice in diverse school settings can be a challenging enterprise. This is because proponents often face resistance from members of school communities. So leaders have to be strategic about the way in which they go about their promotional activities. But given the nature of social justice issues, social justice-minded leaders will have to factor emotions into their strategies. Pearl is a leader who attempts to do just this. She recognises the importance of emotions and does her best to acknowledge them in her social justice strategies.

Pearl is strategic about the way in which she goes about promoting her social justice agenda. She knows that it is important to take emotions into account – both others' and her own – in the process. Like Goleman (2006), she recognises the importance of emotional intelligence; she believes that it is crucial to be able to understand one's own emotions, read others' emotions and comprehend the situations in which they occur. Pearl tries as much as possible to understand the situations that give rise to various emotions. Understanding the way in which organisations work is a central element of strategic action (Ryan, 2010). Understanding the people that she works with – and that includes superiors, teachers, parents and students – and the facts of various situations, are key for resolving issues and promoting particular agendas. Pearl was diligent about looking into the circumstances of the various issues as they arose, figuring out the relationship to people's emotions and communicating with the various concerned parties. For example, she understood why the boy with the parent who had a restraining order was acting out, made sure that she communicated this information to the boy's teachers, and took this into consideration when dealing with the boy's behaviour.

Pearl was also strategic when dealing with emotionally charged situations. She deliberately employed particular tactics to ensure that these episodes turned out in the way she wanted. She has learned that acknowledging others' emotions, being patient and providing support will help her generate preferred outcomes. Pearl contends that distressed people appreciate having their emotions acknowledged; letting people talk, refraining from interrupting and asking questions only when appropriate helps to avoid escalating volatile situations; and supportive gestures and actions will reassure angry and fearful people. She deliberately employs these practices to get through emotionally charged meetings and situations in the short run, but also to promote longer term goals, like instituting social justice practices in her school.

Pearl was perhaps most articulate about the way she managed her own emotions. She has recognised that she cannot express all her feelings, particularly in situations where others are angry or fearful. In other words, she often has to disguise or mask her feelings. Pearl does many of the things that Hochschild (2012) describes when people are engaged in emotional labour activities. Hochschild indicates that there are three techniques associated with these masking activities: cognitive, bodily and expressive. In one way or another, Pearl is involved in all three activities. Most obviously, though, she attempts to adjust her bodily and expressive gestures. She pays particular attention to bodily reactions, including posture, body language and her breathing. She also adjusts her expressions, including attempting to smile, nod her head and use particular kinds of language.

Pearl's cognitive techniques are less clear. She is aware of the emotional component of the interchanges she has with others. She pays close attention to the emotions of others as well as her own, and makes what she believes to be the appropriate adjustments. It appears that this awareness has an impact on her actions. Yip and Cote (2013) have found that those who are aware of how they feel and why are better able to influence their decisions than those who are less aware. Pearl understands how she is feeling and makes conscious decisions to suppress, or at least mask, emotions that she feels will not help her achieve her desired goal. However, it is not clear to what extent Pearl uses this awareness to actually suppress unhelpful emotions, like anger or fear. While there is no doubt that Pearl seeks to disguise these emotions, her statements indicate that she is less successful at suppressing them. Her tendency is to cover them up when she is with others, but to vent – either in her office or later at home – when she is alone. The situation and the identities of those who are involved influences how long these emotions stay with her. She says that she is able to understand and forget certain offensive behaviours when she knows that there is no malicious intent involved. On the other hand, Pearl acknowledges that she has trouble letting go of these feelings when she knows that the intentions of the other parties are not honorable.

In her research about female educational leaders and their experiences managing emotions during an era of change, Blackmore (1996) found that her participants developed strategies to help control their emotions. Their strategies were both similar to and different from Pearl's. In contrast to Pearl's tactics, some of Blackmore's participants distanced themselves from the proposed change initiatives that they opposed. They also employed strategies similar to Pearl's. For example, they kept their own emotions to themselves, refraining from expressing them around those with whom they were dealing. This practice took a toll on these leaders, however; the resulting stress prompted a number of them to leave the profession.

It is also obvious that Pearl's emotional labour took a toll on her. However, she appeared to be able to cope better than some of Blackmore's participants, although it is hard to calculate the actual impact of her efforts to suppress her emotions. Blackmore (1996) concludes that caring professions are most often identified with the positive emotions associated with caring, and not in relation to negative ones. Little mention is made of the costs to leaders associated with managing their own work-associated negative emotions.

Pearl speaks mostly about volatile encounters with others when referring to emotions, no doubt, because they come to mind easily. But she is also occupied with engendering emotions that promote social justice over the longer term. Like some of those who write about activism and emotions (Flam and King, 2005), she attempts to alleviate fear and promote hope. Pearl demonstrates this more through her actions than her words. In the situation with the weak teacher, Pearl had to deal with both her own and the weak teacher's emotions. Given the threatening actions that teachers and parents took, she had to mask her fear and anger, in order to ensure that meetings with both would have a positive outcome. At the same time, though, Pearl tried to change the teacher's fear of change and her anger at being forced into a situation she believed was behind her. By maintaining an even demeanour through some difficult interchanges, and providing the teacher with constant support and help, Pearl was able to give the teacher hope that she could reduce her fear of change and turn her teaching around. In doing so, Pearl stayed faithful to her social justice ideals. Weathering the difficulties in the manner in which she did, she was able to make provisions for appropriate pedagogy for some of the more needy students in the weak teacher's class. More than this, though, her decision not to change the teaching assignments of the other teachers also kept them in situations that best served some of the other less privileged students in the school.

Through all of this, Pearl attempted to generate a particular outcome by controlling her own emotions and engendering particular emotions in others. In other words, she attempted to manipulate situations to generate a desired outcome. When referring to the masking of one's own emotions, Hochschild (2012) prefers not to use the term 'manipulate'. Instead, she favours the terms 'evocation' and 'suppression'. Even though she is alluding to self-emotions more so than others' emotions, the intent of this masking is to evoke a change in others. Hochschild takes a decidedly negative view of this whole enterprise, emphasising the exploitive side of emotional labour and the associated manipulation. Goleman (2006) is more direct and positive about manipulation. He maintains that understanding one's own and others' emotions allows leaders to control the outcomes of particular situations. And he believes that this is a good thing. The moral question here is whether employing the power of administration to manipulate or engender a particular end – in this case, social justice – is justified if those ends are valued enough.

Conclusion

Given the nature of their position, leaders have little option but to attend to emotions. Whether they acknowledge it or not, leaders like Pearl will be immersed in the emotional life of their organisations. Indeed, their mere survival may depend on their ability to understand both their own and others' emotions. More than this, though, their capacity to achieve important goals like social justice may require that they manipulate or shape their own and others' emotions. This raises a number of questions. Is manipulation the right term to characterise how leaders like Pearl deal with emotions? 'Shape'? 'Evoke'? 'Influence'? Regardless of the term used, are education leaders justified in doing what they do to their emotions and the emotions of others? Does the pursuit of a valued end, like social justice, justify these actions? How far can and should leaders go to generate these important goals? And what are the consequences of these actions?

References

Anderson, G. (2009). *Advocacy Leadership: Toward a post-reform agenda in education*. New York: Routledge.

Beatty, B. R. (2000). The emotions of educational leadership: Breaking the silence. *International Journal of Leadership in Education*, 3(4), 331–357.

Bennett, C. (2001). Genres of research in multicultural education. *Review of Educational Research*, 71(2), 171–217.

Blackmore, J. (1996). Doing 'emotional labour' in the education market place: Stories from the field of women in management. *Discourse: Studies in the Cultural Politics of Education*, 17(3), 337–349.

Blackmore, J. (2011). Lost in translation? Emotional intelligence, affective economies, leadership and organizational change. *Journal of Educational Administration and History*, 43(3), 207–225.

Blase, J. and Blase, J. (1997). The micropolitical orientation of facilitative school principals and its effects on teachers' sense of empowerment. *Journal of Educational Administration*, 35(2), 138–164.

Boler, M. (2007). *Feeling power: Emotions and Education*. New York: Routledge.

Dantley, M. (2003). Critical spirituality: Enhancing transformative leadership through critical theory and African American prophetic spirituality. *International Journal of Leadership in Education*, 6(1), 3–17.

Darling-Hammond, L. (1995). Inequality and access to knowledge. In J. Banks and C. McGee Banks (eds). *Handbook of Research on Multicultural Education* (pp. 465–483). Toronto: Macmillan.

Denzin, N. K. (2009). *On Understanding Emotion*. New Brunswick, NJ: Transaction Publishers.

Flam, E. and King, D. (eds). (2005). *Emotions and Social Movements*. London: Routledge.

Furman, G. (2012). Social justice leadership as praxis: Developing capacities through preparation programs. *Educational Administration Quarterly*, 48(2), 191–229.

Goleman, D. (2006). *Emotional Intelligence*. New York: Random House.

Goleman, D. (2014). *What Makes a Leader: Why emotional intelligence matters*. Florence, MA: More Than Sound.

Hargreaves, A. (2001). Emotional geographies of teaching. *Teachers College Record*, 103(6), 1056–1080.

Hochschild, A. (1979). Emotion, work, feeling rules, and social structure. *American Journal of Sociology*, 85(3), 551–575.

Hochschild, A. R. (2012). *The Managed Heart: Commercialization of human feeling*. Oakland, CA: University of California Press.

King, D. (2005). Sustaining activism through emotional reflexivity. In H. Flam and D. King (eds), *Emotions and Social Movements* (pp. 150–169). London: Routledge.

Lambersky, J. J. (2014). Understanding the human side of school leadership: Improving teacher morale, efficacy, motivation, and commitment (unpublished doctoral dissertation). Ontario Institute for Studies in Education, University of Toronto.

Leithwood, K. A. and Beatty, B. (2008). *Leading with Teacher Emotions in Mind*. Thousand Oaks, CA: Corwin Press.

Merriam, S. B. (1998). *Qualitative Research and Case Study Applications in Education*. San Francisco, CA: Jossey-Bass.

Milner IV, H. R. (2010). *Start Where You Are, But Don't Stay There: Understanding diversity, opportunity gaps, and teaching in today's classrooms*. Cambridge, MA: Harvard Education Press.

Natriello, G., McDill, E. L. and Pallas, A. M. (1990). *Schooling Disadvantaged Children: Racing against catastrophe*. New York: Teachers College Press.

Orfield, G. (1995). Metropolitan school desegregation: Impacts on metropolitan society. *Minnesota Law Review*, 80, 825–873.

Ryan, J. (2006). *Inclusive Leadership*. San Francisco, CA: Jossey Bass.

Ryan, J. (2010). Promoting social justice in schools: Principals' political strategies. *International Journal of Leadership in Education*, 13(4), 357–376.

Ryan, J. (2012). *Struggling for Inclusion: Educational leadership in a neo-liberal world*. Charlotte, NC: Information Age Publishing.

Shields, C. (2003). *Good Intentions are Not Enough: Transformative leadership for communities of difference*. Lanham, MD: Scarecrow Press.

Sleeter, C. E. and Cornbleth, C. (2011). *Teaching with Vision: Culturally responsive teaching in standards-based classrooms*. New York: Teachers College Press.

Sweet, R., Anisef, P., Brown, R., Walters, D., and Phythian, K. (2010). *Post-high School Pathways of Immigrant Youth*. Toronto: Higher Education Quality Council of Ontario.

Theoharis, G. (2007). Social justice educational leaders and resistance: Toward a theory of social justice leadership. *Educational Administration Quarterly*, 43, 228–251.

Tremblay, S., Ross, N. and Berthelot, J. M. (2001). Factors affecting Grade 3 student performance in Ontario: A multilevel analysis. *Education Quarterly Review*, 7(4), 25–36.

Yip, J. and Côté, S. (2013). The emotionally intelligent decision maker: Emotion-understanding ability reduces the effect of incidental anxiety on risk taking. *Psychological Science*, 24(1), 48–55.

Zembylas, M. (2007). Mobilizing anger for social justice in education: The politicization of the emotions in education, *Teaching Education*, 18: 15–28.

Zembylas, M. (2010). The emotional aspects of leadership for social justice. *Journal of Educational Administration*, 48(5), 611–625.

Zorn, D. and Boler, M. (2007). Rethinking emotions and educational leadership. *International Journal of Leadership in Education*, 10(2), 137–151.

12

SCHOOL LEADERSHIP IN DIVERSE CONTEXTS

Picking up the thread through the labyrinth

Simon Clarke and Tom O'Donoghue

Introduction

Over twenty years ago, Gronn and Ribbins (1996) argued very persuasively that context needs to be taken seriously in any considerations about educational leadership. In doing so, they suggested that if context should be interpreted not only as the combination of situational, cultural and historical circumstances that 'constrains leadership and gives it its meaning', but also that it is 'the vehicle through which the agency of leaders may be empirically understood' (p. 454). Contiguously, they also suggested that the academic literature in the field, especially as related to the school principalship, was prone to homogenise the role. As a result, they recommended that more research needed to be undertaken to capture the day-to-day reality of schools and the distinctive contexts in which school leaders work. For this purpose, they were keen proponents of an interpretative approach to investigating school leadership on the grounds that it is the most conducive means of revealing the 'lived experience of situationally embedded real world actors' (p. 455).

Since Gronn and Ribbins originally expressed these views, there has been a good deal of academic attention devoted to investigating school leadership according to the context in which it is enacted and including the use of the research approaches that these scholars originally advocated. Some examples of this work have been provided already in Chapter 1 of this volume. The argument in this chapter, while recognising the value of such work, and while not ignoring contemporaneous interest in theorising the complexity of leadership within context, is that many idiosyncratic contexts still remain which are relatively unremarked upon in the extant literature. Indeed, it was our curiosity about the variety of ways in which school leaders define the complexity of their work and the strategies they use for dealing with it across a heterogeneous range of contexts that was the provenance of this book. Accordingly, the main aims of this concluding chapter are twofold. The first aim is to identify motifs emerging from the overall commentary of the book that summarise critical aspects of the ways in which distinctive contexts influence conceptualisations and practices of school leadership. The second aim is to identify variations in these motifs that are germane to individual contexts. In addressing these two aims, we refer back to Braun and colleagues' heuristic device (Braun *et al.*, 2011), described in Chapter 2, as an orchestrating framework for our analysis.

It will be recalled that Braun and colleagues' (2011) heuristic is conceptualised according to four separate but interrelated sets of contexts: the 'situated contexts', the 'professional contexts', the 'material contexts' and the 'external contexts'. Put simply, the situated contexts comprise such dimensions as a school's 'locale, its history and intake and setting'. The professional contexts embrace the dimensions of 'values, teacher commitments and experiences, and "policy management" in schools'. The material contexts refer to such matters as 'staffing, budget, buildings, available technology and surrounding infrastructure'. Finally, the external contexts constitute the pressures and expectations resulting from the influence of broader local and national policies; they include such dimensions as 'local authority support, inspectors' reports, league table positions, legal requirements and responsibilities' (Braun *et al.* 2011, p. 588).

In adopting this heuristic, however, we are keen to avoid the potential implication that we are underestimating the level of complexity associated with the concept of context. Indeed, Braun and colleagues (2011) concede that no attempt at capturing a range of contextual factors can ever be exhaustive. The heuristic does, nevertheless, serve as a valuable framework for investigating some of the exigencies that may be brought to bear on school leadership according to those specific settings that have been portrayed in the preceding chapters. Given the extremely diverse nature of these settings, our exposition will necessarily be selective, with the constituent elements of each set of contexts identified by Braun *et al.* being examined in general rather than in great detail.

Situated contexts

The set of contexts depicted in the preceding chapters which exhibit the greatest amount of heterogeneity is that termed the 'situated contexts'. These comprise a school's locale, its history and intake and its setting. On this, Townshend has emphasised that a school should have a strong sense of its history, its distinctiveness and its difference from other schools. This is clearly the case for his own school that was founded in 1382 and has over the last 700 years, as he has put it, become 'an institution with a strong sense of its prestige and distinctive character and which enjoys, for better or worse, the public perception of being a nursery for intellectuals'. Townsend's depiction of his school serves as a reminder that the situated context is one 'where patterns over time must be considered and where history matters' (Osborn *et al.*, 2002, p. 708).

The situated context of an ancient 'public' school is a far cry from that which applies to the schools located along the political border between Northern Ireland and the Republic of Ireland. Kelly has referred to this unique location as an 'educational fault-line between two different schooling systems, catering for communities and students for whom the border is a meaningless construct'. Not surprisingly, he goes on to comment that this situation presents some challenging professional imperatives. Among these is the desirability to define a school in a way that differentiates it from, rather than reflecting, the context in which it is situated. This, Kelly suggests, is a particularly vital consideration in a post-conflict setting where a powerful statement of intent can have considerable educative purpose for brittle communities and, in the case of the 'borderlands', a community that has suffered forty years of sectarian violence.

Kelly's observation may also apply to schools located in post-conflict Rwanda where, as Karareba and colleagues point out in their account, communities are still coming to grips with the manifold traumas that were inflicted upon them by the genocide that occurred twenty years ago. Moreover, such current intractable problems as student absenteeism and parental apathy that are often encountered by Rwandan schools tend to be magnified by the impact of poverty, especially as it afflicts the more rural areas of the country. This distinctive challenge of working in rural areas is also depicted by Starr in her examination of leadership in Australian small rural schools. Leadership in these environments, as she has observed, has a tendency to be 'complex, diverse and labour-intensive and the exigencies of life in small, rural communities create unconventional leadership circumstances'.

The varied characteristics of the situated contexts portrayed in the preceding chapters also raise the question as to how conventional leadership circumstances may be defined, especially in the wake of newly emerging leadership realities. One such reality which features prominently in the overall narratives is diversity. For example, Ryan and Tuters, in their case study of a social justice-oriented Canadian principal, observe that the school they investigated has a student population in which over 45 languages or dialects are spoken in the home. Likewise, Barnett and Stevenson reported that high poverty urban schools tend to be characterised by a complex array of demographic features, including that of having large numbers of ethnic minorities and immigrants. In these situated contexts the schools' demographic complexity is further compounded by such additional factors as the rapid mobility of families, homeless families, children who are in foster care, incarcerated students and drug abuse.

Those aspects of the situational context considered above are similar, although by no means identical, to the ones encountered by the Canadian First Nation schools which are the focus of the exposition by Walton and her colleagues. Here, once again, the schools' communities are characterised by their low socioeconomic status, but they tend to be rendered even more vulnerable because of the impact that has been made by colonisation and accompanying intergenerational trauma experienced among the Inuit and Métis people. These circumstances, as Walton and colleagues observe, present particular challenges for school leaders in seeking, in their words, to 'break cycles of failure and loss inherited from a difficult past'. In considering such a milieu it serves as a reminder that in schools associated with a history of failure it is axiomatic that convincing parents of the school's capacity to meet their expectations may be thwarted.

Professional contexts

The second set of contexts included in the framework conceptualised by Braun and her colleagues (2011, p. 588) – namely, the professional contexts – encompasses the dimensions of 'values', 'teacher commitments and experiences' and 'policy management'. Here again, it is possible to discern considerable variation according to the ways in which these dimensions are manifested in the range of contexts that has been portrayed. Townsend, for example, has emphasised that an essential aspect of his role as the headmaster of a major English independent school is to provide support and encouragement to all the staff in the pursuit of their professional fulfilment. The teaching staff, in particular, he regards, as he has put it, as being the 'Head's apostles' on the basis that 'the Head looks after them and they, in turn, look after the pupils, academically and pastorally'.

This depiction of a school leader's commitment to developing the intellectual and professional capacity of staff, as well as the academic and social capacity of the students, is in stark contrast to the professional context applying to schools in Rwanda, a country where enhancing the professionalism as well as the motivation of teachers is regarded as a key leadership challenge. In this context, such teacher practices as the use of pedestrian teaching methods, absenteeism and lack of punctuality are commonplace. It is beyond the scope of this concluding chapter to provide a detailed exposition of the contextual barriers that exist serving to impede the enhancement of teacher professionalism in this situation. What does need to be emphasised, however, is that in many post-conflict settings school principals encounter problems well beyond their control and are attempting to lead schools and improve children's education in much more challenging situations than education authorities may acknowledge (Tanaka, 2012).

Starr takes up this same argument in her portrayal of principals' work in small rural schools. In these settings classroom teaching accounts for a considerable proportion of school leaders' responsibilities; often there is limited or no access to those resources that tend to be taken for granted elsewhere, and there is no dilution of stakeholder expectations regarding school improvement, policy accountability or student achievement outcomes. Elsewhere, and along similar lines, Clarke and Wildy (2004) have highlighted the tension that arises in such circumstances between, on the one hand, the professional concerns of teaching and, on the other hand, the demands of management and leadership. This so-called 'double load' (Dunning, 1993) engenders competing demands on teaching principals and may lead to 'role conflict' that can threaten to cause tensions as the requirements of the role are exercised.

As observed already by Barnett and Stevenson in their chapter in this book, given that high poverty, urban schools have a history of struggling to improve student achievement and graduation rates, they have also become prime targets for policy makers in their quest to enhance educational performance. These authors go on to describe the phenomenon of 'turnaround leadership' that has been invoked for this purpose, especially in the United States. There is currently little empirical research available on this practice. However, in order to improve the performance of teachers and students as quickly as possible there appears to be a sequence comprising two distinctive leadership approaches. In their examination of this progression, Barnett and Stevenson note that there is first the implementation of a direct or authoritarian approach. This, they say, entails 'challenging the status quo, demanding that teachers embrace the school's new direction, and forcing recalcitrant teachers to leave the school'. Once positive results start to occur, however, school leaders tend to substitute this authoritarian leadership style with one that is more democratic and collaborative, as well as being more conducive to developing teachers' agency.

A further observation made by Barnett and Stevenson, which is especially apposite to the professional context, is that principals' commitment to leading urban school reform is partly attributable to their rich array of life experiences. These life experiences, they contend, help leaders to acquire the necessary perseverance, tenacity, self-belief and moral purpose to maintain the school's direction. Elsewhere, Harris and Thomson (2006) have made a similar point about principals of schools facing challenging circumstances. According to these authors, the research evidence suggests that principals who work in these types of schools often originate from similar socioeconomic backgrounds and they are inclined to have deliberately chosen to work in schools located in disadvantaged communities. What drives them is a strong sense of moral purpose in seeking to improve the life chances of the young people who live in these communities. In this connection, Harris and Thomson (2006) also allude to the emotional dimension of such an enterprise insofar as school leaders often vacillate between idealism and pessimism about how much is achievable in practice. On this, Ryan and Tuters have presented a more detailed analysis of the emotional investment that tends to be made by social justice-minded school leaders in the chapter they have contributed to this book.

Walton and her colleagues have highlighted that the pursuit of social justice is also a priority in the Inuit and First Nations' contexts of Canada. This priority, the authors claim, requires exceptional school leadership that entails, among other things, an intimate familiarity with the socioeconomic, demographic, cultural and historical composition of the community which governs the intake of the school. They further contend that for this degree of familiarity to occur it is desirable that school leaders should be from the community, thus enabling them to know every student and their families. Likewise, Kelly postulates that effective school leadership in the Irish borderlands is, at least partly, dependent on a desire to engage positively and sustainably with the local community, especially, as he states, by creating a teaching staff '*in* the community and *of* the community'.

Material contexts

It is highly likely, of course, that the professional contexts associated with schools will also be heavily influenced by their material contexts. It is to this contextual dimension that we now turn our attention. According to Braun and colleagues (2011, p. 592) schools' material contexts include such factors as 'staffing, budget, buildings, available technology and surrounding infrastructure'. The heterogeneity of circumstances applicable to this set of contexts is once again apparent in the preceding commentaries. One would expect such an elite school as Winchester College to be particularly well placed as far as its material context is concerned. However, regardless of the somewhat rarefied situation portrayed in his narrative, Townsend places the highest premium on the quality of the teachers in his school. Indeed, in his view, 'good teachers are more important than state-of-the-art buildings'. For this reason, he considers the appointment of teachers to be one of his most important responsibilities as the headmaster of the school in order to maintain a continuous flow of talented teaching staff.

Townsend also goes on to argue that while technology can enhance teaching and learning, it should never eclipse the vital personal dimension that he considers to be integral to these processes. In other words, it is the teachers rather than the futurists, in his view, who must take the lead. For this ascendancy to occur Townsend states that 'Heads [should] have the capacity and the freedom to implement a clear vision of the content, standards, tone and style they want to cultivate and sustain in their schools and are given the resources to pursue their vision'.

The provision of resources for pursuing such a vision, however, is by no means guaranteed. In their account of high poverty urban schools, Barnett and Stevenson present a rather austere portrayal of the ways in which material contexts are likely to have an impact on these institutions. In particular, they contend that dilapidated and unsafe buildings, inefficient data-management systems, and inadequate resources for school improvement, professional development and personnel management disadvantage many schools. As a corollary of these circumstances the recruitment and retention of good teachers can become a constant challenge. Moreover, the frequent occurrence of a 'revolving door' of principals is likely to create instability within the school as well as inconsistent programme implementation. Kelly makes a similar point about schools situated on the 'fault line of conflict' in the Ireland borderlands and poses the question as to how heads can entice the best staff to stay in these deprived and challenging schools. And then, once they have been lured, how they can be persuaded to stay at the school and in the local community.

Starr also comments on the vicissitudes of material contexts as they affect the functioning of small rural schools. When such schools are funded according to per capita formulae they are often forced to operate in somewhat precarious circumstances. In particular, as Starr points out, annual budgets, the number of teachers employed at the school and the overall educational programme are all susceptible to the most minor of fluctuations in enrolments. This degree of unpredictability associated with material contexts of small rural schools can serve to postpone necessary maintenance work and expenditure on resources or new initiatives. A further impact of unpredictability is the threat of closure if schools become too small; a 'sword of Damocles' that can hang ominously over the viability of a school, creating a great deal of anxiety for those principals who are faced with such a spectre.

According to Starr, one way in which principals of small rural schools have responded to an education environment in which the availability of resources appears to be declining is to become more adept at preparing successful funding submissions. Indeed, it appears to have become a trend that schools in these contexts are increasingly dependent on such submissions for their income. Kelly also emphasises that the efficacy of educational leadership in schools that have been affected on a daily basis by socioeconomic decline and political conflict will be enhanced by school leaders' commitment to obtaining all possible sources of financial support on behalf of the school community. Elsewhere, Harris and Thomson (2006) reiterate this point in their portrayal of successful leadership relating to schools facing challenging circumstances. In particular, they contend that successful leaders in these milieux are able to find resources, both time and money, to allow teachers to generate professional knowledge.

External contexts

It would be impossible to divorce considerations of material contexts from the dynamics of the external contexts, which are instrumental in generating pressures as well as supports for schools. It is this dimension that constitutes the final set of contexts as conceptualised by Braun and her colleagues (2011), which is now examined.

Broadly speaking, external contexts take account of the pressures and expectations resulting from the influence of broader local and national policies. More specifically, they include such dimensions as 'local authority support', 'inspectors' reports', 'league table positions', 'legal requirements and responsibilities' (Braun *et al.*, 2011, p. 594). Although one could argue that this is a somewhat British-centric depiction of circumstances, it is still possible to apply such a conceptualisation more generally. Indeed, the accounts provided so far suggest that of all the sets of contexts examined, it is the external environment that appears to exhibit most similarities across diverse settings. One of the main reasons for this is the pervasive influence of the neoliberal thrust that seems to be driving contemporary education policy across a wide range of international contexts. As many of the accounts demonstrate, this policy orientation tends to be characterised by the instrumentalism of government initiatives as well as the marketised environment of schooling. Accordingly, the market values of competition, consumer choice, performance measurement and accountability underpin the politics of education, as does the determination to expand self-management practices in school systems. Some would argue that this agenda is most graphically illustrated by the evolution of an 'academised' system as chronicled by Chapman in Chapter 9.

In the context of a distinguished English independent school, self-management practices are, of course, well established. Nevertheless, Townsend comments that this does not mean such schools have remained entirely unscathed by the escalating requirements that have been introduced for accountability to external authorities. On this, he laments about recent developments occurring in English education, stating that 'it is not the three Rs, but the three Ts – tests, targets and tables – which have become the tightly-imposed orthodoxies in English schools', including his own.

A rather more idiosyncratic aspect of the external context applying to Winchester College (in keeping with other English independent schools) is the government requirement that it should justify the tax advantages it enjoys as a result of being a registered charity. This expectation is made in order that the extent of the school's public benefit is demonstrated. For this purpose, the school has developed a partnership with a local academy. Also, it has forged an access and outreach programme that involves working with primary schools in Lambeth, as well as a community service programme that runs after-school clubs for children in local primary schools (Winchester College, 2013).

Townsend highlights that, in England, it is the state sector that has been most affected by the accountability and performance measurement requirements of recent education policy. He goes on to argue that, as a consequence, heads of 'maintained schools' have experienced an erosion of their discretion over what goes on in the schools for which they are responsible. This observation resonates with Starr's depiction of the ways in which recent policy reforms occurring in Australia have influenced the nature of principals' work in small rural schools. It is clear that the principals on whom she reports are disconcerted about what they perceive to be the escalating demands of mandatory accountability, compliance and administrative work emanating from authorities, and the negative impact that these demands are having on their schools. Indeed, according to Starr, these principals have formed the view that such accountability requirements are often 'unrelated to school-based priorities, take considerable time to execute and are professionally "invisible" and unrewarding'.

These circumstances, Starr contends, tend to be compounded by the principals' general perception that the education bureaucracy at the state and/or district level insufficiently supports their work in schools. In particular, the principals in her study expressed a sense of being marginalised from the main policy agenda, which was thought to be controlled by policy makers and system administrators who are deemed to have little understanding about small rural school life and its accompanying leadership challenges. This phenomenon has been referred to elsewhere as the 'slipstream syndrome' (Dunning, 1993; Clarke and Wildy, 2004). According to this notion, policy makers seldom consider small schools to be discrete elements within a diverse educational system. Such oversight may result in dangerous assumptions being made by system administrators about the capacity of individual units to implement externally mandated changes. Without mentioning the slipstream syndrome directly, Starr has illustrated how it may be manifested according to naive systemic assumptions about the ability of a small school to meet the full range of requirements for school effectiveness with a small teaching staff. It may also be apparent in the use of formula funding resulting in inadequate resourcing levels for small schools.

A context that is unlikely to be automatically associated with neoliberal educational reforms is that of China. Nevertheless, as Qian and Walker have observed, principals in Shanghai are required to navigate with considerable deftness the intersection between the 'lifeworld' and the 'systemsworld' that is brought to bear on their schools. As they point out, the lifeworld in Habermasian terms represents an individual school's culture, traditions, rituals and norms, while the school systemsworld provides management designs, strategic and tactical actions, and policies and procedures. Qian and Walker argue that in China, as in many Western contexts, the systemsworld has increasingly 'colonised' the lifeworld. As a consequence, Chinese schools are subjected to overwhelming control by systemic power. Unlike in the West, however, the systemic power being imposed on schools appears to emanate mainly from the State, with the market playing a more indirect role. It is this complex dynamic relating to the external context, the authors suggest, that warrants further attention in order to develop understandings of the ways in which Chinese principals' work lives are being shaped.

Summing up this rather oscillating commentary is no easy task. It does need, however, to be pointed out that these deliberations cannot be considered to be exhaustive and other contextual nuances exist that have not been referred to explicitly. For example, although it would be somewhat difficult to apply 'individual variables' (Walker *et al.*, 2012) to the heuristic framework that we have used to analyse school leadership in diverse contexts, it is clear that school leaders' personal traits are pertinent to the ways in which leadership practices are assumed within a given setting. In this regard, a number of the expositions presented here are pertinent. Similarly, the influence of societal culture on specific school contexts and the exercise of leadership is a phenomenon that has not been discussed overtly in our analysis. The crucial impact of societal influence is, nevertheless, made especially apparent in the portrayals of school leadership in Inuit and Mi'kmaw contexts of Canada as well as in the three case studies of high school principals in Shanghai.

By way of closure, there are five key and interconnected assertions about leadership in diverse contexts that may be extrapolated from the foregoing discussion – namely, the importance of school leaders acknowledging the complexity of context, the importance of school leaders being sensitive to their own context, the importance of school leaders being flexible in their strategies, the importance of leadership learning enabling school leaders to be flexible in their strategies, and the importance of contextualising research in the field of educational leadership. In accordance with the Latin root of the word 'context', we hope these assertions help to join together the overall commentary and, in accordance with the title of this chapter, enable the reader to pick up the thread through the labyrinth.

The importance of school leaders acknowledging the complexity of context

The first assertion that is suggested by reflecting on the collective commentaries in this book is the importance of school leaders acknowledging that context is far from being a straightforward concept. Although it could be argued that this claim is precariously close to stating the obvious, we believe that it requires constant reiteration. Indeed, the exceptional complexity of context was conveyed effectively by one of the most nuanced definitions that we encountered, quite recently, in a blind review of some of our related work. Unfortunately, this means, of course, that we are unable to cite it, but should the anonymous reviewer in question happen to read this book we wish to acknowledge his/her assistance in developing our thinking around the complexity of educational contexts. It is also a definition that resonates with the significance of context for school leadership that is highlighted so sharply in the preceding chapters.

According to the definition in question, the contexts that shape educational practices, including that of school leadership, are first, multifaceted, unstable amalgams of interdependent material, social, cultural, ideological, political, institutional, historical and geographical factors. Second, these contexts are multilayered, encompassing – for instance, local realities, national policies and practices, and international agreements. Third, contexts are volatile, latent, ambiguous and therefore elusive. It is fair to say that many aspects of the multifaceted, multilayered and elusive manifestations of educational contexts have been illustrated clearly in the portrayal of diverse settings that have been presented here.

The importance of school leaders being sensitive to their own context

It is the impenetrable nature of the concept of context that could well have prompted the oft-quoted comment made by Leithwood and colleagues (Leithwood *et al.*, 1999, p. 3) that 'outstanding leadership is exquisitely sensitive to the context in which it is exercised'. As the preceding chapters have indicated, an exquisite sensitivity to context on the part of school leaders entails an ability to 'read' the complexities of their context, especially the people, the problems and issues, as well as the culture of the school and the community in which it is located. It is this degree of sensitivity to context that facilitates leaders' capacity to determine the school's priorities and interests. At a broader level, it is also clear that it is desirable for leaders to have sensitivity and familiarity with the socioeconomic, demographic, cultural and historical composition of the community which governs the intake of the school. It needs to be further emphasised, however, that school leaders' sensitivity to context should not be confined to circumstances occurring in the micro-context of the school and its community. Rather, it should also be attuned to developments arising in the macro-context of the policy environment (Lovett *et al.*, 2014). In particular, school leaders require a comprehensive knowledge and understanding of international trends and issues in education as well as their implications for national and local arrangements for enabling them to engage as effectively as possible with changes in policy, curriculum and practice at a more parochial level. In sum, and as Kellerman (2013) has so succinctly asserted, contextual intelligence for twenty-first century leadership is every bit as important as all the other intelligences, including that of emotional intelligence.

The importance of school leaders being flexible in their strategies

In keeping with Hallinger's (2011) deliberations on the context of leadership, the depictions of diverse contexts portrayed in the previous chapters tend to challenge the conventional perception as well as the policy imperative that one style of leadership is suitable for all school contexts. Rather, these depictions suggest that approaches to leadership are required which are attuned to the needs of the school and its community as opposed to being determined by normative theories and models of what constitute effective leadership. In such a rapidly changing landscape as that of the academies programme in England, developments in leadership practice considered in this book have been reported as being uneven and unpredictable. This observation would suggest that patterns of school leadership in this extremely fluid educational context remain inchoate. It could, therefore, be some time before it is possible to discern new strategies that may assist leaders to deal with the uncertainties, changes and complexities that tend to be associated with an 'academised' system.

A number of the other foregoing commentaries, however, provide some sharper glimpses of leadership activities that appear to be matched to some extent with their contexts. In response to rural challenges, for example, there is often an adoption of collective approaches by small rural schools in which leadership is distributed not only within and across schools, but within and across communities. Reference has also been made to the efficacy of turnaround leadership for schools located in high poverty urban settings. In these circumstances, as Hallinger has observed (2011, p. 135), there is often an 'urgent need for improvement, a lack of demonstrated success, and uncertain confidence', which require, at least in the short term, a more directive style of leadership to be employed.

The assumption that leadership theories and principles can be applied regardless of the qualities and circumstances of different contexts is especially contentious in relation to schools located in post-conflict settings that are often grappling with multiple intractable problems. It is in these circumstances, perhaps, that adaptive leadership could be most conducive in its adoption and adaptation of more than one leadership style for dealing with the severity of the challenges encountered.

The importance of leadership learning enabling school leaders to be flexible in their strategies

The notion that school leaders should be able to adapt their approaches to suit different sets of circumstances highlights the need for processes of leadership preparation and development to promote flexibility in the employment of leadership styles and strategies (Hallinger, 2011). This is not the place to examine the efficacy of approaches to leadership learning in any detail. Nevertheless, it can be emphasised that in order for leadership learning to enhance leaders' ability to be adaptable according to different contextual circumstances, it is desirable for this process of learning to embrace certain key features (Clarke, 2015). First, it is desirable that processes of leadership learning are carefully constructed to establish a suitable blend between, on the one hand, fostering competencies relating to core management knowledge and skills and, on the other hand, devoting adequate attention to higher order capacities that include 'combining analysis with creativity, developing affective capacity and building authenticity and trust in the leadership of people' (Lewis and Murphy, 2008, p. 22).

Second, it is desirable that leaders should be encouraged to develop self-agency in their learning. In particular, this refers to leaders having the metacognitive awareness to see their experiences as continuously presenting opportunities for learning in order to develop the adaptive capabilities necessary for successful leadership through practice. These observations seem to resonate with the argument that professional learning, in general, needs to shift from a propensity to 'deliver' professional development to supporting authentic professional learning (Webster-Wright, 2010).

The importance of contextualising research in the field of educational leadership

It is likely that supporting authentic professional learning in processes of school leadership preparation and development will be significantly buttressed by adopting a greater commitment to contextualising educational research as a whole, but especially in the field of educational leadership (Thrupp and Lupton, 2006). In this connection, it has been argued (Clarke and Wildy, 2010) that a comprehensive, professional knowledge base embedded in the realities of workplaces found in schools and in the environments in which they are located should be available. For this purpose, it follows that interpretative approaches to research are potentially fruitful insofar as they can help to depict the 'lived' experience of practitioners and describe accurately the realities of their work in given contexts. Hallinger (2011, p. 138), at a more eclectic level, makes a similar point when he states:

> We need to obtain better information not just about 'what works' but 'what works' in different settings. This research will require both quantitative and qualitative studies that describe successful leadership practices across different school levels, at different points in the 'school improvement journey' and across different cultures. This is an ambitious but worthy agenda.

We hope that this book will make a contribution to such an ambitious but worthy agenda, first, through its exhortation to take context seriously in both the practice and in the research of educational leadership, and second by helping to illuminate understanding, analysis and meaning attached to the crucial realm of school leadership in diverse contexts.

References

Barnett, B. and Stevenson, H. (2015). International perspectives in urban educational leadership: Social justice leadership and high-need schools. In M. Khalifa, N. W. Arnold, A. F. Osanloo and C. M. Grant (eds), *Handbook of Urban Educational Leadership* (pp. 518–531). Lanham, MD: Rowman & Littlefield.

Braun, A., Ball, S. J., Maguire, M and Hoskins, K. (2011). Taking context seriously: Explaining policy enactments in the secondary school. *Discourse: Studies in the Cultural Politics of Education*, 32(4), 585–596.

Clarke, S. (2015). School leadership in turbulent times and the value of negative capability. *Professional Development in Education*. Published online 23 March.

Clarke, S. and Wildy, H. (2004). Context counts: Viewing small school leadership from the inside out. *Journal of Educational Administration*, 42(5), 555–572.

Clarke, S. and Wildy, H. (2010). Preparing for principalship from the crucible of experience: Reflecting on theory, practice and research. *Journal of Educational Administration and History*, 41(1), 1–16.

Dunning, G. (1993). Managing the small primary school: The problem role of the teaching head. *Educational Management and Administration*, 21(2), 79–89.

Gronn, P. and Ribbins, P. (1996). Leaders in context: Postpositivist approaches to understanding school leadership. *Educational Administration Quarterly*, 32(3), 452–473.

Hallinger, P. (2011). Leadership for learning: Lessons from 40 years of empirical research. *Journal of Educational Administration*, 49(2), 125–142.

Harris, A. and Thomson, P. (2006). Leading school in poor communities: What do *we know and how do we know it?* Paper presented at the International Congress of School Effectiveness and Improvement (ICSEI), Fort Lauderdale, 3–6 January.

Kellerman, B. (2013). Leading questions: The end of leadership – redux. *Leadership*, 9(1), 135–139.

Leithwood, K., Jantzi, D. and Steinbach, R. (1999). *Changing Leadership for Changing Times*. Buckingham: Open University Press.

Lewis, P. and Murphy, R. (2008). *Review of the Landscape: Leadership and leadership development. A review of what is known about effective leadership and leadership development*. Nottingham: National College for School Leadership.

Lovett, S., Dempster, N. and Flückiger B. (2014). Personal agency in leadership learning using an Australian heuristic. *Professional Development in Education*. DOI: 10.1080/19415257.2014.891532.

Osborn, R. N., Hunt, J. G. and Jauch, L. R. (2002). Toward a contextual theory of leadership. *The Leadership Quarterly*, 13, 797–837.

Tanaka, C. (2012). Profile and status of untrained teachers: Experience in basic schools in rural Ghana. *Compare: A Journal of Comparative and International Education*, 42(3), 415–438.

Thrupp, M. and Lupton, R. (2006). Taking school contexts more seriously: The social justice challenge. *British Journal of Educational Studies*, 54, 308–328.

Walker, A., Hu, R. and Qian, H. Y. (2012). Principal leadership in China: An initial review. *School Effectiveness and School Improvement*, 23(4), 369–399.

Webster-Wright, A. (2010). *Authentic Professional Learning: Making a difference through learning at work*. Dordrecht: Springer.

Winchester College (2013). *Investing in the Future. Annual Report*, 2013. Winchester College.

References

INDEX